The Greening of the Church

By the same author

To Care for the Earth: a call to a new theology (Geoffrey Chapman/Bear & Co.)

The Greening of the Church

Sean McDonagh SSC

ORBIS BOOKS
Maryknoll, New York 10545

GEOFFREY CHAPMAN

Published in Great Britain by **Geoffrey Chapman**
An imprint of Cassell Publishers Ltd
Villiers House, 41/47 Strand, London WC2N 5JE

Published in the United States by **Orbis Books**
Maryknoll, NY 10545

The Catholic Foreign Mission Society of America (Maryknoll) recruits and trains people for overseas missionary service. Through Orbis Books Maryknoll aims to foster the international dialogue that is necessary to mission. The books published, however, reflect the opinions of their authors and are not meant to represent the official position of the society.

First published 1990
Reprinted 1990

British Library Cataloguing in Publication Data
McDonagh, Sean
   The greening of the church
   1. Environment. Conservation—Christian viewpoints
   261.8'36

Library of Congress Cataloging in Publication Data
McDonagh, Sean, 1935–
   The greening of the church / by Sean McDonagh.
   238 p. 21.6 cm.
   Includes bibliographical references.
   1. Human ecology—Religious aspects—Christianity.   2. Nature—Religious aspects—Christianity.   3. Creation.   I. Title
   BT695.5.M42   1990
   261.8'36—dc20   90-33049
                                                         CIP

ISBN 0-225-66586-7 (Geoffrey Chapman)
     0-88344-694-4 (Orbis Books)

Typeset by Area Graphics Ltd, Arden Press Way, Letchworth
Printed and bound in Great Britain by
Biddles Ltd, Guildford and King's Lynn

Contents

ix   Preface and Acknowledgements

1   Introduction

PART ONE: When the trees are gone

9   1 International debt is killing the poor and the earth itself

38   2 Will there be too many mouths to feed? *Human population and the carrying capacity of the earth*

74   3 When the trees are gone

PART TWO: Creation in scripture and tradition

109   4 And God saw that it was good *A theology of creation*

126   5 The covenant tradition

144   6 Prophets of Israel, the Psalms and wisdom literature

158   7 Jesus — 'I have come that they may have life and have it to the full'

165   8 Christian witnesses through the ages

175   9 The environment in the modern Catholic Church

204   *Appendix 1:* A new Decalogue

207   *Appendix 2: What Is Happening to Our Beautiful Land?*

217   *Notes*

For my sister, Maire

Preface and Acknowledgements

The reader will realize very quickly that *The Greening of the Church* emerges from my missionary experience on the island of Mindanao in the Philippines during the past 20 years. A person is transformed by the land, the culture and the people among whom he or she works. Little of what follows could have been written were it not for my experience of almost ten years living among the T'boli people of southern Mindanao. I am deeply indebted to many T'boli people for their friendship and insights.

The tribal peoples of South Cotabato have been faithfully served by the men and women of the Santa Cruz Mission for the past 30 years. The experiences of these development workers and missionaries are also reflected in these pages. Many of the ideas here have been teased out with the director of the Santa Cruz Mission, Fr Rex Mansmann CP, as we prepared for training programmes or sat around at night chatting. I am also grateful to Flor Mamon and Alice Swawa of the T'boli Study Center who typed much of the text and tirelessly researched references.

The missionary does not plough a solitary furrow. The various Christian Churches and missionary groups, like the Society of St Columban, have attempted to flesh out and engage more seriously the social dimensions of the gospel of Jesus in recent years. At the Columban General Assembly in Pusan, Korea in 1988, the delegates built on these foundations and insisted on the ecological dimensions of the missionary's challege to live in solidarity with the poor today. Many of my Columban colleagues have developed an ecological apostolate during the past decade in different parts of the world.

I am particularly grateful to Frs Kevin McHugh and Rufus Halley, who laboured over different parts of the manuscript. Thanks also to Joan Longmore FMM for her valuable comments; to Robert Kelly and Ruth McCurry of Geoffrey Chapman, whose encouragement and gentle prodding guided *The Greening of the Church* from the realm of general ideas to the present text; and to Brian Davies of CAFOD for advice and help.

Biblical quotations are taken from the Revised Standard Version Bible, Catholic Edition, copyright 1965 and 1966 by the Division of

Introduction

The new face of mission today

I am an Irish Columban missionary priest who has spent the past 20 years on mission on the island of Mindanao in the Philippines. I arrived in the Philippines just three years after the Second Vatican Council ended, and so I have had the privilege of living in one of the most exciting periods of missionary activity in the history of the Catholic Church. During this time, individual missionaries and missionary congregations have gradually redefined the role of the missionary in today's Church. He or she is no longer that distant figure of popular imagination who stalks across Africa wearing a pith hat and baptizing 'black babies'.

Modern missionaries, in continuity with their predecessors, are still bearers of Good News. But preaching and witnessing to the Good News of Christ takes a variety of forms today. Missionaries are still challenged to understand the language and culture of the people among whom they work and, together with the people, to respond to the challenges that face particular communities. In some situations this will still mean providing education, health care and even emergency relief, especially for those people who are forgotten in society or marginalized by local or global economic systems. But an adequate response does not end with attempts to solve social, economic and ecological problems. No, there is also the challenge to understand why widespread poverty is still spreading in Third World countries after three decades of 'development' and to change this inequitable and iniquitous situation.

A phrase attributed to the French microbiologist and environmental campaigner, René Dubos, 'think globally, act locally', sets one dimension of the agenda for modern mission. Poverty and environmental degredation in the T'boli hills on the island of Mindanao in the Philippines springs from a variety of sources. Some may be discernible in the immediate locality, as people lose their lands to local land speculators or transnational agribusiness corporations, or are forced to grow cash crops instead of food crops. But the deeper reasons for the impoverishment of the countryside and consequent hunger, pain and suffering often lie in a distant capital city like

Manila or in the offices of multilateral lending agencies like the World Bank in Washington, DC.

On this world stage, where the destiny of cultures and countries is becoming more closely intertwined, the missionary is seen as an agent of dialogue between cultures and local churches. Within the past 20 years, for example, missionaries who have experienced economic oppression, political brutality, social inequality and grinding poverty in Latin America and Southeast Asia, have brought back the praxis of liberation theology to First World countries. This, in turn, has helped a growing number of First World Christians to become more critical of the global, political, economic structures which are oppressing the vast majority of human beings and destroying the fertility of God's creation. Despite upsets and the concerted efforts of some people to put back the clock, the dialogue has borne fruit within the Catholic Church and the World Council of Churches. Significant areas of this teaching on economic, social and ecological issues have gradually made their way into the mainstream of the Church's official teaching. In the Catholic Church this has recently been enshrined in the 1988 Encyclical Letter of Pope John Paul II called *Sollicitudo Rei Socialis* ('On Social Concerns').

The Santa Cruz Mission

A missionary's perspective on social, political, economic or ecological problems does not derive primarily from flow-charts, annual reports or graphs. It emerges from an experience of living with another culture, with the daily struggles of a faith community trying to live out the Gospel in faithfulness to their own culture and in the footsteps of Jesus. Since 1981, I have been a member of the Santa Cruz Mission which is located in the province of South Cotabato on the island of Mindanao.

The story of the Santa Cruz Mission began when Fr George Nolan CP responded to a request from five T'boli chieftains to build a school at Lake Sebu, which at that time was a remote tribal settlement, eight hours' walk from the nearest road. In 1962, the present director, Fr Rex Mansmann CP, took charge of the Mission, and he gradually expanded its work.

The integral development policy which is a central tenet of the Santa Cruz Mission philosophy grew out of the experience of responding to the needs of the people and their environment. The education component has now expanded to include a high school and a modern college. Every effort is being made to pursue modern education in a way that is sensitive to the particular culture of the people and is relevant to the tasks that need to be faced so that the community can survive and prosper. Health care is crucial to human well-being, so the Santa Cruz Mission has developed an extensive community-based health programme which focuses on both preventive and curative medicine. Food production, agriculture and the protection of the environment through reforestation programmes have assumed increasing importance over the past ten years as forest destruction and soil erosion became a growing major problem for the T'boli people.

Other elements are also important. Very often the poor, especially tribal people, are exploited in trading relationships even by those a rung or two above them on the socio-economic ladder. They receive the lowest prices for their produce and are charged the highest prices for commodities they wish to purchase. A network of marketing centres established by the Santa Cruz Mission has helped to minimize this exploitation. But more work in this area is called for as the farms become more productive and there is some surplus. Unless co-operative financial institutions are set up to plough back the community's savings into projects beneficial to the tribal people, this money could bring disaster. For example, it could be invested in lowland Filipino commercial banks and used to finance projects detrimental to the welfare of the tribal community.

Two final components, religion and community organization, draw together many of the other threads of development into an overall tapestry. By being sensitive to the social, cultural and religious traditions of the people, they provide the psychic energy that will enable the T'boli and other tribal groups to confront the problems that face them and build a better, more sustainable society.

What can be learned from tribal people?

Apart from a curiosity about the culture and way of life of tribal people, is there anything which Westerners or people living in other parts of the world can learn from tribal people? It seems to me that in many ways the problems facing the tribal peoples of the Philippines are a kind of microcosm of the problems facing other Third World people, the rest of humanity and the earth itself. In our modern world, because tribal peoples are so vulnerable, they play a role in our common effort to survive akin to that played by the canary in nineteenth-century collieries.

The canaries were sensitive to odourless toxic gases, so if a canary became agitated or, worse still, died, the miners fled from the mines before they, too, were asphyxiated. This book argues that myopic worldwide economic policies are impoverishing people and destroying the natural world of South Cotabato, the Philippines and the earth itself. It invites people to take stock of what is happening and to plan a new way of living in the context of our common solidarity for survival. If the natural world of South Cotabato cannot support tribal peoples in this decade, within another decade or two it will not support the lowland Filipino settler population either, and in a few short decades beyond then, current policies could make the earth uninhabitable for any human society.

The greening of the Church

Part One of this book looks at the relationship between environmental issues and Third World poverty. Chapter 1, *International debt is killing the poor and the earth itself*, looks at both poles of this debate. It is generally recognized that the burden of international debt is draining Third World countries. Some of the gains made during the 1970s in bringing down the rate of infant mortality are rapidly being lost because of debt-related policies. Many restructuring policies forced on Third World countries by multilateral lending agencies are forcing governments to cut back on their already inadequate level of services. In the process the poor suffer. So does the earth; only by cutting down more trees or planting more cash crops can Third World governments service their debts. The chapter looks at some suggestions which might help stop the haemorrhaging caused by the debt crisis and devote local and international aid to supporting social and environmental programmes in poor countries.

Chapter 2, *Will there be too many mouths to feed?*, addresses the problems which a rapidly growing population is posing for the world as a whole and especially for Third World countries. This chapter discusses the question of rapidly increasing populations within the context of justice and the carrying capacity of the earth or local bio-region. In this way it aims at moving the morality debate over fertility control away from an exclusive concentration on individual acts to a broader discussion as to what population levels are sustainable within local regions and for the earth as a whole. The discussion takes off from a challenge which we have experienced at the Santa Cruz Mission. It moves on to question whether the present policy of fertility control promoted by the leadership in the Catholic Church is really pro-life when looked at from a wider angle.

Chapter 3, *When the trees are gone*, looks at the importance of the rainforest for the local, national and global environment. Details of attempts in the Philippines to save or replant rainforests are intertwined with the larger role of the rainforest within the biosphere. Some of the 'small print' may seem a little tedious to some readers, but it brings an important dimension of realism to the debate. It also illustrates many similar controversies which are raging over rainforest issues in Latin America, Australia and Africa as well as Asia.

Part Two, *Creation in Scripture and Tradition*, looks at environmental and social problems in the light of the Hebrew and Christian scriptures and the traditions of the Churches. Since I write from the perspective of a Catholic missionary, I deal primarily with that tradition.

I am well aware that the World Council of Churches has been much more to the fore on this issue than the Catholic Church. Chapter 4 re-examines the Genesis accounts of creation with special emphasis on what might be intended by the command to 'subdue the earth'. Chapter 5 begins with a discussion of the covenant tradition of Israel. In the light of the covenant Israel was called upon to be accountable before Yahweh and to be a good steward. This chapter asks how Christians today can be stewards of God's creation in the light of the challenges which this generation faces. It calls for a more eco-centred morality and for concerted efforts to change key political, social and economic institutions. In Chapter 6, the focus is on what we can learn from turning our attention once more to the Prophetic tradition, the Psalms and the wisdom literature.

Chapter 7 is entitled *Jesus — 'I have come that they may have life and have it to the full'* (John 10:10). Life to the full was at the heart of the ministry of Jesus. The chapter examines how the example and teaching of Jesus can challenge our throw-away, consumer society. Healing, which is also central to the ministry of Jesus, is of particular significance today. Personal, social, and earth healing are so essential for the survival of human societies and of planet Earth itself.

Chapter 8 holds up for our inspiration and imitation *Christian witnesses through the ages*. It includes a rapid schematic survey of some writings of the early Fathers, the Celtic monks, the Benedictine and Franciscan traditions and Hildegard of Bingen.

Chapter 9, *The environment in the modern Catholic Church*, begins by looking briefly at the contribution to creation theology made by Teilhard de Chardin, Thomas Berry and Matthew Fox. It recognizes that positive things are happening. A number of Bishops' Conferences have made significant statements on the environment, and the World Council of Churches has given a creative lead by linking together peace, justice and the integrity of creation. This chapter recognizes that Christian people are joining together to defend the environment and create human communities that live in a more sustainable way with the environment.

It goes on to examine some of the reasons why the leadership in the Catholic Church has been so slow to respond to the environmental crisis. It ends with a plea for ecumenical action to defend and nurture life on earth.

I am told that the Chinese ideogram for 'crisis' includes the characters for 'breakdown' and for 'opportunity'. There is no difficulty convincing most people that we are living in a time when 'things are falling apart'. We have seen it in Bhopal, at Chernobyl; we have seen fish killed in our rivers, oil spills on beaches, the depletion of the ozone layer and a host of other social and environmental problems. But it is also a time of great promise. In the Christian context this is a crisis or *kairos*-filled moment. The events unfolding in front of our eyes call for a choice between living in a way that enhances all life or continuing to hurtle down the road to disaster.

The crisis is heightened by the realization that this generation of people is in a unique position in relation to all other generations who have lived before us and those who will live in the future. We received the blessings of a healthy natural world with clean air and water, fertile soil and an abundance of life — a world in full flower. The decisions taken now will determine whether we will hand on this precious heritage intact to our children or whether we will irreversibly destroy earth's fruitfulness. Ensuring that we do the latter is surely the religious task of this generation of Christians.

PART ONE

When the Trees are Gone

International debt is killing the poor and the earth itself

The indebtedness of Third World countries has many, many faces. First World bankers see the huge sums of money continuing to grow — by mid-1989 the combined Third World debt totalled $1.3 trillion. They are aware of the possible impact of this on the world economy unless something is done to alleviate the burden, yet they will engage in almost any kind of financial juggling in order to avoid writing off debts. They sometimes hint at doomsday scenarios of financial collapse to scare off politicians from taking political action. On the other side of the divide, Third World countries complain about how in the 1970s they were lured on to the slippery road of debt by bankers making false promises. They point to high interest rates in First World countries, depressed commodity prices, protectionist policies and a host of other unfair trading arrangements which make debt repayment impossible. Much of this jargon belongs to the domain of economists, which is why many people would prefer to leave them to get on with untangling the present mess. But the debt crisis is not just played out in the various columns of bankers' ledgers; it has a human and an earthly face which the average missionary in a Third World country confronts every day, whether he or she is aware of the connections or not.

The story of Dodong — a Filipino farmer on the island of Mindanao — caught up in the debt crisis, illustrates many of the economic and political mechanisms which today are working in tandem to kill the poor and the earth itself. This chapter will examine the human suffering and ecological degradation which is caused by the debt crisis and look at some solutions which really confront the crisis and promise to establish a more equitable economic order to protect humans and our planet, earth.

Dodong Balayon is a typical Filipino farmer — in fact he has much in common with other farmers in many Third World countries. In 1989 Dodong is in his mid-forties, though he looks much older. He is a *kainginero*, a slash-and-burn farmer. Each planting season Dodong burns down a further half hectare of the dwindling rainforest in order to grow rootcrops and corn. This is how he feeds his wife and six children and earns a few pesos with which to buy the necessities of life. On a few occasions I have shared with him my concern at watching him burn down this dipterocarp forest. I point to soil erosion and the heritage of a wasteland for his children and grandchildren unless the forest is protected. He is not unaware of this, but he insists that his scramble to meet today's needs is his primary concern. Tomorrow will have to take care of itself.

Once, when I took shelter from a shower in a hut which he had built, he shared with me the ups and downs of his life. As I listened, it became clearer to me that his plight is a direct result of economic and commercial decisions which are taken on the other side of the world. Though Dodong is not aware of it, problems associated with debt repayments are high on that list.

Dodong's downward slide is so similar to that of millions of peasants in Third World countries that it is well known to most missionaries and development workers. A few background details will set the scene. Dodong's father, Bert, migrated to Mindanao from one of the central islands of the Philippines in the 1950s. Through the government's Homestead Programme he acquired a 4-hectare farm in a fertile valley. He cleared the land and planted corn, root crops and rice. In the early 1960s Dodong remembers that everyone worked hard, but at least the family made ends meet. When Dodong married in 1965 his father split the farm and gave him two hectares to work. Dodong assured me that he worked hard and knowing him I believe it, even though peasant farmers are often characterized as lazy and shiftless. Anyone who has worked with them knows that there is nothing easy about their lives. Day after day they face the continual grind of preparing land, planting seeds, weeding and protecting the plants and finally harvesting and milling the crop. Nevertheless they derive satisfaction from working with their own land, whilst cultural and religious festivals lighten the load and bind the community together.

In the early 1970s something happened that seemed to hold much promise; in fact, it changed Dodong's life for the worse. He was advised by technicians of the Department of Agriculture to abandon the mixed farming that his father practised and to concentrate all his efforts on planting new high-yielding varieties of rice. He was assured that the increased yield would be substantial and that financially his lot would improve dramatically. Experiments on adjacent farms seemed to corroborate this and so, despite reservations expressed by his father, he decided to join the programme.

For a number of years things went really well. However the loss of two crops through a prolonged drought and pest infestation threw him heavily into debt. It seemed to him that one misfortune rode on the back of another, as the price of fertilizers climbed steadily, especially after the 1979 rise in oil prices. The last straw was the increase in interest rates to 22 per cent in the early 1980s. His debt continued to grow, and the banks began to knock on his door more insistently. His land was surety for the various loans: with no escape in sight, he was finally forced to sell his holding to a transnational agribusiness corporation. He admits that he received a fair price for his land, but once he had paid his debts there was precious little left. Inflation and the demands of a growing family quickly ate into the rest. Before he knew it he was almost penniless and forced to move to the hills as a kainginero.

Dodong knows that many of his friends are in the same position as himself and yet he tends to blame himself for what has happened. He is aware, of course, that he had a run of bad luck, but in his cultural world bad luck is linked to behaviour which is considered morally or culturally reprehensible. From talk shows on the radio and conversations with his friends he realizes that some local factors contributed to his downfall. Like most Filipinos, he heard of the thousands of shoes and bras that Imelda Marcos had stored up in the Presidential palace. He presumes that Imelda's extravagant ways were in some way financed by money taken from poor people like himself. He has not, however, been apprised of the wider picture: how international banks recklessly lent money to the Philippine government, and now that the day of reckoning has arrived, servicing these loans has contributed greatly to his plight.

Dodong believed the government technician who promoted the Green Revolution. Increasing the food supply and improving oneself economically seemed worthwhile and achievable goals. It also appeared to herald a bright future for his growing family, since he would have sufficient money to send them to school in the nearby town and buy medicines for them if they became sick. In those heady days when the banks were flush with borrowed money and petrochemical products were still relatively cheap, the government agent did not spend much time discussing the problems which indebtedness would bring if the rosy future which he was painting suddenly turned dark. Needless to say, the agricultural adviser did not draw attention to the long-term adverse affect on the land of inorganic fertilizers and pesticides. The evidence of huge harvests was there to quieten any worries about possible long-term side-effects. Finally, not a word was said about the fact that the chemical package which is an essential ingredient of the Green Revolution is an expensive drain on foreign exchange for the Philippines as a whole. The only way the country could continue to import chemicals after the threefold price rise in 1979 was by borrowing more foreign money.

The party is over, not only for Dodong, but for the Philippines itself. The financial costs of borrowed money soon began to haunt the country as foreign creditors sent telegrams demanding repayment. The International Monetary Fund's team also moved in and counselled austerity measures. These included removing some subsidies on fertilizers and boosting agricultural policies to favour agribusiness corporations which were growing export-oriented crops. This seemed to be the only way that the government could generate the $1 billion that was needed annually to service the national debt. Dodong and his rice farm and hundreds of thousands like him are the direct casualties of these policies.

Dodong and his family are not alone in paying the price for ill-conceived and unjust policies; the earth itself is suffering. Deprived of his land and unable to acquire land through real land-reform initiatives, Dodong has no choice but to head for the mountains and eke out an existence there. Yet as we will see later on, lumber companies and slash-and-burn farmers like Dodong are wreaking havoc on what remains of the tropical rainforest in the Philippines and many other Third World countries.

The debt crisis

Unfortunately Dodong's story is not unique. There are millions of stories like his in Third World debtor countries. In fact it is like an endemic plague in every Third World country today. Many countries are at this moment spending the bulk of their foreign earnings merely servicing their external debt. In May 1988 the Philippines owed $28.9 billion to 483 foreign banks.[1] 44 per cent of the national budget was being siphoned off to pay external creditors.[2] In many cases, the funds which made up these debts were either embezzled by corrupt political leaders, used on grandiose and useless projects, or funnelled into buying arms and expanding the armed forces. The conspicuous waste of the Marcos regime in the Philippines is legendary. Millions, if not billions, were stashed away in foreign banks by Marcos's relatives and supporters.[3] Much of the money which did reach the country was spent on luxury hotels and resorts, an expensive experimental Film and Conference Center in Manila, a useless nuclear power plant built in an earthquake zone on the island of Luzon at the cost of $2.2 billion, and a fourfold increase in the armed forces. This extravagance took place in a country where 70 per cent of the people are undernourished, over 30 per cent are unemployed or underemployed and where poverty-related diseases like tuberculosis and gastroenteritis combine to kill large numbers of people. Despite the deteriorating health profile, only 18 per cent of the 1989 budget was allocated for social services.[4] Even a relatively simple and curable illness could mean death for Dodong or any member of his family, since they have little money for medicine or hospital expenses.

A brief history of the present crisis

In the early 1970s many Western banks, flush with petrodollars, vied with one another in encouraging the borrowing spree. There are scores of stories of bank officials waylaying Third World finance ministers at international conferences in order to offer loans on easy terms. Now these same banks are hounding any country that attempts to renege on its debt, declare a moratorium, or even move to limit repayments to a certain percentage of foreign earnings. Peru and Brazil spring to mind. In February 1988, Brazil was forced to suspend its debt moratorium and take on board austerity measures inspired by the International Monetary Fund (IMF) in order to secure credit to buy much-needed imports.

Currency fluctuations and high interest rates

Before succumbing to housekeeping rhetoric— 'what you borrow you must pay back, those are the rules of the game' — it is important to remember that there is a huge difference between the amount of money that was originally borrowed and the subsequent increase in the level of the debt. These increases are largely due to currency fluctuations and sharp rises in interest rates. Brazil, which leads the table of Third World debtor nations ($130 billion), is an excellent illustration. Its various borrowings amounted to around $20 billion during the last decade or so. Much of the money was borrowed when interest rates were 5 or 6 per cent; then suddenly, interest rates started to climb. By the late 1970s the interest rates had jumped to 16 per cent and in the early 1980s they even topped 20 per cent. This, together with the compound interest factor, sent the foreign debt rising out of control. By 1978 it had climbed to $35 billion, and still further to $82 billion four years later. In 1989 it stands at around $130 billion.

This rising debt might suggest that Brazil has not paid a cent to its creditors during the past 15 years. Nothing could be further from the truth. In fact, it paid a staggering $80 billion in interest and principal repayments between 1978 and 1985. This outflow of financial resources is tantamount to cutting an economic artery for a country with a rapidly growing population and a high percentage of its people living below the poverty line. It desperately needs every dollar it earns in order to meet the food, medical and housing requirements of its people and to protect the environment.

The Philippines is also shackled in the same way. Between 1987 and 1992 it is estimated that there will be a net outflow of $16.2 billion from the Philippines to First World banks. Altogether it is estimated that during 1988 Third World countries paid an estimated $43 billion back to creditors. This is not a one-off occurrence; in fact, 1988 was the fifth consecutive year in which there has been a financial flow from poor to rich countries. The total is something in the region of $143 billion. This huge financial haemorrhage has undermined the economies of most debtor countries, making it well nigh impossible for them to feed their people let alone pay the international debts.

The role of the US economy

It is easy to blame the victim, but in order to understand the mechanisms which increased the debt it is important to remember that Brazil and its Third World counterparts have no control whatsoever over the interest rates or currency markets which have caused such a phenomenal escalation of their debts. The major factor determining the upward surge of interest rates was the deficit in the US economy in the 1970s and 1980s. The US government decided against raising taxes to pay for its rising standard of living and the largest increase in military spending during peace time. It felt that tax increases would fuel inflation and probably alienate the voters who had put them in office. So the only way to keep the economy expanding was to borrow huge sums of money from overseas and leave it to the next generation to pay. That was not too difficult. Foreign investors felt their money was secure in American banks and government bonds and the high interest rates gave them a good return on their money.

Worse still, Third World countries are not equal partners in the process that sets commodity prices. In this period the prices for sugar, coffee, soya beans, minerals or other commodities which are exported in order to pay off the debt have fallen dramatically, especially during the past decade. In the Philippines the value of four primary commodities which account for a sizeable 20 per cent of exports fell by 20 per cent between 1980 and 1985. The impact of falling commodity prices and the rising cost of manufactured goods is easy to grasp when one realizes that a Third World country has to export three or four times as much coffee in 1989 as it did in the early 1970s in order to buy the same piece of machinery.

How did Brazil come by the $80 billion which it used to pay its creditors? It was not scooped off the cream generated by the booming economic growth of the 1970s in ways which would not wreck the economy or injure and oppress the people. The debt was repaid by cutting spending and promoting export-oriented growth. The bankers' prescription for indebted economies are a mix of free-market and monetarist policies. They include currency devaluations, restrictions on imports, the removal of government subsidies on food and energy, an increase in indirect taxation and an aggressive export drive in every sector of the economy, with special support for agribusiness. To date almost 70 countries have had to put on the IMF strait-jacket. The letter of intent (LOI) signed between the Philippines government and the IMF in March 1989 contains almost all the above provisions. The bottom line in the strategy is to force Third World countries to spend less and to generate more dollars so that the government can pay the foreign debt, no matter what the social or ecological costs may be.

Together with the World Bank, the International Monetary Fund was established at the Bretton Woods Conference in 1944. It was designed as a lender of last resort, one that might be willing to make available bridging loans for countries which are temporarily caught in a short-term balance-of-payments problem. Since the emergence of the debt crisis in the late 1970s, the International Monetary Fund has assumed a much more prominent role in attempting to regulate Third World economies. It is often disparagingly referred to as the 'policeman for the capitalist world', since countries find it impossible to borrow from private banks unless the IMF endorses the country's economic policies.

World Bank–IMF policies create social unrest and mass poverty

The IMF uses temperate and innocuous images to describe the economic policies which they force on debtor countries. Two such images predominate. The first is that of belt-tightening. This comes from the world of health clinics where overweight Western men and women are encouraged and cajoled into shedding a few pounds here and there in the interests of improving overall health and developing a better figure. Alternatively, the consultants present themselves as doctors who are called to administer an essential but bitter medicine to a patient. In the short term the medication is distasteful, but the long-term results are presumed to be good. The patient can be expected to be back on his or her feet within a short period of time.

These words hide the appalling reality of suffering and death which these policies are wreaking on Third World people. In reality, as we saw in the case of Dodong, the debt burden is murderous. Thumbscrews and the garrotte would be more appropriate images for the savage reality. Attempts to repay the debt are strangling the poor in Third World countries and scarring the earth. The debt can only be paid by taking food out of the mouths of the poor, especially women and children, and by irreversibly damaging the environment. Efforts at repayment set in motion economic, political and social changes which very quickly lead to a curtailment of personal and political freedom and draconian labour laws, and end up playing into the hands of the torturers and the death squads.

One does not need a sophisticated knowledge of economics to understand the main signposts on the downward spiral set off by the debt crisis. Small-scale, subsistence agriculture suffers as governments shift their support from small farmers who grow staples to large-scale export-oriented agriculture. As a direct consequence the price of staple foods increases and the poor must manage by eating less. The removal of subsidies from food and energy, together with a wage freeze, results in hunger and starvation for landless people and the rural poor who already have little or no money. It can also lead to rioting, looting and a breakdown in law and order as hungry people take to the streets in protest. IMF-inspired increases in food and gasoline prices caused three days of riots in Caracas, Venezuela, in February and March 1989. When the tear gas had lifted and the gunfire died down, over 300 people had been killed, 1,000 injured, thousands gaoled and millions of dollars-worth of damage done to property. At a press conference the Venezuelan President, Carlos Andrés Pérez, said that 'the crisis Latin American nations are undergoing has a name written with capital letters — foreign debt'.[5] There are justifiable fears that the letter of intent (LOI) signed between the Philippine government and the IMF in March 1989 will lead to a threefold rise in the price of rice from 5.50 pesos per kilo in 1989 to 16 pesos in 1990.[6]

Austerity measures also slow down economic activity. Currency devaluations are designed to stimulate local industry to produce goods which will be more competitive on the international markets, but in the process spare parts and new machinery become prohibitively expensive. Many small and medium-sized industries cannot afford these costs and so they are quickly driven to the wall. Unemployment soars and government revenue plummets. People who lose their jobs have no financial reserves or social security to fall back upon. They are forced to have recourse to unscrupulous moneylenders in order to purchase the necessities of life, or to depend on relatives and friends who are themselves little better off. With inflation and devaluation even those with jobs are forced to work longer hours to make ends meet. This mass impoverishment of a people is, of course, fertile ground for the drug barons and drug smugglers in many Latin American countries. People who are hungry and destitute will grow and sell drugs. Western governments must be made to see that the IMF-inspired economic policies inevitably lead to the smuggling of illegal drugs into their countries.

So the belt-tightening financial policies which are devised by well-fed bankers in the comfort of their boardrooms in New York, Washington, London, Tokyo or Basel mean a downward slide of pain, suffering, malnutrition, loss of self-esteem, sickness and finally death for many people in Third World countries. It is estimated that between 1980 and 1986 there has been an annual 2.4 per cent drop in income in most of the heavily indebted countries of Latin America. The results are stressed in the 1988 UNICEF report which was published on 20 December 1988. Writing in *The Guardian* (1 January 1988), Victoria Brittain quotes James Grant, the executive director of UNICEF, as saying that

for one sixth of humanity the march of progress has now

become a retreat. In its annual report UNICEF estimated that
the debt crisis was responsible for the deaths of 500,000
children world-wide during the year 1988. Because children
are both the more vulnerable members of any society and the
hope for the future, UNICEF appeals for international action
to resolve the debt crisis.

I am not attempting to exonerate the Third World governments of
all blame; they borrowed the money and have often spent it foolishly.
It is, nevertheless, a tragedy that the Aquino government in the
Philippines or the present government in Argentina are expected to
carry the can for debts that the former corrupt and oppressive regimes
ran up. These governments are now caught in a very delicate situation which may lead to their downfall. The revenue which is lost as the
economy contracts must be made up elsewhere. This means increasing the cost of basic services like electricity and water, raising taxes
and devising new ones like the ubiquitous value added tax (VAT).
The increase in taxation, in turn, leads to a further slowing down in
the economy; the revenue out of which the debt must be paid also
falls. The end result is that the debt continues to grow until it
threatens to consume the people, especially women and children who
are hardest hit by these cuts, and the land itself. The combined debt of
Latin American countries rose from $75 billion in 1975 to $360 billion
ten years later. Politicians, economists, religious leaders and now
even many bankers realize that these debts will never be repaid.
However, rather than tackle the problem in a comprehensive and
radical way, bankers and First World politicians stumble along from
one stop-gap solution to another. The present policies are motivated
by selfishness on the part of the banks and cowardice and indecision
on the part of First World political leaders.
    The political and social fall-out from such short-sighted policies is
obvious. It fuels a growing unrest and swells the ranks of insurgency
movements. In response to the unrest, many Third World governments abandon any attempt at democracy and adopt a mailed fist
approach to dissidents. Repressive labour legislation often leads to
social unrest. Debtor governments respond by calling in the army and
suspending civil liberties. Often martial law is declared and the
military brush aside the civil government. Even as a temporary
measure this can only be done by expanding the army considerably
and wasting scarce capital on military salaries and hardware. Increased oppression, human rights abuses and curtailment of personal
freedom follow. It is generally agreed that debt repayments were a
significant element in the proliferation and continuation of military
dictatorships in Latin America and in the Philippines in the 1970s.
The fragile democracies which have emerged in some Latin American
countries and the Philippines will not survive unless there is some

relief from debt payments. President Alfonsin of Argentina said succinctly that 'increased debt payments can only be taken out of the account of democracy'.

The social repercussions are also evident. Countries saddled with a huge debt, like the Philippines and Brazil, have no money for expanding and improving education. In the 1989 Philippine budget a mere 10.9 per cent was allocated to education.[7] It is generally recognized that the present educational services are totally inadequate to meet the needs of the people. With an annual growth rate of 2.7 per cent, the population is expected to double within 30 years. This means that the government must double its educational services just to keep them at their present level. Yet today it is estimated that there are 5.8 million Filipinos who can neither read nor write.

Education is not the only service which is suffering. Health services are rudimentary and declining in effectiveness. A visit to a barrio health centre or provincial hospital will leave one in no doubt about the present deplorable state of the health services. At the root of much of the problem are present budgetary constraints which means that the salaries of health workers are low, especially in the rural area. The high salaries available in First World countries and the Middle East attract an increasing number of Filipino doctors and nurses. Once again the Third World effectively gives aid to First World countries. The overseas drain on medical personnel leaves only 1,155 rural health officers to take care of 40,000 local communities. Clinics and hospitals lucky enough to have health workers are hampered by lack of medical supplies and drugs. Diseases which can easily be cured, like tuberculosis, pneumonia, malaria, cholera, typhoid, dysentery and other intestinal diseases, take a huge toll. Beyond the medical care there are no adequate programmes to help the 70 per cent of the population who are suffering from some degree of malnutrition.[8] The present monetarist policies of the International Monetary Fund will not improve the health or educational status of the poor in Third World countries.

Against this background a document from the Vatican's Pontifical Commission for Justice and Peace entitled *An Ethical Approach to the International Debt Question*,[9] insists that industrialized countries and international banks cannot act 'without regard for the effects of their own policies on other nations'. Such pleas from religious leaders and Third World peoples have, so far, fallen on deaf ears.

To date it appears that bankers are more interested in presenting their investors with a glowing quarterly report of increased profits than in alleviating the misery and pain which their policies are causing. Few bankers are willing to face the stark fact that their policies are causing starvation and squalor for millions of people. Perhaps they are not fully aware of how their policies simply empty the already depleted food basket of the majority of Third World people.

As they are set up at present it is impossible for the World Bank and the International Monetary Fund to serve the interests of the poor. They are controlled by First World countries and were moreover designed with the needs of First World countries in mind. If these run into trouble with their fiscal policies they can readily bargain with the fund. Third World countries are not in such a strong position and thus they have little room for manoeuvre. These countries usually have no option but to pay their debts, otherwise international financial institutions turn off the tap and starve the country of the foreign currency which is essential to keep their economies ticking over. Without it they cannot pay for needed energy, agricultural inputs or industrial spare parts.

The case of Jamaica

A look at Jamaica shows that the medicine is in fact killing and not curing the patient. In her book *A Fate Worse Than Debt*, Susan George discusses what has happened in Jamaica over the past decade and a half. The economy should be in robust condition since, in many ways, it is a showcase of IMF orthodoxy. In the 1950s and 1960s the government encouraged an export-orientated economy based on bauxite mines, fruit plantations and tourism. Initially the strategy seemed to work: the economy expanded at an annual rate of 5 or 6 per cent, and the government made significant gains in the social and educational fields. Few noticed the hidden costs involved in this transformation of the tropical paradise. To fuel the export boom the government was forced to borrow so heavily that Jamaica has now one of the heaviest per capita debts in the world.

The quadrupling of oil prices in the early 1970s, combined with the drop in commodity prices, suddenly punctured the Jamaican economy. Investment dried up, jobs vanished, wages dropped and poverty increased. The government of Michael Manley, which was perceived to be left of centre, especially by the US administration, attempted to initiate policies and programmes in the area of health, education and land reform design to benefit the majority of the people. The rise in oil prices, coupled with plummeting commodity prices, the international recession and the flight of capital, resulted in the foreign debt jumping from $150 million to $813 million between 1971 and 1976. The government simply ran out of foreign exchange and was forced to suspend all payment.

The IMF stepped on to this stage wielding its surgeon's scalpel in one hand to cut social spending; whilst with the other it pursued the interests of free enterprise. It demanded huge cuts in public spending and a reversal of the government's policies aimed at redistributing wealth. The results were predictable: an increase in unemployment and inflation, a downturn in economic activity, a dramatic rise in the foreign debt itself and a defeat for the Manley government which had been forced to undertake such a U-turn on its social commitments.

In 1980, the right-wing government of Edward Seaga was elected. This coincided with the arrival of President Ronald Reagan in the White House. President Reagan welcomed the defeat of a left-wing government in the Caribbean, in what he termed 'the US's backyard'. His administration therefore helped to secure a package of foreign aid, soft loans and access to the US markets for Jamaican goods. The aim was to make Jamaica a showcase of how a strengthened private sector could lead a country to economic recovery. By 1985 the Jamaican government was claiming a huge victory as the balance of payments had been turned around from substantial deficit to a major saving. It takes some deft financial footwork to claim that a balance of payments saving is really a sign of a healthy economy when, at the same time the national debt has more than doubled to $3.3 billion, basic services have been cut or become prohibitively expensive and the indicators of malnutrition have risen steadily. The bankers and the rich minority of Jamaicans, who have undoubtedly reaped higher profits, were delighted with the direction in which their package of adjustments steered the economy, but the poor are burdened by massively increased food prices and there is no let-up in sight. The landslide victory for Michael Manley in February 1989 is perhaps an indication of the scale of the suffering. It is, however, significant that he has had to soften his left-wing stance considerably.

Ecological impact of the debt crisis

While the impact of the debt crisis on health, housing and education are often discussed by economists, politicians, trade unionists, religious leaders and farmers, the ecological implications of what is happening was overlooked until very recently. This is most unfortunate because the ecological consequences are really the most serious and enduring. When the earth is disfigured and its fruitfulness impaired, then every succeeding generation of people living in the affected areas is automatically condemned to poverty. In the long term, as I have said, even First World countries will be condemned to a similar fate. No bright tomorrow can be built on eroded wastelands, toxic rivers or lifeless oceans.

This is clearly recognized by the Catholic bishops of the Philippines in their January 1988 Pastoral Letter on environmental degradation entitled *What Is Happening To Our Beautiful Land?* (see Appendix 2 below, pp. 207–16.) In the introductory paragraph the bishops state that the present social and economic decline is intimately linked to a deteriorating environment and that the damage is both extensive and often irreversible and thus will adversely affect every generation of Filipinos yet to come.

The Philippines is now at a critical point in its history. For the past number of years we have experienced political instability, economic decline and a growth in armed conflict. Almost every day the media highlight one or other of these problems. The banner headlines absorb our attention so much so that we tend to overlook a more deep-seated crisis which, we believe, lies at the root of many of our economic and political problems. To put it simply: *our country is in peril*. All the living systems on land and in the seas around us are being ruthlessly exploited. *The damage to date is extensive and sad to say, it is often irreversible.* (Emphasis mine)[10]

The international debt is contributing to the destruction of the tropical rainforest in Latin America, Africa and the Philippines. The destruction of the forest is a biological catastrophe for the Philippines and the community of the living. Thousands of living species will be lost for ever. This is what makes the destruction so damaging and irreversible. Since we do not see it happening in our backyard we tend to be unaware of its magnitude and implications. The flora and fauna of the tropical forest, especially in some of the highest debtor countries like Brazil, Mexico, Colombia and Indonesia, are rich in food, in medicinal plants and animals. Writing in *The Guardian* (7 February 1989), Peter Montagnon estimates that 40 per cent of all prescription drugs sold in the United States are derived from tropical forest plants or animals. Yet only a small fraction of the riches of the forest has been put under the microscope and classified. The extinction of hundreds of thousands of species will effectively deprive the human community of potentially valuable and still largely unexplored sources of food and medicines. There are an estimated 80,000 species of edible plant, none of which has been cultivated, in the tropical rainforests of the world.[11] In recent years a drug derived from a plant in the forests of Madagascar has provided new hope for young leukaemia sufferers. Cures for many forms of cancer and possibly AIDS may well come from the tropical forest, and its destruction closes off fruitful avenues of possible research.

The long-term effects of sterilizing planet earth are not predictable. Biological and geological history tell us that it is sheer madness recklessly to tear apart the fabric of the living world and not expect trouble. We know already that important and even essential ecosystems like rainforests and mudflats will be permanently impaired and may even collapse altogether. Any creature that depends on these, including ultimately ourselves, will go down in the crash.

Apart from losing species and genetic diversity, the ruin of the forest sets in motion a disastrous pattern of events which is discussed in more detail in Chapter 3. Deforestation leads to soil erosion, flooding in built-up areas, destruction of the marine environment, climatic changes and desertification.

The problem of irreversible damage

As I have repeatedly pointed out in this chapter, much of the damage being inflicted on fragile ecosystems is irreversible in historical time, especially in tropical countries. This fact is not being faced up to sufficiently in the majority of the current books and articles on the effects of the debt crisis. Most of these recommend a mix of measures which are designed to ease the problem and turn around ailing economies. The proponents believe that a judicious mix of debt cancellation married to more equitable fiscal, monetary and trading policies could accomplish this within a few years. According to the present economic calculus there is no reason why indebted nations cannot once again become prosperous. There are numerous examples of this happening in recent economic history. Japan, Germany and the newly industrialized countries of Taiwan, Korea, and Singapore immediately spring to mind.

But there is one important proviso which will spoil this bright scenario. There is no hope for survival, let alone for prosperity, if the natural world is permanently impaired. Any wealth that is not based on the preservation of a healthy and sustainable environment is illusory and will not survive. For too long our industrial and economic policies have been detached from the realities of the natural world. Every now and then we are brought back down to earth with a jolt. The 1988 drought in the US heartland revived fears of another dust-bowl in the breadbasket of the world — with all the dire consequences for the poor, who will face inevitable ruin as food prices increase. Farmers are conscious that, while they may not have too much control over the rains, they do have control over their farming methods and they know that stripping trees and vegetation from their farms opens the way for dust storms and the loss of precious topsoil. Unfortunately, memories are short and the lessons of the dust storms in the US in the 1930s, and in Melbourne in the 1970s, seem to have been forgotten by government officials, most of whom live in cities. When a particular crisis passes, government officials and farmers quickly forget the danger and return to viewing the world as a bottomless mine to be recklessly exploited in the pursuit of short-term profits. Unless we abandon this way of thinking immediately, the mine will soon be exhausted.

AIDS of the earth

Many people are rightly concerned about the rapid spread of the AIDS virus in this decade. This plague is now threatening large population groups in Africa, America and Europe. Governments and private organizations have responded in a variety of ways. Vast sums of money have been made available for research into the disease with a view to developing a vaccine to halt its spread and a cure for those who are already suffering from it. Extensive educational campaigns have been mounted to tell people about the disease and to allay unfounded fears. This co-operation, which transcends national boundaries, is a very positive sign. It shows a willingness to commit resources and human energies to a project which threatens a vast number of human beings. This is very laudable, and I would like to see more resources made available to combat AIDS and to care for those who are suffering from the disease.

It is worth pointing out that the interlocked web of destruction which is presently being inflicted on the earth is akin to AIDS. All the elements which underwrite life for the body of nature are being weakened in very real and serious ways. The immune system of the earth is under attack. The consequences will be felt, not just by a single species, but by all our fellow creatures and by the water, the air and the land. For some it will mean not merely a reduction in numbers, but extinction. The roll-call of extinction signals that the land which underpins our survival is now under threat.

Cutbacks scuttle environmental protection programmes

I was very conscious of the role the international debt plays in undermining environmental protection during a four-hour meeting between the Minister for the Environment and Natural Resources, Mr Fulgencio Factoran, and thirteen bishops which took place on 12 May 1988 in Davao City. The meeting arose out of the Philippine bishops' concern for the widespread deterioration of the environment which was expressed in the pastoral letter quoted above. As meetings go, this one was quite cordial with both sides sincerely trying to understand the concerns of the other. Though the debt crisis was not mentioned directly it hovered like an invisible hand guiding almost every exchange between the parties.

Every one of the bishops expressed serious reservations about the impact of the logging industry in their diocese. Alarmed by the cycle of destruction which is now clearly visible even to town and city people, many Christian leaders, including the bishops, favour a total ban on large-scale commercial logging. Without the logging ban, all the remaining forest will disappear within a decade or so. But a logging ban is not feasible for political and economic reasons. This is not due entirely to the formidable political clout which the logging industry can wield. It is due to the fact that the industry brings in some foreign exchange. One cannot lay everything at the door of the debt crisis. It is possible that the Philippine government would still support logging and mining interests even if there was no debt crisis;

still the debt is an albatross around the government's neck which does not allow it the luxury of exploring alternative economic policies even if it wished to.

At the Davao meeting the bishops also expressed concern about the quantities of mercury being dumped in the river systems of Mindanao as a result of the recent gold rushes in various parts of the island. Once again regulatory controls cannot be imposed because of the need to generate foreign exchange *now*. The government is forced to champion almost any venture that will rake in foreign exchange, which is tantamount to extending invitations to polluting and toxic industries which are no longer welcome in First World countries.

A glaring local example is the approval which the Assistant Secretary for Local Government, Saidanen Dangarunan, gave to an American company, LPT Developments Inc., to build a toxic-waste incineration plant at Iligan City. At a public meeting in October 1987 called to oppose the plan, speaker after speaker pointed to the known health and environmental hazards of such a plant. The by-products of such high-temperature incineration include oxides of sulphur and nitrogen and organometallic compounds which are known to have mutagenic and carcinogenic effects. For this reason strict environmental laws and public opinion make it very difficult to build such incineration plants in the USA. Since American companies produce 264 million tons of hazardous waste every year according to Winston Porter of the Environmental Protection Agency (EPA), some place must be found to dispose of it. The easy solution is to export it to Third World countries where the environmental laws are less stringent.[12]

Cutbacks due to debt adjustment policies are also hampering environmental protection programmes in Brazil. 1988 witnessed the most extensive burning ever to have taken place of the Amazon forest. In fact, it was one of the largest fires ever to burn on planet Earth. The scale of the despoliation — to make way for cattle ranches — drew protests from ecological organizations from all over the world and even from First World governments. The protests do not spring completely from altruistic motives. Westerners are beginning to realize that the Amazon fires pump billions of tonnes of carbon into the atmosphere. This is contributing significantly to the greenhouse effect. A warming of the earth's climate could spell disaster for low-lying countries like Bangladesh, Holland and part of England. These countries will have to spend billions of dollars protecting themselves from rising sea levels. It could also trigger climatic changes which would create a desert in the US breadbasket. This awareness of the interlinked nature of worldwide ecological problems is beginning to dawn on many nations right around the world.

In September 1988, in response to the international outcry, President Sarney announced a series of measures to protect the Amazon.

Nevertheless, within a few days of this announcement the President closed down Brazil's Forest Protection Service (IBDF), the only agency which could do something to curtail logging and stem the annual burning. The agency was abolished as part of an austerity, anti-inflationary package. Environmental agencies are one of the softest targets for budget cuts even when they are desperately needed. Mexico City, for example, is notorious worldwide for its poor air quality, yet the pollution control centre was one of the first agencies to be targeted for cutbacks in 1985.[13]

As we have seen, countries with huge debts like Brazil and the Philippines have less capital available to monitor what is happening to the environment and to heal the damage that has already been done. Any serious attempt to regenerate the dipterocarp forests on the bald hills and mountains of the Philippines will take billions of dollars. Over 16 million hectares should be replanted. This scale of expenditure is essential to guarantee the future of sustainable agriculture in this tropical archipelago. Rehabilitating coral reefs and replanting mangrove forests will also be expensive. The mix of measures needed to curb soil erosion and to move agriculture away from its present reliance on dwindling petrochemicals will cost further billions. These programmes cannot remain forever on the back burner. Unless they are begun soon a black future looms ahead for many Filipinos.

Even the truncated land-reform bill which finally made its way through a reluctant Congress in May 1988 will not be implemented without a huge infusion of capital. *Time* (20 June 1988) quotes a government source as stating that it will eventually cost $70 billion to implement the programme and this presumably does not include the cost of promoting organic, ecologically sound farming methods and improved markets for farmers.

Solidarity for survival

In the light of this extensive and growing threat to the biosphere, a phrase in a recent Vatican document on *An Ethical Approach to the International Debt Question* captured what people are challenged to do today. It speaks of the necessity of global co-operation and 'solidarity for survival'. The authors are thinking primarily of economic, political and cultural survival, since the ecological dimension of the debt crisis is not highlighted in the document. In the light of the foregoing presentation it is obvious that solidarity for survival must also include this basic biological and ecological dimension. The loggers who thoughtlessly cut down the tropical forest are killing the earth; so too are the merchants who deal in toxic waste and palm it off on unsuspecting Third World countries. Meanwhile, Dodong and millions like him are chipping away at the very web of life. The first three are driven by the need for higher profits while Dodong is forced to do what he does in order to survive today. All — in one way or another — are driven on by insane economic policies dictated by debt repayments.

Some solutions to the Third World debt crisis

Extricating First World financial institutions

A number of solutions have been put forward to solve the Third World debt crisis. By now it should be clear that the IMF-inspired approaches involve enormous hardships for people, exacerbate the debt and destroy the environment. Other similar approaches have been proposed by representatives of the First World in recent years. The best known is the Baker Plan, which was proposed at the 1985 meeting of the World Bank IMF in Seoul by the then Secretary of the US Treasury, James Baker. The plan encouraged commercial banks and multilateral lending agencies like the World Bank and IMF to make more loans available to indebted countries in order to help them to work their way out of debt. Very poor African countries were earmarked for special attention. Eligibility for the new loans required a willingness to agree to further IMF-style economic remedies.

The Baker Plan found favour with First World bankers and governments. The bankers were happy to see their risks being reduced since under the plan they would be working in tandem with the various multilateral lending agencies. There was little in the plan, however, for debtor countries to enthuse over. The amount of new loans involved in the plan paled in comparison with the size of their debts. Their experience of ten years under the tutelage of IMF-inspired economics had taught them to be wary. Instead of alleviating their debt, the plan could lead to more indebtedness and the impoverishment of their people. As a result, few of the major league debtor nations chose to avail themselves of the plan: only Ecuador, with a relatively small debt of $8 billion, joined the programme.

Another plan devised in the North is that of US Senator Bill Bradley. Though he was critical of the Baker Plan, Bradley's primary aim was to protect the Western financial system and particularly US markets. In order to benefit from relief, countries would have to liberalize their trading arrangements and allow free entry of US-produced goods into their country. Bradley's hope was that debt relief would allow countries to relax a little and not expend so much energy producing goods which in the previous decade had virtually wiped out traditional US markets through an exclusively export-oriented drive.

In March 1989, Nicholas Brady, the Treasury Secretary in the administration of President Bush, announced a new plan to tackle the Third World debt. The Brady Plan had the familiar extra $20 billion new loans package to be made available through the World Bank–IMF with the usual greater austerity strings attached. In one area the plan signalled a departure from the Baker Plan. It began to face up to the need for substantial debt forgiveness. It suggests that this might run to between 20 and 35 per cent of the debt of individual countries. The riots and deaths in Venezuela, which any astute political observer could see spreading to other Third World countries unless the debt burden was reduced, may well have tipped the balance in favour of this new realism. Some people, however, point out that the percentage of debt forgiveness envisaged in the Brady Plan is not enough to allow these economies to grow and thus pay back their debt. Despite the initial favourable reaction from some indebted countries, by August 1989 it seemed that the Brady Plan was destined to follow the Baker Plan into the wastepaper basket of financial initiatives. Most indebted countries were cautious about the plan; in fact, only Mexico had agreed to it and the private banks were still loath to begin writing off debts. It seems that the banks only joined in the Mexico deal because of pressure from the US Treasury officials.[14] The banks are more interested in juggling the debt money in new ways. Profits are being made from Third World debts being sold on First World financial markets at discounts, some debts for 30 per cent of their face value.[15] Traders on these debt markets can make a killing. The value of the Venezuelan debt, for example, rose by 48 per cent between March and July 1989.[16]

Debt-for-equity swaps
Debt-for-equity swaps are favoured by banks as another way of squeezing as much money as they can out of debtor nations. Under the scheme, a person or corporation interested in investing in a foreign country or expanding his operation there can negotiate with private banks who hold some of the country's foreign debt to buy that debt at a discount rate. The investor now turns creditor and sells this debt back to the Third World country. He is paid the full dollar value of the debt in local currency which he can then invest in equity in existing firms or in new local ventures. It is easy to see how this mechanism allows transnational corporations to invest cheaply in highly profitable operations in debtor countries, taking over national industries and other assets eg land. Ford and other US car manufacturers used debt-for-equity to buy cheap car plants in Mexico.[17] Some debtor countries, like the military dictatorship in Chile, have seen this as an acceptable way to privatize moribund state corporations. Yet the bias against the Third World country is clear from the fact that the country itself cannot buy back its own debt at knockdown prices. This gives First World countries more direct control over Third World economies. The Peruvian historian, Heraclio Bonilla, points out that a debt-for-equity swap in the late nineteenth

century between Peru and British bond-holders resulted in the 'complete economic colonization of the country'.[18]

The debt-for-equity swap also fuels inflation in Third World countries — there is an understandable urge to print more local currency to redeem the debt which is denominated in 'hard' currency.[19] Raising funds locally to buy foreign debt will also push up interest rates and turn the foreign debt into a ballooning domestic one. This in turn will cut available financial resources for social, education and medical programmes.

The most pernicious aspect of the debt-for-equity swap is that it presumes that the debt is legitimate and that the present economic order is fair and just and that a solution to the present crisis must emerge from playing according to the present rules. The truth is that the rules are drawn up by First World countries and that they are heavily stacked in their favour. This chapter argues that the present worldwide economic system is, in fact, stealing precious resources from the poor and at the same time bankrolling the destruction of the biosphere. This is the real bottom line, so any solution to the debt crisis demands drastic changes in the current international economic, social and political order.

Some swaps can operate in a positive way as long as they are not seen as a panacea for solving the debt crisis and they do not distract attention from the underlying causes which provoked the crisis in the first place. An agreement signed between the Sudanese government and the Midland Bank (Britain's fourth largest commercial bank) may well pave the way for a new, more creative way for the banks to cope with a certain percentage of the international debt. Under the agreement the Sudanese government will exchange the debt, with a face value of $800,000, for local currency which will then be used to finance a UNICEF health, reforestation and water programme in the drought-stricken central Kordofan area of the country. It is estimated that about 5,000 villagers will benefit from this scheme.

The growth of the Green Movement worldwide has given impetus to one form of debt swap known as the debt-for-nature swap. This has received cautious support from environmentalists. In a speech at the *International Citizens' Conference on the World Bank*, during the 1988 World Bank/IMF meeting in Berlin, the Brazilian ecologist José Lutzenberger recommended that the World Bank should help arrange agreements between borrowing and lending countries in which some portion of the Third World's debt is forgiven in return for guarantees to protect the forest and other important wilderness areas.

A number of such relatively small transactions have already taken place. A group called Conservation International purchased $650,000 worth of the Bolivian debt for $100,000. The equivalent money in local currency will be used to expand and maintain the reserve at Roi Beni. Critics of this project, however, insist that the money has not been used to protect an endangered wilderness area. Rather it was used to 'develop' an area where logging is still being promoted. Also the scheme was devised and implemented without real consultation with the indigenous people of the area.[20] In Costa Rica, the debt-for-forest swap has been used to finance reforestation projects at Guanacaste. The World Wildlife Fund (now the World Wide Fund for Nature) purchased $10 million worth of Ecuadorian debt at a discount. A local ecological organization, Fundación Natura, will oversee the use of this money for research and the protection of biodiversity.

Apart from the proper management of funds to ensure that it does not end up in the wrong pocket, critics of the debt-for-nature swap say it has a whiff of a new kind of paternalism and colonialism about it. Here again are First World people, who have often destroyed their own environment, lecturing Third World people about how to preserve their environment which, incidentally, is being destroyed by First-World-driven economic policies. If the boot were on the other foot and foreigners, for example, the Japanese, decided to use their financial power as the US's largest creditor to buy the Grand Canyon and administer it in a way that the Japanese thought fit, there would be a public outcry in the United States.

One cannot overemphasize the need for sensitivity when dealing with the sovereignty issue. One way to defuse it is for First World nations to make substantial financial and other resources available to Third World countries outside the context of the debt-for-nature mechanism. In fact, the debt-for-nature swap can only operate on a relatively modest scale, whereas the need for environmental rehabilitation is extremely serious in most Third World tropical countries. Remedial action will not come cheaply. Dr Norman Myers, writing in *The Guardian* (30 October 1988), estimated that an effective reforestation programme worldwide would cost over $120 billion. Many would consider this a small price to pay by way of global insurance.

It is also important to remember that the sovereignty argument is often used by the elite in Third World countries to protect their right to plunder their own environment. The ordinary Filipino or Brazilian citizen has gained little and lost much by the exploitation of the rainforest. Many would appreciate a certain amount of outside leverage to support their claims for land reform, improved social services and more protection of the environment.

Given the environmental costs of the debt crisis, support for debt relief and environmental protection is one of the best long-term investments which First World governments and multilateral funding agencies could make at this time.

As I have argued consistently, the Third World debt is not just an economic problem. Any single strategy, for example, the debt-for-nature swap, cannot solve the debt problem. There are political, social, ecological and trading dimensions to the problem which need to be faced. Transferring ownership from private banks to non-government aid, environmental organizations or Church-related groups is not going to improve matters for the poor of Third World countries. Any lasting solution demands a new economic order, one which espouses a reorientation of development priorities away from the Western model. Hence a fair price for commodities produced in Third World countries is essential, as well as lower and more stable interest rates internationally. In addition, a world development fund to be administered by countries from the North and the South and to be spent on providing food, health services, water for the poor and protection of the environment could also be considered.

There is strength in working together

Political co-operation among debtor countries is also important. Creditor countries are already united in their demands to pay up, speaking through agencies like the IMF. To date, the multilateral funding agencies and private banks prefer to deal on a case-to-case basis with debtor countries, which amounts to little more than the traditional colonial tactics of divide and rule. This policy is aimed at ensuring that, if any country wishes unilaterally to repudiate its debt or restrict payments — as Brazil tried to do in 1987 — then the international financial community can simply gang up on the culprit and frog-march it back into line.

There is also need for flexibility and pragmatism since no single strategy will solve the crisis. While there are commonalities in the problems facing individual countries and hemispheres, the problems facing sub-Saharan Africa are not exactly those facing Latin America. Compromises will also be necessary. Some oil-exporting countries like Nigeria, Mexico and Venezuela would benefit from a stiff rise in oil prices. This would exacerbate the debt problem for the Philippines and Brazil which have no oil.

Debtor countries can help sustain and co-ordinate the demands for debt cancellation which are now emerging among their own people and from First World non-government organizations and Church-related groups which are working to promote justice and peace. Only through such co-ordination and efficient organization of networks can sufficient pressure be brought to bear on the banks and on First World governments. In particular the connection between Third World debt and the loss of jobs and environmental repercussions in First World countries must be made clear. If ordinary First World citizens can be made to see that the only ones really profiting are the banks, their shareholders and the Third World elite, then they will more readily exert political pressure on First World politicians.

A rising clamour to cancel the debts

Increasingly many people's organizations in Third World countries themselves see debt cancellation as the only effective way to help most debtors to recover from the present crisis even when their governments, for example the Aquino administration in the Philippines, are still intent on marching to the IMF/World Bank drum. The Freedom of Debt Coalition (FDC) in the Philippines insists that Filipinos need a respite to get back on their feet. This coalition of 100 organizations is planning to move simultaneously on a number of fronts.

It has challenged the Aquino government's subservient attitude towards multilateral lending agencies (the IMF/World Bank) and supported a bill in the Philippine Senate which would limit debt service to 15 per cent of foreign exchange earnings. The FDC is particularly insistent that banks which often encouraged the borrowing should also be forced to assume responsibility for their reckless behaviour. The University of the Philippines economist Dr Manuel Montes, who is prominent in the FDC, argues that each claimant on the debt should be forced to produce all the papers relevant to the particular debt to determine who is really responsible for it. Much of the debt benefited Marcos's supporters and it is they who should be held responsible for it, not the government, since it will have to use the taxes of the poor to guarantee and repay the debt. Until many of the questions relating to who really owns the foreign debt and whether the country has the capacity to pay are investigated more thoroughly, the FDC insists that the Philippines government should declare a moratorium on the debt.

The poor should not be forced to pay for the folly and luxury of the rich. No taxpayers' money, particularly money extracted from the poor through indirect taxation, should be used to service the debt on the nuclear plant in Bataan or any of the debt which is tainted with fraud.[21] In its rather uninspiring language the Vatican document on debt leans in this direction when it exhorts multinational financial organizations to recognize the subhuman living conditions in which the poor are forced to live because of debt repayments. The document states that 'there is always the danger of remaining on the level of theoretical, technical or bureaucratic solutions, while at stake are human lives, the development of peoples and solidarity among nations'.[22]

Non-government aid organizations, Church and environmental groups in the First World can help indebted countries in a number of ways. Again a variety of strategies are essential. One important role is to support research activity on the indebtedness of each country. The Philippine Resource Centre in London prepared a paper on *'The UK banks and the Philippine debt'*.[23] This information is vital when it comes to more direct lobbying of any of the actors involved in the debt drama — the Philippine government, the British government, the multilateral lending agencies or the private banks. It is also crucial for an effective media campaign in both First and Third World countries to inform people about the consequences of the present debt crisis. Much more political pressure needs to be applied to First World governments and to the banks. The leaders of the seven major Western industrialized economies felt no urgency to solve the Third World debt at the economic summit in Paris in July 1989, primarily because the First World public do not see it as a major issue. The media need to highlight the social and environmental cost of the debt to the planet and also the cost to ordinary workers in First World economies.[24] An editorial in *The Australian* (20 March 1989) asked whether 'by insisting on payment the West is not cutting off its nose to spite its face'.

The banks and First World governments, however, are wary of debt cancellations. They say that it will rock the financial system to its foundations and bring everything down in one gigantic crash. Yet one wonders whether this argument really holds water. On a single day in October 1987 more money was wiped off the price of shares than is contained in the combined debts of all the Third World countries, yet the financial system survived that trauma.

Pay debts into a development fund

Susan George in her book *A Fate Worse Than Debt*[25] does not recommend outright cancellation of debts because that would benefit the Marcos cronies and make the debtor country an economic pariah. She feels that the debt, which is at present sucking the life-blood from poor countries, could be transformed into an instrument for promoting genuine development and democracy. Approaching the problem this way, moreover, would forestall First World countries' washing their hands of any responsibility for the plight of Third World people once unpayable debts were forgiven. George envisages negotiations taking place between a debtor country and a body somewhat like the IMF. It goes without saying that this body would need to be much more representative of Third World countries and interests and more sensitive to their needs. These negotiations might then determine what percentage of the country's GNP might be used for debt servicing. This money could then be lodged in a national development fund to be administered by local people chosen or elected in a democratic way. There is a twofold goal here: first to promote genuine democracy by having ordinary people participate in the process, particularly at local levels, and secondly, to ensure that new money is not squandered once again on grandiose projects, but rather used to promote genuine development with pride of place being given to meeting the basic needs of the people, especially the need for locally produced food.

Her second suggestion is along the lines of the debt-for-nature swap. It would include using the money to preserve the environment and local cultural and artistic traditions. This might help to atone for the sins of colonialism and also help to build real bridges of concern and friendship between First World and Third World countries. The knowledge and mutual understanding which might be expected to result from this effort to understand and share the riches of a variety of human cultures would also be a major stimulus to peace. The various undertakings involved in these programmes from, for example, conserving a biologically rich area of forest or collating local knowledge of herbal medicine, could be assigned a monetary value and the debt written down accordingly. According to Susan George,

> The ultimate goal of repayment in kind and in [local cash] is to strengthen the peasantry, the pastoralist and the agricultural sector and thus work towards the elimination of hunger, and the poverty on which hunger thrives, to rehabilitate the environment and to provide income-generating activities for people who live in it.[26]

The above process would involve abandoning the traditional capital-intensive, export-oriented development model which most developing countries have been pursuing since World War II. This has often amounted to little more than a new form of slavery. Workers are paid a pittance, as little as 10 per cent of what their counterparts in First World countries receive, they are forced to work in conditions which are a health hazard and are often not allowed to go on strike. The only feasible approach in the future is to pursue the kind of development which will benefit the vast majority of the people and not endanger the environment. This means abandoning plantation agriculture in favour of a return to small-scale, ecologically sound family farming. A thriving rural market fully integrated into the local economy would once again be the focus of commercial attention rather than the external markets with the prices for commodities which have been fixed in some foreign capital. It would also mean investing in people and providing basic health care and adequate nutrition, especially in rural areas. It entails supporting small-scale local industries which are designed to meet local needs for household goods, agricultural development, transport and energy and the use of appropriate technologies. The major pitfall with this strategy is that, unless it is carefully managed, it could easily fuel inflationary pressures — particularly if the government simply prints money with little consideration for the long-term effect on the economy. Personally, I would like to see a central role for non-government organizations in all of this. Government bureaucracies rarely change their spots!

Additional money needs to be made available to speed up these goals, otherwise Third World economies will languish in a dangerous economic and social limbo. Beyond that we need to take seriously the renewed call of Pope John Paul II to redouble our efforts to develop a more just economic order.[27] No time should be lost. The human pain of mounting debts is plain for all to see. It can only increase as the debt burden grows and stop-gap solutions, like those contained in the Baker Plan, are seen to be ineffective. Rescheduling and lengthening the periods of maturity for loans only postpones the day of reckoning. Beyond this the pain of the earth, in terms of environmental degradation will haunt the world for ever unless remedial action is taken now. This generation is blessed in that we have the means to do all of this. What we lack thus far is simply the will.

The year of grace

Many religious leaders, like Bishop De Jong of Zambia, call for the cancellation of their country's foreign debt.[28] There is a solid biblical basis for this approach, which is designed to alleviate intolerable poverty and growing despair in Third World countries. The Year of Jubilee was seen as an attempt to re-establish a just social order at regular moments in the history of Israel. The excess land which had been accumulated by the rich and powerful often through questionable means was to be restored to the original owners (Lev 25:23–31). Verse 28 states explicitly, 'In the Jubilee Year, the latter [the purchaser of property] must relinquish it [the property which he has bought] and return to his own property.'

The Jubilee Year also involved the cancellation of debts:

At the end of every seven years you must grant a remission.
Now the nature of the remission is this: every creditor who
holds the person of his neighbour in bond must grant him
remission; he may not exact payment from his fellow or his
brother once the latter appeals to Yahweh (Deut 15:1–2).

This was considered essential if Israel was once again to become a real community united in the service of Yahweh and not just a nation where the few who owned everything flourished and the have-nots lived on the verge of starvation. Verse 5 of the same text exhorts the Israelites 'Let there be no poor among you'.

Exodus 22:25 warns those who lend that they must not impoverish the poor and grind them into the ground:

If you lend money to any of my people, to any poor man
among you, you must not play the usurer with him: you must
not demand interest from him.

If you take another's cloak as a pledge, you must give it back to
him before sunset. It is all the covering he has; it is the cloak he
wraps his body in; what else would he sleep in? If he cries to
me, I will listen, for I am full of pity.

This desire to transform society did not emerge from a vague sense
of pity for the poor; it was seen as a demand of God's justice. His
Covenant did not envisage a community where a few would live in
abundance and the rest in misery (Deut 15:4–11). A lively concern for
the less fortunate which expressed itself in concrete action is to be the
hallmark of the community of God's people. The earth, after all, is the
Lord's (Ps 24:1) and he wishes all people to share the goods of the
earth to meet their basic needs. Cardinal Arns of Sao Paulo has
pointed out that when interest rates rise, 'thousands die in the Third
World because the money that would be used for health care and food
is sent outside these countries to pay the debt'.[29]

Economic activity should be organized to meet the basic needs of
all people. Writing to the Corinthians, Paul was not shy about asking
them to help out their less well-off brothers and sisters in Jerusalem:

I am not trying to relieve others by putting a burden on you;
but since you have plenty at this time, it is only fair that you
should help those who are in need. Then, when you are in need
and they have plenty, they will help you. In this way both are
treated equally. As the scripture says, 'The one who gathered
much did not have too much, and the one who gathered little
did not have too little' (2 Cor 8:13–15).

It is not difficult to see that Third World debts are having similar
effects on those described above, not just on individual poor people
but on vast population groups. They are losing their cloaks, their
homes, their food, their very way of life and the world that sustains all
life. This is why someone like Fr Eugene Thalman insists that the
present debt crisis is not unlike the situation which the 'year of
release' addressed to Israel.[30] Now is the opportune moment for
political and financial leaders in First World countries to initiate a
Jubilee in regard to Third World debtor countries.

In October 1989 the Catholic Bishops' Conference of the United
States issued a lengthy statement on Third World debt. *Relieving Third
World Debt* argued that 'both the nature of the original agreements
and the attempts of some debtors to repay them lead us to the
conviction that no single principle can govern all the different
situations of indebtedness. We believe that in many instances the
presumptive obligation to repay should be overriden or modified
because of the social costs imposed on the poor.'[31]

Grounded on the principles of Catholic social teaching enunciated in recent encyclicals and pastoral letters, especially on justice, solidarity and the obligation to promote the common good of all, the bishops put forward the following recommendations to resolve the Third World debt crisis.[32]

a. The primary objective ought to be to assist in revitalizing the economies of debt-burdened countries and to help poor people participate in their economy and improve their quality of life; in general, the greatest help should be provided for the greatest need.

b. Any debt solution ought to preserve the basic human rights of the people and the autonomy and independence of the debtor nation.

c. Responsibility for the solution ought to be shared equitably by both creditors and debtor countries, especially by the wealthier segments of their societies; the burden should not continue to be borne disproportionately by poor people.

d. The solution should not increase the debt; generally, less money going out of the country is better than more money coming in.

e. Some immediate benefit should be obtained by the debtor country, especially for poor people.

f. Criteria established for adjusting debt should take into account the extent to which those responsible are accountable to their people and how human rights are fostered and protected in the debtor country, what the money was borrowed for, how it was used, what kinds of efforts the country has made or is making to develop as well as repay, and how the debtor nation proposes to reform its economy, including how to deal with capital flight.

g. Any acceptable solution ought to recognize and attempt to relieve external factors beyond the control of the debtor country which tend to aggravate or perpetuate the burden — e.g., interest rates, commodity prices, trade barriers, budget deficits, and geopolitical considerations. The global economy should be managed in the interest of equity and justice; participation of the poor ought to be a central test of the morality of the system.

h. Proposed solutions ought to enhance the ability of the debtor nation to pursue independent, self-reliant, participatory, sustainable development. This consideration should receive high priority in any judgement as to the country's ability to service a discounted debt — i.e., the amount of debt the country can reasonably be expected to manage fairly.

In common with many other individuals and groups who view the debt from the under side of the poor, the bishops point out that the debt, which has mushroomed in the past decade and a half, is a symptom of deeper problems which are affecting the international economic order in a way that continually impoverishes the poor. Even if all debts were cancelled tomorrow, unless the economic system is radically changed, it will continue to benefit the rich and beggar the poor. Economic systems do not change of themselves; people must will them to change. This calls for the promotion of alternative values and political will to devise new, more equitable economic structures which enshrine these values of justice, solidarity and interdependence.

Bold political decisions are called for at the local, national, regional and global level on exchange rates and interest rates, investment, aid, the role of transnational corporations, commodities prices and access to markets, if the debt crisis is to be resolved in a satisfactory and lasting way.

Relieving Third World Debt envisages something analogous to another Bretton Woods round of negotiations, except that this time the Third World and the interests of the poor must be represented. This comprehensive restructuring of the world economic system must not become an excuse for industrialized countries to drag their feet and not face the crisis. The problem can be seen every day in villages, towns and cities of the Third World when poor people, especially women and children, are unable to purchase food or medicine and slowly starve to death. Repaying Third World debts is literally killing the poor and costing the earth.

Chapter 2

Will there be too many mouths to feed?

Human population and the carrying capacity of the earth

Many people are worried about the rapid rate of population increase in the countries of the Third World. They question whether a particular region, or the earth as a whole, can support in a sustainable way the projected increase in human population. In this chapter I will attempt to show that there are solid grounds for this questioning. I begin with a concrete example. The rapid increase in the population is seriously affecting a small community with which I am familiar. I go on then to look at the wider population picture as it relates to the Philippines and the earth as a whole. It goes without saying that the parameters discussed in this case study are flexible. Nevertheless they signal the kinds of factors which government and Church leaders must take into account in any realistic discussion of the potential carrying capacity of any geographical region.

The case of Tablo[1]

Tablo is a T'boli village of 177 families — 969 inhabitants in all — located at the foot of Mt Talili on the shore of Lake Sebu, which is a municipality in the province of South Cotabato in southwest Mindanao. Tribal peoples in this part of Mindanao had very little contact with the outside world until about 40 years ago, when a government-assisted migration programme encouraged tens of thousands of lowland Filipinos from the islands of Luzon and the Visayas to migrate to Mindanao.

Traditionally, the T'boli of Tablo were hunters and gatherers, slash-and-burn farmers and fishermen. Though there were seasonal food shortages, and hunger during prolonged droughts, their way of life provided a nutritious and balanced diet for the inhabitants. However, with the loss of some of their best lands, a curtailment on their fishing activities on Lake Sebu and the destruction of wildlife in the forest, the nutritional quality of their diet steadily declined.

A lack of sanitation and no ready access to modern medicine meant that epidemics of infectious diseases took a heavy toll, especially among the children and the elderly. It is estimated that, until recently, about 33 per cent of the children died during the first five years of their lives.

Resources of the community

The primary resource of any rural community is its land. Tablo consists of around 950 hectares of land. (This excludes several thousand hectares of dipterocarp forest.) Out of this total, however, only 76 hectares of the land area is sufficiently flat for agricultural use. The soil is fertile though stony. Moving up from the flat land, a sizeable proportion of the area — about 280 hectares — consists of slopes of between 20 and 80 per cent gradient. This soil is of poor quality since much of the topsoil has already been eroded. Finally, the remaining 594 hectares is covered with cogon (a species of grass which proliferates on deforested lands). Severe erosion has rendered this area very unsuitable for agriculture, although corn, rice and camote (sweet potato) is now grown there. In recent years, 40 hectares of this land has been reforested using a variety of indigenous and exotic trees.

In terms of water, Tablo is well served by two springs and five rivers of varying sizes. In the past, these have always provided an abundant supply of water for domestic and other uses. However, with the destruction of the forest, the water supply can become scarce and even dry up. Water sources dwindled to a trickle during the long drought of 1983–84.

Tablo is one of the traditional tribal communities served by the Santa Cruz Mission. From the mid-1960s personnel came from the mission centre at Lem Ehek; in 1985 a separate community centre was set up within Tablo itself. Teachers, paramedics, development workers and agriculturalists now live there. They provide and organize educational, health, agricultural, village craft and community services for the community. The range and quality of these services means that Tablo is much better served than the average tribal or lowland village community in the Philippines.

The two services which have an immediate bearing on the present discussion are the agricultural and health programmes. The goal of the agricultural programme is to promote sustainable, ecologically sensitive, family farms. Already ten two-hectare organic farms have been established, whilst a further 16 families, formerly landless, cultivate half-hectare 'mini-farms'. The primary aim in both the ecological and the mini-farms — often called food gardens — is to provide food for consumption within the family and the community. Otherwise a cash-crop mentality will develop. Most of the best land will be devoted to growing cash crops. Initially, landowners may have more money, but the whole community will be more vulnerable if they are dependent on outside food. In 1989, for example, the price of coffee plummeted while food prices continued to rise. In such a situation, a community which had planted all its land to coffee would be seriously impoverished.

The health programme strives to promote good health through

better sanitation, immunization against communicable diseases, better nutrition and readily available modern health care when necessary. One of the staff members living in Tablo is a trained paramedic who takes care of the common health problems. More serious cases are referred to the Mission hospital about two kilometres from the village. Despite these intensive efforts, however, the general health profile of the community is still not satisfactory. 53 per cent of the children between the ages of one and three are underweight by national standards. Using the same national criteria, the majority of the children are malnourished.

The most successful aspect of the Santa Cruz Mission health programme is that it has significantly reduced the rate of infant mortality from an estimated 33 per cent in 1978 to 10 per cent in 1987. This compares well with the Philippines' national average of 8 per cent. Naturally, the drop in infant mortality has led to a rapid increase in population. In 1987, for example, there were 55 live births and 9 stillbirths. For a population of 969 people this works out at a 4.54 per cent annual increase. If this rate of growth remains constant, the community will double its population in just over 15 years. Clearly, prudent planners should be asking themselves whether Tablo can support such a population increase.

In looking for a tentative answer, a number of factors must be kept in mind. First, some inhabitants might migrate to other areas in the Philippines. This will undoubtedly take some of the pressure off Tablo, but it will, of course, add to the problem elsewhere, since almost every community in the Philippines is now feeling the pressure of a growing population. Second, it is unrealistic, however, to project a massive migration of tribal people to lowland areas. They would not be able to secure land, and as tribal people they would face a certain level of discrimination in applying for jobs in an already crowded job market. Third, it is also unreasonable to project such a major increase in industry in the area that it will draw people off the land and supply them with a steady income.

Given these preconditions, Tablo will, in the main, have to survive on its own horticultural and agricultural resources. To do this in a sustainable way, certain principles will have to be followed. First, no so-called development strategy must be allowed to disrupt the balance of the ecosystems in the area. For example, the people of Tablo could be assured of a certain prosperity for a number of years by cutting the remaining forest. This, however, would have long-term adverse effects on the soil, the lake, the various rivers and thus the survival of the people of Tablo. Moreover, all the communities downstream from Tablo would also be jeopardized. Its location in the watershed of the Allah river means that it is of paramount importance that the existing forest be preserved and the residual forest enriched by the planting of mainly indigenous species. Apart from the intrinsic value of preserving one of the richest life-systems on earth and the advantages for irrigation in the lowlands, the forest will be able to provide fruits and other forest products which can be harvested on a sustainable basis. Timber cutting in the residual forest will have to be ruled out for the 40 to 60 years that it takes many dipterocarp species to mature. As things stand for the next 40 years, the people of Tablo cannot look to the rainforest for a regular source of income.

Moving down on to the denuded cogon grass slopes, about 125 hectares of this area is suitable for establishing agroforestry. If properly developed — through planting a variety of lumber, fruit and fibre trees and other plants like coffee and cacao — this area can produce a substantial income, especially for those people who at present do not have land. The processing of these products will also add to the employment possibilities of the community. It is important to note, however, that the initial production from this area can begin, at the earliest, only five years after planting. It takes that long for many trees and plants to bear fruit. It will take between 10 and 15 years for the area to arrive at full production. Trees like falcata or gemelina take that length of time to mature. To establish and operate facilities like processing plants or furniture shops demands capital and a range of managerial and marketing skills. Initially, at least, considerable outside help will be needed to develop an integrated approach which will reap maximum benefit from the resources of the area in a sustainable way.

In approaching the use of land resources a few factors must be kept in mind. First, the land must be worked intensively in order to feed the present and projected population. Second, the fertility of the soil must be preserved. In practice, this will mean using erosion-control techniques, minimizing the use of agrochemicals and planting nutritious food crops which give a high return for the land they occupy. Fallow periods and crop rotation are also essential. It will be necessary to build up food reserves so that the community can move beyond the present hand-to-mouth existence. The need for this was underscored in 1983–84 when the people of Tablo experienced a seven-month drought. Without substantial food aid from abroad at that time, the community would have experienced a major famine and many people would have died.

Drawing on five years' experience devising appropriate agricultural programmes in the area, the Santa Cruz Mission personnel have learned that a tribal family can survive on 0.45 hectares by using intensive methods of cultivation. Traditionally, the T'boli staple food was composed mainly of root crops, which are more efficient in terms of land use. Rice or corn (the cereal preferred by lowland Filipinos) requires more land — a hectare of land for upland rice or a quarter-hectare for paddy rice. In many studies on population levels in relation to land area and crop use, optimum yields are often used as a basis for projections. A word of caution is appropriate here. Although many of the methods of cultivation which the Santa Cruz Mission agriculturalists use are based on traditional tribal planting patterns, the intensity of the operation will, nevertheless, demand major cultural changes. It will be necessary to generate a work ethic that encourages the tribal community to adopt this mix of traditional and modern farming methods. When one remembers that traditionally a tribal couple only spent, on an average, three hours a day working to collect food with which to feed the family, one can hardly expect 100 per cent success immediately from the new programme which will demand much more extended work periods.

Based on the above experience and stated in purely mathematical terms, 177 families require 79.6 hectares of arable land in order to attain a minimal standard of comfort. So even today the 76 hectares of flat land referred to in the general description of Tablo (p. 39) is not sufficient to give each of the 177 families the basic 0.45 hectares of land. Matters would improve if and when the proposed 125 hectares of agroforestry began to produce in a sustainable way.

The real problem is with the rate of increase in the population. With a 4.5 per cent annual increase, Tablo will double its population to 354 families in a mere 15 years. Ideally, they will need 159.3 hectares of arable land to support them. The harsh reality for Tablo is that while the human population continues to grow, the land area remains constant.

This discussion of the relationship between population and land resources in a given community is theoretical. In the real world, land areas cannot be neatly divided up into equal plots; some people own much more land than others. This is especially true in the Philippines as a whole where a small percentage of the population own the bulk of the productive land. Still, in comparison with the national situation, the land in Tablo is distributed fairly evenly. In Tablo in 1987, for example, 83 families owned 199 hectares of land. Their holdings averaged between 2.3 and 4 hectares. Sixteen families own less than one hectare of land, much of which was severely eroded. It is clear that the existing land cannot be stretched too much. The 67 families with over one hectare have some land which could be distributed to others. Most of these people will probably hold on to it in order to pass it on to their married children in the years to come.

The discussion thus far has centred on the capacity of the arable land to support the present and future population. There are other resources, as I mentioned above. Agroforestry and the industries based on it can offer a livelihood for a section of the population. This, as we have seen, will take time to realize. Nevertheless, our present calculations for processing items like coffee, vegetables, lumber and handicrafts indicate that one hectare of agroforestry in conjunction with the added value from ancillary processing industries could support one family. The mix of produce will mean that the ratio of one to one will probably remain stable. Some items like lumber may rise in value in response to the expected national and worldwide shortage of lumber within the next decade. The price of other items like coffee, cacao and coconuts has been volatile on world markets in recent years. Within a 15- to 20-year projection, their value may not keep step with inflation or currency devaluations. So it is fair to assume that if everything works out as planned, the 125 hectares of agro-forestry project at Tablo should provide sustenance for an additional 125 families.

If these figures are correct, and if there are no major catastrophes, Tablo should be able to support the increase in population until about the year 2010. It is at this point that the crunch will come. From that moment on Tablo will not be able to support the increase in population in a sustainable way. Faced with demands for food and shelter there will be a strong temptation to over-work the land, cut the forest or over-fish the lake in order to satisfy immediate human needs. This, of course, will involve eating into the resources. By doing this the people of Tablo will be undermining the possibility of their continuing stability and prosperity. In the long run they will be digging their own graves and the graves of their children and their children's children.

In view of this Fr Mansmann CP (who has lived in the area for 27 years) remarks, 'the simple conclusion is that there cannot be a stable livelihood or sustainable community without population control'.[2]

Some of the people of Tablo, especially the mothers, are quite aware of the problem, albeit in a general way. Education in family planning, basic child care and nutrition have been part of a mothers' programme organized by the health personnel over the last eight years. In a warm, friendly atmosphere which facilitates discussion, some of these problems have been broached. Beyond the level of recognizing the problem, efforts have been made to teach the young mothers a variety of natural family planning methods. In this respect, Fr Mansmann writes:

> Looking back over the years of this educational process, the religious sister-nurse in charge of the programme feels that the programme could have been presented more effectively. That is, no doubt, true. But the fact remains that not a single family, even those with whom the sister had daily contact, was able to effectively apply the natural birth control system. The four married T'boli assistants of the sister-in-charge have a total of twenty-six children. All these women are still in their twenties or early thirties.

They were disturbed and depressed by their third and

succeeding pregnancies. One eventually had herself ligated by the government doctor.

Fr Mansmann concludes, 'this experience throws a shadow of serious doubt on the effectiveness of natural birth control methods in the tribal setting'.[3]

From the preceding discussion, it is reasonable to argue that Tablo has a population problem and the time to do something effective about it is now.

The global picture

What is happening in Tablo and many other communities is of recent origin in the history of the human race and of the earth itself. Because of a delicate system of checks and balances in the living world, the population levels of most species have remained constant, at least in the recent life-history of the planet. Humans are the only exception. Even here the rapid growth in the human population is a recent phenomenon. This can been seen at a glance from Table 1.

Table 1

Years ago	People living on Planet Earth
300,000	1,000,000
10,000	5,000,000
2,000	250,000,000
100+ (AD 1870)	1,000,000,000
37 (AD 1950)	2,510,000,000
(AD 1988)	5,000,000,000

A number of factors are responsible for this dramatic increase in recent decades. These include better nutrition and more control of infectious diseases through immunization programmes and improved sanitation. Together these have caused a dramatic decrease in the level of infant mortality and have also contributed to the greater longevity of the population as a whole.

These developments are all good in themselves and have contributed in no small way to the quality of life. As we have seen in the case of Tablo, the resulting rapid increase in population does, however, create problems for particular communities, primarily in poor countries where the population growth rate is high. Within the next few decades, it is almost certain to generate difficulties for the world as a whole. Common sense dictates that this situation should be addressed now, instead of waiting until the level of human population exceeds the capacity of the land either in particular areas or in the world as a whole to support it.

Population increases in the Philippines

Worries about the impact on a rapidly growing population are particularly acute in Third World countries like the Philippines which have a high birth rate, widespread malnutrition and limited, even shrinking resources. The increase in recent decades is very noticeable. In 1900 the population of the Philippines was 6 million. By 1949 it had jumped to 19.2 million; 1970 saw the population pass the 38.5 million mark and in 1989 it was estimated to be 63.8 million.[4] The particular population profile of the country — 50 per cent of the people under the age of 18 — means that the figure will shoot past 100 million within three decades. This rapid increase in population within a very short period of time has placed an immense strain on both the living world of the Philippines and on the economic and political stability of the country.

Finding land on which to produce food for the expanding population is a major challenge. It is important to remember that 17.6 million hectares or 59 per cent of the total land area of the Philippines has a slope of 18 per cent or more, and thus is not suitable for agriculture. Other areas with more gentle slopes can be cultivated in a sustainable way, through the use of soil conservation methods. Soil conservation has not been a high priority in agriculture programmes, so much of the land area is now heavily eroded. In fact, there are only 2.8 million hectares of flat lowlands which can produce more than one crop per year.[5] During the 1940s and 1950s the average annual population growth rate was 3.1 per cent. However, since the annual average of newly opened land for cultivation was 3.8 per cent, population increase did not appear to be a major problem. This changed in the 1960s, when the average annual increase in cultivated land fell to 1.4 per cent. This was far short of the annual population increase of 3 per cent.[6] In response to this situation the Philippine government encouraged the introduction of high-yielding varieties of rice in the late 1960s. But high-yielding varieties do not thrive without fertilizers — most of which are imported. Between 1960 and 1983, fertilizer use jumped from around 200,000 metric tons to 878,000 tons annually. The increase in yield enabled the Philippines to move from being a rice importer to becoming a rice exporter.[7] But the respite in terms of population to land and crop-yield ratio was short-lived as fertilizer prices increased in the 1980s and crop yields began to fall again.

It must also be recognized that not everyone in the Philippines owns land. In 1987 there were over 7 million landless agricultural people, hiring out their labour whenever they could find work in order to get food or money. Many landless poor people have moved to overcrowded cities like Cebu and Manila in search of work. But the manufacturing sector is not able to absorb the 800,000 people who each year are now entering the job market.[8] In 1990 the number of people who neither have land on which to grow food nor money to buy it is increasing as the population increases. The potential for mass starvation if crops fail or the economy goes into recession is already there.

One can easily understand why some authors, like Paul and Anne Ehrlich, view overpopulation as the fundamental cause of ecological destruction.[9] Others, like Robert Repetto of the World Resources Institute, present a much more subtle picture of the interrelated factors which are destroying the earth. These include the consumption patterns of the rich, the inequitable distribution of resources, and the concentration of power and wealth in the hands of a few. Nevertheless, in reflecting on current population projections in the overview to the book *The Global Possible*, he suggests that 'population growth at the high end of the projected range . . . would exacerbate already serious problems in many developing countries'.[10]

Prudence and foresight counsel that the problem should be tackled now, before a crisis point is reached. The crisis can come about in two ways. The first signs of crisis occur when the food which is produced is not available for people. The poor, since they have no land on which to grow food or money with which to buy it, go hungry and starve. Aside from this lack of access to the resources of the earth, a second element is now entering the equation. This involves the sharp decline in crop yields and a consequent drop in food production which take place when fertile lands become depleted, and rain patterns are disturbed by environmental degradation and climatic change. In 1987 and 1988 there has been a sharp fall in world grain production.[11] These two factors are contributing to an increase in malnutrition, particularly among children in many Third World countries. In sub-Saharan Africa they have been responsible for famine which has resulted in a sharp rise in the death rate, especially among infants. It is this kind of scenario which has led public authorities to adopt drastic measures in order to bring down the birth rate and thus avoid an impending catastrophe. The one-child-family policy now current in the People's Republic of China is one such response. Many people will rightly condemn the curtailment of human freedom involved in this policy, and the fact that the authorities promote abortion. Nevertheless, most demographers recognize that China has a population problem, in terms of the relationship of people to the country's land and resources. The population cannot continue to double every few decades. From the time of the establishment of the People's Republic in the late 1940s until the mid-1970s, the growing population was not seen as an important issue. If efforts had been made in the 1950s to promote extensive family planning, there would be no need for the draconian measures which are now being taken.

The carrying capacity of the earth

In recent years, ecologists have often used the notion of 'carrying capacity' in discussions about the optimum levels of human population in particular areas. It is important to note that, while the concept is helpful as in the case history above, it does lack rigour; many interrelated factors must be taken into account in attempting to determine what the parameters of the carrying capacity might be for a particular area. Still, many ecologists now argue that the carrying capacity of the earth as a whole or of local bioregions involves a delicate balance between the population levels of all species in the bioregion, the ownership and productive use of land and other food sources, human creativity and access to other resources. The nub of the problem can be stated simply. An increase in the human population is likely to place more strain upon the life-support systems of the earth. In recent years, this has led to widespread disregard for many members of the earth's community. It has caused the extinction of many species already and threatens the same fate to many more which do not, at present, seem to serve human needs.

Although we live on a planet with an abundance of living forms, the resources of the earth are finite. Of course, as human history amply illustrates, the above relationships are not static or rigidly predetermined. A society pursuing intensive agriculture can support a higher population density than one engaged in hunting and gathering. Human labour and activity thus become important factors in increasing the availability of the resources for the community. Nevertheless the continual expansion of agriculture to wetlands, mountains, forests and marginal areas tends to degrade that habitat for other species and, in the process, endanger their survival. It may also damage the land to such an extent that agriculture is no longer possible within a few years. This is particularly true of the land formerly covered by tropical rainforests, especially in the Amazon basin. There, the soil only supports a few harvests before the nutrients are exhausted and the land becomes barren. Extensive cultivation, clearing of forests and burning fossil fuels are also causing major climatic changes which will affect everyone on earth for generations to come.

One must not forget, of course, that a more equal distribution of the goods of this world, more careful management of its life-systems and resources and some technological innovations can greatly increase the carrying capacity of the earth or a given region. Despite this elasticity, if the pressure continually grows, there will undoubtedly come a time when the limits of a particular region will be reached. This will happen sooner rather than later, if large populations double in a little over 20 years, which is what we fear in the case of Tablo and many other similar communities in the Philippines. At present there are numerous warnings that pressure on the environment is reaching a crisis point. *Time* magazine for 2 January 1989 departed from its usual practice of naming a Man or Woman of the Year and instead named 'the endangered earth' as the 'Planet of the Year'. Various articles in this issue covered the destruction of the rainforest, the climatic changes which appear to be caused by humans burning fossil fuels and using chemical products, soil erosion, toxic waste, deteriorating water supplies, waste disposal, and the population pressures. Many of these changes to the biosphere, like the destruction of species, are irreversible.[12] Once again it must be emphasized that the despoliation of the earth cannot simply be laid exclusively at the door of population growth, but results from the numerous factors that go to make up our modern industrial society.

Getting the balance right

Our bodies require food, clothing and shelter for survival. Since we do not create our own food or sources of energy, we depend on other creatures and resources to meet these basic needs. Without sufficient food, water and clean air we die. Yet this dependence on other creatures is disputed by some people. James Schall, for example, in his book *Welcome, Number 4,000,000,000!* writes that

> there is no reason to suppose that man is at all ultimately
> dependent on plant and animal life. Space technology already
> has pioneered ways to bypass many of these natural systems,
> or imitate them in man-made environments. In the last
> analysis, plants and animals may be destined for our
> enjoyment and pleasure, not for our survival by consumption.[13]

Few biologists would agree with this attempt to place human beings outside the web of life which links together all the creatures of the earth. It appears to be grounded rather on the Cartesian dichotomy between spirit and matter. In this perspective humans are seen as superior to every other creature on the earth and not linked organically with them. Like its antecedents in Gnosticism and Neoplatonism, this view recoils at the thought of humankind being firmly rooted in the earth.

Mere survival, of course, is not an adequate goal for individuals or societies. All people yearn for sufficiency and enough comforts to allow them to enjoy a reasonable standard of living. In practice this means that our emotional, aesthetic, intellectual and spiritual needs must also be catered for. This calls for education, an extensive communications network, economic, political and social structures which are responsive to human needs, adequate health care and a host of cultural and religious organizations. In most countries, individuals, a variety of associations and public authorities attempt to meet these needs as best they can from the wealth which people create and the resources which are available to that society. But meeting all of these needs also requires healthy and sustainable life-systems, adequate resources, capital and, of course, human ingenuity.

In the Philippines, as we saw above, the population has doubled almost four times in this century. This is putting huge pressure on its resources. The basic services have to be doubled to maintain them even at their present inadequate level. A concrete illustration of this pressure in the field of education came in an announcement from the Department of Education and Sports (DESC) in June 1987 that an additional million students had entered the public school system over the previous year. Figures of this magnitude are so large as to be meaningless to most people, so a local example from my experience in South Cotabato might help to give some understanding of what this might mean in practice.

In the town of Marbel, South Cotabato, the Notre Dame Catholic complex in 1987 had a population of around 10,000 students. It had taken over 40 years of dedicated work by the Marist brothers and the Dominican sisters and their respective staffs to build up this institution. Bearing this in mind, the government of the Philippines must provide, from scratch, the equivalent of 100 such institutions merely to meet the needs of the additional students for the year 1987–88. The same addition is expected in 1988–89. With a 29-billion-dollar foreign debt and scarce funds, there is no way the government will be able to meet these targets. So as the population increases one can presume that the school system will lag further and further behind in its ability to educate the people. In this kind of situation the people who will suffer most will be the poor. The rate of illiteracy can be expected to rise dramatically in the years ahead.

Affluence consumes the natural world

When looking at population levels for a country or worldwide one must not forget the fact that in an interconnected world the life style of a small segment of humanity, in either First World or Third World countries, should not be so extravagant as to eat up a lion's share of the earth's resources. The demands which people in industrialized countries and the elite in the Third World make on these resources are often ten to 20 times higher than those made by the poor. As more and more communities are sucked into the international economy everything is measured in purely financial or economic terms. People living in any part of the world now have access to the resources from any other part. This often leads to a beggar-my-neighbour behaviour among nations. For example, forests are protected in Japan, yet the Japanese have played a significant role in plundering the forests of Southeast Asia during the past two decades. Industrialized countries are also exporting their dirty industries or toxic waste to poor countries that will do almost anything to acquire foreign currency.

Despite these considerations, it is still important to insist that there must be a balance between the population level and the resource base of any society, and also that the world take seriously the demands of social justice and the rights of other species. To achieve this it seems prudent to avoid the extremes of either under- or over-population.

If, for example, there are too few people living in a given area, it is difficult to utilize the resources in a creative way and also to build human communities where economic, social, aesthetic, cultural and religious needs of all people can be adequately met. In some First World countries, planners fear that the low birth rate and increased longevity in recent decades will mean that the working population in the next decade will not be able to support the retired population.[14] In the Philippines, the drop in numbers among many tribal people endangers their survival as integral cultures. So for the survival and enhancement of any species, especially humans, a certain level of population is essential.

Boom/bust syndrome

On the other hand, if a population is growing too rapidly there is a danger that it will spin through what biologists call a boom/bust syndrome. This happens when the population expands dramatically within a very short space of time, while the resource base on which it depends remains constant or may even shrink. The expanded population must feed itself and meet its other basic needs from the same limited resources. The situation is further aggravated by the fact that a significant minority in the society may have rising expectations which will place an additional strain on the resource base.

In an attempt to meet these expanded needs, people will tend to exploit the environment more intensively and, in the process, further degrade it. For a while everything may appear to be prospering. Modern technology allows humans to exploit the earth and it can even camouflage the long-term ecological consequences of over-exploitation. But, as we are seeing more and more today, the day of reckoning cannot be put off indefinitely. Tropical forests are being laid waste with the consequent loss of hundreds of thousands of species, prime agricultural land is being degraded through soil erosion, desertification and chemical agriculture; the atmosphere itself is under attack through what is called the 'greenhouse effect' and the depletion of the ozone layer, and the oceans, lakes, rivers and ground-water systems of the world are being polluted and rendered unsafe for human consumption. It is increasingly obvious today that, at a certain point, over-exploitation interferes with the self-renewing processes of the life-systems of the earth as a whole and exhausts or irreversibly damages the living world. Once again I am not arguing for a direct cause-and-effect relationship between the growing environmental crisis and population growth. It is, however, a significant factor in the equation.

The boom/bust phenomenon can be seen in Third World countries like the Philippines in the growing scarcity of specific items. The needs of an expanding population for firewood is contributing to the destruction of what remains of the tropical forest. Kerosene took the pressure off wood for a while in towns and cities in the 1960s, but as the price of fossil fuels increased during the 1970s, many poor people were forced to return to a traditional supply of energy and to utilize what remained of the forest. The same pattern can be seen in the area of food production and energy. The demand for more food and energy to supply a growing population calls for a more intensive use of marginal land. This, in turn, leads to greater encroachment into the forests and a consequent increase in soil erosion and land degradation.

During the 1980s, for many countries in the Third World, ecological deterioration is translating directly into economic decline for the poor who are the first to experience the consequent hardships. This statement is not meant to buttress, much less canonize, the present economic order. It merely recognizes the fact that the continued impoverishment of the environment can and does spark a fierce scramble for scarce resources which inevitably leads to social disintegration and a breakdown in peace and order. What has happened in Africa in recent years should be a lesson that this cycle can quickly lead to a return of high birth and high death rates — through increased malnutrition, illness, outright famine and starvation.

This will inevitably lead to a reduction of population levels, but given the suffering involved it is hardly the way that sensitive and, particularly, religious people would like to see populations being controlled. It is important to emphasize that this route involves a double tragedy. The first is immediately visible, especially on television screens, in the pain and suffering of famine victims, and the starvation and death of millions of poor people. It is heart-rending to see young children die of hunger, or to be left so stunted by hunger that they will never be able to live normal lives.

However, the suffering does not end with the pain of the present generation. In a desperate struggle for survival, hungry people cause further ecological degradation and often irreversibly destroy the life-support systems by cutting more trees, grazing marginal land and farming steep slopes. If the damage to the environment is irreversible, the life-support systems will never again be able to support a population even at previous levels of density. This point should be emphasized because it is the crux of the argument from a carrying capacity.

So, in the boom/bust syndrome, the scythe of death does not merely sweep through a single generation; it cuts into every succeeding generation. These too will have to pay a heavy price for the lack of foresight and justice displayed by one or two generations of human beings.

It is worth repeating again that it would not be correct to lay all of the ecological problems at the door of population growth. Repetto is correct in insisting that while it does contribute significantly to the pressure on the environment, it may not be as important as the inequitable distribution of land which affects so many poor people in many Third World countries.[15] More access to fertile lands now used for cash crops by the local elite or transnational corporations would transform the life of the rural poor. Still, even in a more socially just society, the rapid growth of population can also be a problem.

In the meantime, poor people must survive in today's less than perfect world. While it is good to dream of a more just society and to work to bring it about, it is important to remember that the present distribution of land and resources makes rapid population increase a serious problem here and now.

In the province of South Cotabato, the annual rate of population increase is 6.2 per cent achieved through new births and migrations from the northern and central Philippines. With this level of increase the population of almost every rural community is poised to double in the next 20 years. These people will draw little comfort from being told that if transnational corporations involved in agribusiness move out they will have plenty of land. The transnationals are there, and it will take more than pious rhetoric to move them. In the meantime the rural communities will continue to exhaust their lands and chop down their trees in order to meet today's needs.

The petrochemical era

As we have seen, the rate of population growth is an important component in any discussion of carrying capacity. Another glance at Table 1 (p. 44) will show that the time frame for population doubling has decreased considerably in recent decades. It took from the end of the Neolithic era until the sixteenth century — over 11,000 years — for the population to double. Then the pace quickened, and the doubling time was cut to a few hundred years. The last doubling was achieved in 37 years. To a great extent this was made possible through a single non-renewable resource: crude oil. Oil and petrochemicals were the crucial factors in generating the necessary food and energy which made possible the doubling of the human population. A remarkable fivefold jump in the use of petrochemical fertilizers in agriculture fuelled a 3 to 4 per cent annual increase in the world's food supply between 1950 and 1973. This increase was well in advance of the rate of population growth. The most spectacular gains were seen in world grain output which doubled in this period. The successful package linked hybrid cereal strains, irrigation, the increased use of petrochemicals and wholesale farm mechanization. The key to this success lay in cheap oil — around $2 a barrel for most of this time.

But the benefits of oil were not confined to agriculture. Cheap oil also favoured the replacement of natural fibres (cotton, wool and rubber) by synthetic products derived from petrochemicals. The cumulative effect of all of this was to release more and more land for crop production. In the USA alone 24 million hectares formerly used to produce grain and fodder for horses were released for other purposes when tractors replaced horses.

There were other more indirect ways in which the oil bonanza increased the available food supply: better boats powered by gasoline or diesel increased the supply of fish. The 1950s, 1960s and 1970s saw an average 6 per cent per annum increase in world fish supply. Animal feeds derived from petrochemicals also increase the worldwide production of beef and fowl.

The first jolt to this rosy picture came abruptly in 1973 when the world's oil producers dramatically increased the price of their product. Further increases throughout the decade culminated in another major increase in 1979. It is worth mentioning that in the process the producing countries were only getting a fair price for their oil which until then had been controlled by Western oil companies. The immediate effect of these increases, especially in Third World countries, was to raise the price of agricultural chemicals and therefore to put the brakes on agricultural output. Even though these countries borrowed heavily, they could still not afford the higher oil prices.

The fall-off in the use of chemical fertilizer quickly translated into a drop in agricultural production. World grain production, which had jumped from 623 million metric tons in 1950 to 1,219 million metric tons in 1973, increased very slowly during the following years. By 1982 it had only reached 1,523 million metric tons. Before the first oil price rise, world grain output per person had been rising more than 1 per cent per annum, but since then it has barely kept pace with world population growth. In the past two years, as we saw, world grain production has fallen sharply.

The heavy dependence on oil as an important ingredient in sustaining population growth is increasingly worrying to demographers for two reasons. First, oil is a non-renewable resource. There are geological limits to the world's reserves. As the world approaches the end of the petrochemical era and extracting oil becomes more and more expensive, so the widespread use of cheap petrochemicals for agriculture and other areas of life will decline. Many analysts expect oil production to peak in the mid-1990s. Secondly, the petrochemical era in agriculture, while producing huge yields, has led to a deterioration in the biological support system for agriculture. It has contributed to massive levels of soil erosion, depletion of nutrients, poisoning of the soil and the pollution of rivers and lakes. It is now becoming clear that this kind of agriculture is non-sustainable in the long term. In the future the food needs of a rising population must be met by agricultural methods which are sustainable over the long term.

Food exporters and importers

Another factor worth keeping in mind is that low-fertility countries are both food exporters and food donors while most high-fertility countries cannot satisfy their food needs. They have to use foreign currency to pay for their imported food. The outflow of foreign exchange to buy food and energy has contributed to the huge foreign debt which many developing countries have run up. Paying the interest on these debts, not to mention repaying the capital, places unbearable strains both on the human population in Third World countries and on the natural world. The only way this can even be attempted is by exploiting the forest, soil and natural resources, which in the long term exacerbates the problem.

Population increase is not uniform

Population increase is not uniform around the globe. In many richer countries, like West Germany and other European countries, the population is stable or even falling, but in Third World countries there is a runaway growth. Countries like Syria and Kenya are close to the top of the table. The latter, with an annual growth rate of 4 per cent, will increase from the present 23 million to an estimated 79 million within 30 years. Demographers estimate that when the annual growth rate is 2 per cent the population will double in 35 years; when it is 3 per cent the time-frame is 23 years and when it increases to 4 per cent the time shrinks further to 17 years. First World countries in general have a less than 2 per cent increase, while in African, Asian and Latin American countries the figure often runs between 2.5 and 3.5 per cent.

In an effort to calm the fears of Third World countries, some people suggest that their population growth will follow the trajectory of European countries and stabilize over time. But Third World countries draw little comfort from this for a number of reasons. First of all their rate of increase far outstrips the European experience. They double in less than half the time it took European countries to double. Even at the height of the industrial revolution, the population of Britain was doubling only every 70 years. Secondly, even today, in almost all of these less developed countries a significant proportion of the people are suffering from malnutrition and in some cases outright famine. These countries are saddled with enormous debts and they can ill afford the pressure which high population growth places on their natural environment and on their financial resources. Thirdly, during the nineteenth century massive emigration helped siphon off the excess European population to North America, Australia, New Zealand and South Africa. So the situation facing developing countries is very different from the nineteenth-century European experience. For this reason they must attempt to bring their populations under control within a single generation. If not, they risk destroying the self-renewing life-systems in their region in a frantic effort to feed this generation.

Huge growth in the population of Third World cities

Third World cities are top of the league as far as population growth is concerned. With the high fertility and the influx of landless rural workers in search of work, many Third World cities are bursting at the seams. In 1950 only 18 per cent of the urban population of Third World countries lived in cities with a million or more inhabitants. By 1980 the figure had jumped to 35 per cent. None of these cities has the infrastructure of roads, schools, clinics, sewage disposal, water and electric power to meet this phenomenal growth. Mexico, where the 1984 United Nations Conference on Population was held, illustrates what has happened very starkly. In 1940 there were 1.5 million people in the city; by 1960 the number had climbed to 2.7 million; by 1984 it had jumped to 14 million, and the projected number for the year 2000 is 25 million. The picture is much the same for Manila. At the turn of the century it had a population of about 250,000. In 1989 the population was around 9 million and is expected to jump to 16 million by the end of the century. Merely feeding these huge populations will be a gigantic task. One wonders where the money will come from to provide even a minimum level of basic services. For example, the present sewage system in Manila was constructed in 1905 when the population was only a fraction of what it is now.

Is rapid population increase a neutral factor?

In these circumstances it is hard to see how population can be called a neutral factor. At the 1984 United Nations Conference on Population in Mexico City, this was the position expressed by Mr James Buckley, the US delegate. His paper reworked some of the themes of US economic policy of the time: population growth itself is a neutral phenomenon, and populations will stabilize when free rein is given to free trade, and market forces are allowed to work unimpeded. Third

World countries, tottering under the burden of growing populations and economies which have been devastated by neo-colonial economic policies and huge debts, drew little comfort from his remarks. The rural poor have little to gain from the economics of greed which place company profits before the well-being of people or the long-term fruitfulness of the earth. Effective policies to distribute wealth and resources more equitably were foreign to supply-side economics, yet they are essential for the twin task of building a more just society and caring for the earth.

It should be emphasized that much of the data used to support this position and downplay the need for concerted family planning emanate from economists of the New Right like the late Herman Kahn of the Hudson Institute, and Professor Julian Simon. Both are defenders of the US view on population presented at the Mexico Conference in 1984. Simon argues his case in great detail in his book *The Ultimate Resource*, and both Kahn and Simon joined together in producing a report entitled 'The resourceful earth'. Both studies set out to refute the argument of the *Global 2000 Report to the President*. This report was prepared during the administration of President Carter, and attempted to document the devastation of the environment which was taking place worldwide. The letter of transmittal to the president read as follows: 'if present trends continue, the world in 2000 will be more crowded, more polluted, less stable ecologically and more vulnerable to disruption than the world we live in now'.[16] Simon and Kahn questioned both the statistics and the perspective of *Global 2000*. In 'The resourceful earth' they parodied the words quoted above and insisted that 'if present trends continue, the world in 2000 will be less crowded (though more populated), less polluted, more stable ecologically and less vulnerable to resource supply disruption than the world we live in now'.[17]

The first point worth making is that events since 1984, which include Chernobyl, the pollution of the seas, the devastation of the Amazon rainforest, the damage to the ozone layer and the climatic changes set in motion by the 'greenhouse effect', do not support Simon and Kahn's conclusions. On the contrary, the chorus of voices support of the general thesis of *Global 2000* is constantly increasing. The 2 January 1989 issue of *Time* magazine (which I quoted earlier) is a case in point. In the 1960s and 1970s environmental concerns were a peripheral interest for most political and religious leaders. In the late 1980s all that has changed. Even a conservative politician like Mrs Margaret Thatcher shared her apprehension about what was happening to the earth in a speech to the Royal Society in September 1987. Pope John Paul II also raised the ecological issue in no. 34 of his encyclical letter *Sollicitudo Rei Socialis* ('On Social Concerns'). In the 1970s and early 1980s, Simon and Kahn's view would have found extensive support among the central planners and leaders in Marxist countries. Not so in 1989, as the Soviet Foreign Minister made clear in his address to the 43rd General Assembly of the United Nations in October 1988.

> Faced with the threat of environmental catastrophe, the
> dividing lines of the bipolar ideological world are receding.
> The biosphere recognizes no division into blocs, alliances or
> systems. All share the same climatic system and no one is in a
> position to build his own isolated and independent line of
> environmental defence.

In their writings Simon and Kahn use economic indicators like price-indices and historical price trends to attempt to project future supply patterns. While it is true, for example, that in recent years most prime commodities were less expensive relative to wages than they were at any time during the last century this fails to take into account the simple fact that the earth is finite. There is a limit to what a biological or geological system can support. Even if the price tag of commodities is kept artificially low (through political pressure and inequitable trading mechanisms), all the gold in the world will not buy oil once the well runs dry, nor buy food if the land is eroded, nor timber once all the forests have been felled.

But not every economist would share the bright scenario of the future that Simon presents. Hall and Hall, summarizing recent studies, have this to say: 'the last decade was characterized by a measurable increasing scarcity of important natural resources'.[18] Projected use is also an important index which must be kept in mind. If the world population stabilized at 11 billion, for example, and everyone used minerals at the per capita rate that North Americans used them in the mid-1970s, all the estimated reserves of more than half the basic items would be exhausted in about 30 years. How long would the world's forests survive if even a fraction of the projected 11 billion people were to subscribe to the Sunday edition of the *New York Times*?

Let me repeat what I have said many times; it would be fallacious to point the finger exclusively at population growth as the main cause of environmental degradation, since much of the damage is done by people and corporations who represent only a minute fraction of the population. Still, as I have also reiterated, it would also be incorrect to discount population growth as a contributing factor. The activities of landless people who burn down the forest in order to grow food or make charcoal in order to earn a little money together leave huge scars on the surface of the earth. Similarly the cumulative effect of many small fishermen using dynamite or poison to increase their catch is devastating.

Monetarist economics as propounded by Simon and Kahn is not

very interested in creating caring societies where the basic needs of everyone are met and the well-being of people takes precedence over company profits and the accumulation of capital. The monetarist perspective is quite hostile to the social vision of papal social encyclicals like *Populorum Progressio* ('The Development of Peoples') or, more recently *Sollicitudo Rei Socialis*; that is why some New Right Catholics like Michael Novak, the author of *The Spirit of Democratic Capitalism*, were rather upset by Pope John Paul II's critique of capitalism in *Sollicitudo Rei Socialis*. Population growth is not a problem for Simon and Kahn, mainly because they see each person as a potential consumer of goods and services. The needs of the poor and the weak, or the carrying capacity of the earth, is not taken seriously into account. Considering such a blind spot about social justice, it is disconcerting to find that some Catholics are using the arguments of Simon and Kahn to support a position on population which springs more from a philosophical or theological source. James Clad writes in the *Far Eastern Economic Review* (20 October 1988) that the Center for Research and Communication (CRC), a Manila-based research institute with close links to Opus Dei, shares such a perspective.

The need to face the population issue

To avoid the tragedy which is even now staring us in the face in so many Third World countries, planners and those responsible for forming public opinion must come to terms with the fact that we live in a finite world which has a limited carrying capacity. This does not mean concentrating exclusively on birth control, much less using deceptive means or bribery to inveigle people into being sterilized or accepting IUDs. Attempts to regulate fertility without efforts to transform inequitable political, social and economic institutions and cultural values exacerbate the exploitation which many women experience in both traditional and modern societies. What is called for is a sustained attack on the root causes of poverty, adequate provision of of food, health care and special services and programmes to strengthen and improve the position of women in society. The World Fertility study carried out in 1980 concluded that policies which provide cheap and effective mother and child care and which enhance the employment opportunities of women outside the home are more closely correlated with fertility decline than any other social factor.

But it also means helping people to limit the size of their families through education and making diversified family planning options open to them. In any mix of fertility control techniques, breast-feeding and natural family planning should have an important place. But other methods should not be excluded from a public programme since many people cannot use the natural methods for either medical or personal reasons.

One cannot help wondering how history will judge political or religious leaders who, for whatever reason, refuse to acknowledge the strains which rapidly increasing populations are placing on the earth. To date many of these leaders have not encouraged people to respond in a responsible way to the new experience of living with limits.

The Catholic Church and population

Many people feel that the Catholic Church has been particularly slow to tackle this issue seriously and thoroughly. In *Familiaris Consortio*, the document which Pope John Paul II wrote after the 1980 Synod on the family, the population issue is addressed twice in nos 30 and 31. The first reference questions whether the increase in population is really a problem at all and warns against 'a certain panic deriving from the studies of ecologists and futurologists on population growth, which sometimes exaggerates the danger of demographic increase to the quality of life'.[19] No one will deny that some predictions may well be exaggerated, but even Robert Repetto (who can hardly be accused of being neo-Malthusian) acknowledges that 'there is a consensus that the human population must become stable, as it was for most of human existence. Rates of population growth even remotely approaching those experienced in this century are unsustainable over the next.'[20]

In article 31, the Pope briefly admits that there is a problem by saying that 'she [the Church] also recognizes the serious problem of population growth in the form it has taken in many parts of the world and its moral implication'. The same single-line acknowledgement is found in *Sollicitudo Rei Socialis*, no. 25. Once again there is no in-depth discussion of what the ecological, social and moral implications of the statement might be. It is essential that all aspects of this complex and delicate issue be treated in a thorough way and that Church leaders realize that the problem will simply not go away.

The Catholic Church is rightly concerned about the fact that the widespread dissemination of contraceptives might undermine the sanctity of marriage and lead to a contraceptive and anti-life mentality. One cannot deny that for some couples, mainly in First World countries, material possessions and love of luxury sometimes take precedence over their willingness to have children. But to be fair, selfishness and hedonism are not always the reasons why people choose to have fewer children today. Most people do not have the financial or psychological resources to support large families.

Humanae Vitae

A brief history of the birth control controversy in the Catholic Church during the past few decades may be helpful at this point. The problem first surfaced in a serious way in the 1950s when artificial contraceptives became readily obtainable in Western countries. In 1963, Pope John XXIII established a commission composed initially of four priests and four laymen to examine the Church's teaching on birth control. The commission was later expanded to include doctors, demographers, sociologists and theologians from a variety of cultures and backgrounds. With the election of Pope Paul VI the commission continued to meet and grapple with the complexity of the birth control issue. Gradually it became clear to the majority of the commission that the absolute ban on the use of artificial methods of birth control embodied in traditional teaching, especially *Casti Connubii* of Pope Pius XI, no longer seemed to respond to the contemporary needs of married couples. The Council Fathers who were meeting in Rome around the same time seemed to be moving in the same direction. In *Gaudium et Spes* they dropped the traditional dichotomy between the primary and second ends of marriage and affirmed instead that conjugal love lay at the heart of marriage. According to the Council Fathers, 'this love is uniquely expressed and perfected through the marital act' (no. 49). Eventually 64 members of the Commission voted for dropping the ban on the use of contraception. Only four commission members voted to retain the traditional teaching.

Finally, in July 1968, the long-awaited encyclical *Humanae Vitae* was published. The encyclical is a rich source of Christian teaching on marriage and incorporates many insights from modern psychology and scriptural studies. Nevertheless, on the crucial issue of contraception, Pope Paul VI reaffirmed the traditional teaching that 'each and every marriage act (*quilibet matrimonii usus*) must remain open to the transmission of life'. Given the fact that the majority report had been leaked to the press, the encyclical came as a shock and a disappointment to many Catholics.

Bishops' conferences around the world found it difficult to explain the teaching to the priests and people who had expected a change in the teaching. The German, Dutch, French, Italian, Australian and Indonesian episcopal conferences interpreted the encyclical broadly. According to these conferences, the teaching represented an ideal at which couples should aim, but they should not feel themselves cut off from the Church if they could not live up to this ideal.

From the day it was published, *Humanae Vitae* has created a huge controversy in the Church. Few priests have preached the encyclical and many Catholics have simply ignored it. During a speech at the Synod on the Family in 1980, Archbishop John Quinn of San Francisco presented statistics on the acceptance of the encyclical by US Catholics: 71 per cent of the priests, 84 per cent of lay people and 91 per cent of young Catholics have refused to accept the teaching. Comparable statistics are available from much of Western Europe.

The 1978 Philippine Fertility Survey found that 48.6 per cent of Catholic women of child-bearing age were using contraceptives at the time of the survey.[21] Mercedes Concepcion quotes Laing's (1981) findings that 'there was no difference in religious stance on contraception between Catholics and Protestants'. The survey also found that 'the most frequent attenders [at Church] had the highest proportion of contraceptive use'.

For a while in the late 1970s the controversy died down and it seemed that the encyclical might share the fate of *Veterum Sapientiae* (which discussed the use of Latin in the Church) and be simply forgotten. All that changed with the election of Pope John Paul II to the papacy in 1978. He has vigorously espoused the teaching of *Humanae Vitae* during his pastoral visits to various countries including those with a high population growth like Kenya and the Philippines. He has also reiterated the teaching in *Familiaris Consortio* and *Sollicitudo Rei Socialis*, as we have seen above.

In the early 1980s there were signs that Pope John Paul was willing to adopt a more sympathetic approach to those who were living in poverty and wished to limit their families by using artificial means. In a message to the Second International Conference on the Family of the Americas held in Acapulco, Mexico, in August 1982, the Pope praised those who promote and practise natural family planning and went on to say:

> We cannot conclude these considerations without recalling
> that there are, in spite of everything, many families living in
> such [difficult] circumstances — we think, for example, of vast
> sectors of acute poverty in the Third World — that the putting
> into practice of moral laws expressed in the Christian ideal
> may appear impossible. While continuing to maintain its
> validity, great pastoral efforts should be made to strengthen
> the faith of these persons, while leading them gradually to the
> knowledge and putting into practice of the gospel ideal
> *according to the possibility of their strength*. (Emphasis mine.)[22]

This more realistic statement of the problem facing many couples seems to have receded recently in papal pronouncements. In September 1983 the Pope told an audience in Rome that 'those who practise contraception or even believe it to be lawful are refusing objectively to acknowledge God'.[23]

One thing should be clear from this discussion. Despite this robust championing of *Humanae Vitae* by Pope John Paul II, the majority of Catholics in the Western world and many Third World countries do not believe that each use of artificial methods of birth control is 'intrinsically evil'.[24] Neither do the vast majority of Christians from the other Christian Churches. In view of this comments like those made by Monsignor Caffarra of the Pope John Paul II Institute for the Family are not helpful. Speaking at the Lateran University in Rome in October 1988. Caffarra claimed that those who do not accept the strict interpretation of *Humanae Vitae* are 'anti-life, anti-human and anti-God'.[25] Fr Bernard Haring, the well-known moral theologian, took grave exception to the position enunciated by Mgr Caffarra, in an article which he wrote for the 15 January edition of the Italian Catholic magazine *Il Regno*. A few months later, in an interview in an April 1989 issue of the Italian newspaper *Il Corriere della Sera*, he said that the tactics used by the Vatican to muzzle dissident theologians are 'shameful', and likened them to those used by the Nazis during World War II. These 'unfair' and 'unchristian' pressures were responsible for the 'psychological schism' which was now prevalent in the Church.[26]

The theological status of *Humanae Vitae* figured prominently in the Cologne document signed by 163 German-speaking theologians in 1989. The theologians criticized the present tendency in Rome to equate the teaching of *Humanae Vitae* with central truths of the Christian faith. Any understanding of a hierarchy of truths espoused by Vatican's II Decree on Ecumenism is simply abandoned when Rome speaks about *Humanae Vitae*. The theologians added that 'the dignity of the papal teaching office' was damaged by bans on thinking and teaching. 'Furthermore we regret the intense fixation of the papal teaching office on this problem area.'[27]

Given this level of widespread dissent among the laity and theologians, what place should an understanding of *Humanae Vitae* play in the broad discussion in this chapter of the need for family planning facilities in Third World countries to stabilize population levels as soon as possible? First of all, I recognize that though it is not widely accepted by Catholics or other Christians,[28] *Humanae Vitae* is still the teaching of the Church and, at the moment, it carries the personal authority of the Pope.[29] According to the Second Vatican Council, Catholics are required to give 'religious submission' (*Lumen Gentium* 25) to the teaching.[30] Couples who wish to follow the dictates of the encyclical must use natural family planning methods only. There are many positive benefits to be gained by practising natural family planning on the personal level. Because these methods actively involve both husband and wife, they tend to enhance their married life. At a public level, the Church should continue to promote these methods and support research aimed at making them more reliable. Catholics should also urge public authorities to have these methods included in government birth limitation programmes. But given the fact that many Catholics do not share the Pope's position on the morality of other forms of fertility control, and the success rate to date of natural family planning programmes in reducing population growth, one can legitimately question whether Catholic leaders have a right to insist that governments support these methods only, particularly in a pluralist society?

It is also clear that Catholic couples themselves wish to have access to a broad variety of methods. The 1978 Philippines Fertility Survey reported that 70 per cent of the women surveyed in the 15 to 49 years age bracket approved of modern methods of family planning which included the pill, IUDs, condoms and sterilization.[31] One wonders whether this general approval by Filipino Catholics of a wide variety of contraceptive methods was taken very seriously by Cardinal Edouard Gagnon when he met with a number of legislators in Manila in June 1988 in order to lobby against having artificial methods included in the government's birth control programmes.[32]

What about the vast number of Catholics who dissent from the teaching or find it impossible to practise natural methods? It is clear that most of these people have not taken their stance simply to defy Church authority. They usually have given the matter serious consideration, remembering that it affects their lives intimately. They will contend that, in their deliberations, they have attempted to follow the teachings of the Lord and that they too are guided by the Spirit (1 John 2:27 and John 14:26). These people can also appeal to other Church documents: no. 33 of the Constitution on the Church in the Modern World states that 'the Church . . . does not always have the answer to particular questions'. The same point is made in no. 43 of the same document. In no. 52, the Fathers say that 'the Christian sense of the faithful can contribute to addressing modern problems in the areas of marriage'. When such a high percentage of Christians who are actually married feel unable to follow a particular teaching, this surely raises serious questions about the teaching.

It is also important to state that *Humanae Vitae* is not an infallible pronouncement. This was clearly stated at the press conference which was called to mark the publication of the encyclical.[33] Therefore the teaching is reformable. Changes in Church teaching regarding beliefs, moral values and behaviour have occurred in the past. The change in the condemnation of usury is often quoted as an example. There is another example which is closer to home in the T'boli hills where polygamy is still practised. In 1866 two questions were put to the Holy Office by Bishop Guillelmus Massaia from Ethiopia. He asked whether he could baptize polygamists, and whether he could give the sacraments to those involved in the slave trade. The answer of the Holy Office to the first question was No, and to the second question Yes, since slavery was 'permitted by the natural law'. The latter answer will embarrass most Catholics today, and even in the 1860s there was an extensive body of opinion that maintained that slavery was against the gospel of Jesus.[34]

Unfortunately, in recent years divergent views regarding *Humanae*

Vitae have hardened into fixed positions. This is a pity because, even if one accepts the position of the encyclical, there is in practice a need for a more subtle understanding of the morality of contraceptives. All forms of birth control and all situations in which people use contraceptives should not be bracketed together. Writing in *The Furrow*,[35] Nicholas Ayo says that *Humanae Vitae* does not state 'that all circumstances in which contraception arises as a moral problem are identical or that even the wrongdoing, if wrongdoing there must be, is of equal gravity or sinfulness'. There is quite a difference morally between having an abortion and using contraceptives. There is also a difference between the couple who freely choose to use contraceptives and the couple who have them forced on them by unscrupulous medical personnel or through implicit or explicit threats. Studies have shown that where safe, reliable contraceptives are widely available and easily affordable, induced abortion rates are typically much lower than elsewhere.[36]

It is easy to close one's eyes to the widespread practice of back-street abortions to which many pregnant women have recourse. It is estimated, for example, that 32.4 per cent of all deaths from infection at the Philippine General Hospital in Manila are directly related to pregnancy.[37] Theologians and Church leaders who pronounce on the relative morality of individual methods of birth control must also recognize that, unless there is a slowing down of current trends in population growth, a significant number of deaths in Third World countries will be caused by famine. The irreversible destruction of the natural world caused by over-population is also a moral issue.

We need to ask how much time, energy and resources Church leaders have invested in trying to understand all the facets of these crucial questions. Are they content to repeat established positions and wash their hands of any responsibility for the suffering and chaos that will almost certainly follow another doubling of the population? How dedicated have they been in working for solutions which meet the problem head-on while respecting people's freedom, culture, religious traditions, as well as the limits of the earth? Fr Bel R. San Luis SVD in his column in the *Manila Bulletin* (22 December 1988) appears to both Church and State leaders in the Philippines to join hands in seeking solutions to the problem.

What does pro-life really mean?

In the context of the entrenched positions which are now found in the Church, the pro-life argument (which is often interpreted as an acceptance of a strict interpretation of *Humanae Vitae*) is often presented in an emotional, simplistic and partisan way. This approach tends to dismiss those with genuine questions and concerns and thus terminates any fruitful dialogue. Within the context of discussion of the carrying capacity of the earth, the pro-life argument needs to be seen within the widest context of the fragility of the living world. Is it really pro-life to ignore the warnings of demographers and ecologists who predict that unbridled population growth will lead to severe hardship and an increase in the infant mortality rate for succeeding generations? Is it pro-life to allow the extinction of hundreds of thousands of living species which will ultimately affect the well-being of all future generations on the planet? At present some scientists maintain that one species — homo sapiens — uses 40 per cent of the solar energy which is transformed into living tissue through photosynthesis. These same scientists question whether at this point in history, human beings can be considered the ultimate resource. Through our almost total control of all the earth's resources we are acting more like a cancer on the rest of the biosphere. Is it pro-life to ignore the increase in population levels to such an extent that the living systems in particular regions are becoming so impoverished that they will never recover?

Is there not the danger of narrowly pursuing a single goal and in the process falling into the trap of what one writer calls the paradox of conscious purpose? In setting out to defend human life in a narrow anthropocentric context, we might be creating the conditions that will, in fact, endanger all life on earth. These are important questions which were not faced by *Humanae Vitae* or any document from the Church *magisterium* since then. There is no denying the painful dilemmas involved here. The moral obligation to value life, which in a way has been so constant since the beginning of human history, now appears to be translating into a moral obligation to live with the limits of the natural world. This involves serious efforts to stabilize population levels.

A natural law grounded in an 'understanding of the kinds of beings which we are, and the ways in which we interact with our environment' might help us out of the present dilemma, which has risen in part from a static understanding of the natural law.[38] Fr G. J. Hughes, writing in *The Month* (March 1987), states that ethics should be based on the study of our nature in its natural environment. It follows that ethics is at the root an empirical study, something we find out about, in the way that we might find out about astronomy or physics or psychology or medicine. And just as further information will, as a matter of course, call in question previously accepted conclusions in these sciences, so too further information about human nature and its environment can call in question previously accepted conclusions in ethics.[39] I think it is arguable that recent understanding about the role of human beings within the natural world, coupled with our present knowledge of the extent of the damage to the biosphere, should throw open again the whole question of what are acceptable methods of controlling human fertility. This crucial knowledge has made its way very slowly into the central decision-making process of the Church. It was only in 1988, with the publication of *Sollicitudo Rei Socialis*, that the Roman authorities began to wake up to the reality of environmental degradation. Even in that document the problem is not faced in its magnitude or urgency. Lastly, as I have said before, population pressures will not go away with our refusal to face them. And in facing them, emotional slogans are no substitute for rigorous enquiry and intelligent discussion.

The Philippine Catholic Church and population increase

I feel that the Philippine Catholic Church is caught in the same dilemma as the universal Church, and that it has not faced the population issue squarely. In the mid-1970s, the Jesuit anthropologist, Fr Frank Lynch, felt compelled to challenge Catholic bishops and priests to 'speak out openly and often against the false morality of those who extol large families and abandonment to Divine Providence as prima facie evidence of supreme value'.[40]

Fr Lynch's words are even more relevant today than they were when he made them, as the following brief discussion of the Philippine population will show. The Philippines is now one of the most densely populated areas in the world, with over 173 persons per square kilometre. As we saw earlier, there was a fall in the growth rate in recent years, from a high of 3.01 per cent in the early 1960s to 2.4 per cent in the 1970s. A report in the *Manila Bulletin* (13 October 1987) indicates that the population increased by 2.7 per cent in 1987. This is attributed to the slow-down in family planning services which took place after President Aquino came to power in 1986. The life-expectancy of Filipinos has also contributed to the growth in population. This has jumped from 53 years in 1960 to 61.8 years in 1980.

In the Philippines, as in many other Third World countries, there are powerful social, economic and political reasons for people to have large families. In the rural Philippines, where a subsistence economy is still intact, each child is a potential source of labour and therefore an asset for the family. The situation changes drastically in a cash economy, where every additional member is another mouth to be fed. One important cultural reason often advanced for the high birth rate is that in the absence of an adequate social security system, people have large families so that parents can have someone to look after them in their old age. This is an additional reason why efforts to improve the socio-economic conditions of the majority of people and to provide adequate education are crucial in helping to stabilize population levels.

I began this chapter by pointing out that Tablo and many other communitites in the Philippines cannot afford to ignore this runaway growth in population. Immediate steps must be taken gradually to stabilize the population. These might include discouraging early marriages and encouraging breast-feeding. But the question must be asked: will these steps in addition to natural family planning methods significantly affect Tablo's population growth without having recourse to artificial methods? I do not know of any country which has reduced its population without using artificial methods.

But unless the growth is arrested, a sustainable future is a pipe-dream as far as Tablo and most other Philippine communities are concerned. This chapter has argued that all the life-support systems of the country — the forests, the soil, the marine and aquatic resources — are being irreversibly destroyed, even in sustaining the present population. It is true that better management of these life-systems, a more equitable distribution of wealth, and living more lightly on the earth will help alleviate some of the pressure. Techno-logical inventions and the substitution of one material for another will help lessen the pressure on non-renewable metals. But recent decades point to the fact that more people speed up the degradation of the environment.

We should also remember that some of the traditional safety valves for rising populations, like massive migration, are no longer available, as every region of the Philippines is now heavily populated. Migration was a major factor in population distribution in recent decades. Millions of people from Luzon and the Visayas moved to Mindanao to establish new homes. In the move to the new frontiers, the rights of tribal Filipinos and Muslims were often trampled upon. Today there are no more new frontiers; the possibility of migrating to First World countries will only be open to a minuscule portion of the rich and middle class.

Need for a new realism regarding population growth

This calls for a new realism regarding our population growth. It means being aware of the role that cheap oil played in spurring the increase in earlier decades and that we are in the twilight of the petrochemical era. No longer can we expect to have cheap petrochemicals available for agriculture. It will be very difficult to feed the people if the population continues to grow unabated. Present figures show that the population may double to 120 million by 2010 and double again to 240 million before the end of the twenty-first century. As the Tablo study illustrates, these demographic projections sit poorly with agriculturalists, ecologists and those involved in projecting the future needs of public services. The carrying capacity of the country will be reached long before these figures become a reality, and malnutrition, starvation and death will become a central mechanism for population control.

Those who maintain that population is not a serious problem for the Philippines must be asked to present a realistic picture of the future with a population of 200 million people. How will they be fed, clothed and sheltered? A study among industrial workers in Metro Manila in 1988 revealed that the majority of the respondents were not receiving a living wage. This study (conducted by the School of Labor and Industrial Relations of the University of the Philippines) found that a family of four members needed a minimum of 185.33 pesos per day in order to enjoy a reasonable standard of living (*Manila Chronicle*, 18 December 1988). This is more than double the present minimum wage of 69 pesos for industrial workers in Metro Manila. Any discussion about future population projections needs to take these figures seriously. If the present population is not being adequately cared for in terms of a living wage, what chance is there that double the present population will fare any better?

The same is true of public expenditure on social and educational services. What kinds of services can people expect from public authorities and where is the money going to come from to provide these services? Statements about optimum or possible levels of population tend to be based more on entrenched dogmatic positions than on a careful analysis of available data. They also ignore what the carrying capacity of a particular area might be.

This wider dimension of the population issue moves beyond the confines of individual families and looks at the impact of population growth on society as a whole. Many people feel that family planning should be left entirely in the hands of married couples. This is the position which Bishop Jesus Varela espouses in a letter to his fellow bishops dated 24 October 1988. He was writing as Chairman of the Episcopal Commission on Family Life of the Catholic Bishops' Conference of the Philippines, enunciating a possible position to be adopted by the Philippine hierarchy at their January 1989 meeting. He insists in bold capitals that 'GOVERNMENTS SHOULD NOT BE INVOLVED IN FAMILY PLANNING SERVICES'. But as Repetto (who for some curious reason is quoted in an earlier part of the letter as supposedly opposing family planning) points out in his essay:

> Individual households fail to take into account the effects of their decisions, individually small but powerfully large in the aggregate, on the community and the entire globe. These neglected effects may reverse the benefits households foresee in

having larger families: to the individual many sons may mean many earners and greater security; to the entire community it may mean only more unemployment, stagnant real wages, and greater educational burdens.[41]

It is for this reason that any government will hotly contest the position enunciated by Bishop Varela. According to his article in the bulletin of the Catholic bishops of the Philippines, *The CBCP Monitor*, Bishop Varela wonders whether there is a population problem at all in the Philippines.[42] Many people in Congress and the government are convinced that there is a major problem looming for the country and the government which has public responsibility for all the citizens has an obligation to respond to it. This responsibility includes ensuring that the population does not outstrip the resources of the country and that effective methods of fertility control be made available to the people. In the light of the earlier discussion on *Humanae Vitae* and the researches of Mercedes Concepcion, it is important to bear in mind that many Catholics feel the need for these services and resent the political lobbying of bishops aimed at denying them these services.

In order to be successful, family planning calls for major social and cultural changes. For this reason it needs the support of the religious and political leaders at both the national and local level. The overt or even tacit opposition from religious leaders of the dominant religious tradition will seriously compromise the success of family planning programmes in the country, especially when it influences government policies. At a seminar on Public Health and Population organized by the magazine *Solidarity*, Chester L. Hunt articulated the widely held feeling that the 'usual Catholic reaction is not to recognize the existence of a population problem'.[43] The same point is made by James Clad, writing in the *Far Eastern Economic Review* (20 October 1988): both Cardinal Sin and Cardinal Vidal telephoned senators to lobby against Senator Shahani's resolution which urges giving 'all men and women of reproductive age access to information and services'.

Population growth not a problem?

In the March–April edition of the Catholic Bishops' Conference of the Philippines (CBCP) *Monitor*, Fr James Reuter SJ lauds an initiative of George Winternitz of Opus Dei and Families for Family. He summarizes the content of George Winternitz's fortnightly population seminar as follows: 'For the world and for the Philippines, there is no population problem. For the world and for the Philippines, there is no problem with food. For the world and for the Philippines there is no problem with space.'[44] Few current data are presented to support any of these sweeping assertions.

Both the seminar presenter and Fr Reuter fail to take the present damaged state of all the living systems in the Philippines into account. This seems strange since human beings depend on these for their sustenance, clothing and shelter. Since 1950, for example, the tropical rainforests have dwindled from 17.5 million hectares to less than 1 million hectares. Yet experts insist that long-term agriculture in a tropical archipelago like the Philippines demands over 50 per cent forest cover. As a result of forest denudation and inappropriate agricultural techniques, much of the best land in the country is already serious eroded. Crop yields are down and the trend is expected to continue. Coral reefs and mangroves, the breeding grounds for fish, have virtually disappeared in recent decades. The repercussions are already being felt by many Filipinos. Traditionally fish was an important component in their diet; now it is much more expensive, difficult to come by and the situation is expected to deteriorate as environmental damage increases. Many rivers and springs, essential water sources for towns and villages, have been either polluted or have dried up altogether.

Some action, but not enough

It would be unfair not to mention the number of urban and rural family planning centres which have been set up by religious, priests and bishops in the Philippines. Even so, these centres are not meeting the extensive needs for family planning services nationwide. In 1973 the Catholic hierarchy of the Philippines published a pastoral on *The Population Problem and Family Life*. The document acknowledged that there was often a need to limit families (p. 4), but felt that a more just distribution of the goods of the earth was more important than controlling fertility (p. 5). It comes down heavily on the side of accelerating economic and social development as the most significant factors in bringing about fertility reduction. As we have seen, these involve a more equitable distribution of land and access to better employment, especially for those on the lower rungs of the socio-economic ladder. But, to quote Repetto once again, 'the two are complementary, and both contribute to the changes in the birth rate. Rapid fertility decline depends both on strong motivation and on access to suitable means for fertility control.'[45]

The above document did not look at the then current demographic data or discuss population levels in relation to the life-support systems of the country which, after all, must sustain the human population. There was no attempt to estimate the carrying capacity of the country or to understand what exponential rates of growth really mean. Nor did it look at the distribution of the population throughout the country and the overcrowding and growing slums in cities like Manila. In fact the greater part of the document deals with the morality of differing methods of population control and the response of *Humanae Vitae*.

The Episcopal Commission and population statements

In February 1987, the Philippine government, in its population policy statement, claimed that

> If such trends continue [a population characterized by rapid growth] the pursuit of these objectives [improved quality of life] will become more and more difficult in the future, as rapid population growth exerts more and more pressure on scarce resources as well as on an environment that is already showing signs of strain.

On 29 April 1989, the Episcopal Commission on Family Life challenged this claim. In paragraph 3 it asserted that 'the demographic reading of the situation of our people does not reflect recent findings on the nature of the relationship between population levels and socio-economic development, and between population and the nature of resources'. The statement goes on to challenge the government's claim that 'rapid population growth exerts more and more pressure on resources'. This, according to the Episcopal Commission, 'repeats an outdated 1969 view. Malaysia, Taiwan, South Korea, Israel enjoy economic growth despite some of the fastest rates of population growth.' The paragraph ends by quoting the US statement to the Second World Conference on Population (Mexico, 1984) that 'population growth is of itself neither good or bad'.

The above seem to me to be a highly selective reading of the literature on the challenges associated with rapid population growth. As I pointed out above, the USA was a minority voice at Mexico. The Secretary General of the Conference, Rafael Salas, himself a Filipino, spoke of the need to 'stabilize the global population within the shortest period possible before the end of the next century'.[46] The report of the World Commission on Environment and Development, published in 1987 under the title *Our Common Future*, states that

> the present growth rates cannot continue. They already compromise many governments' abilities to provide education, health care and food security for people, much less their ability to raise living standards. The gap between numbers and resources is all the more compelling because *so much of the population growth is concentrated in low-income countries, ecologically disadvantaged regions, and poor households.*[47]

This is the position espoused by the Philippine government's policy statement. While people are free to disagree with it, it is hardly fair to dismiss it in a cavalier fashion as a 1969 view.

One important service the Church could render is to insist that projections and judgements about population, food supply and the condition of various ecosystems be based on accurate data. The Episcopal Commission's statement quoted above is not based on current data. Three of the four countries which are said to enjoy fast economic growth do not, in fact, have high birth rates. The 1986 World Population Data Sheet records that Israel and South Korea have a 1.6 per cent increase and Taiwan 1.5 per cent, while the Philippines is credited with a 2.5 per cent annual increase. The doubling period in one case is 43 years, while for the Philippines it is 28 years. Statistics like this should be double-checked. Misuse, or patently partisan use, of data will only result in the erosion of any moral authority which the Episcopal Commission and the Bishops as a group have.

Fr Joaquin Bernas SJ approaches the Philippines population debate in a more realistic way in the *Manila Chronicle* (21 February 1989). Fr Bernas is a constitutional lawyer and brings his legal expertise to bear on the discussion of population control in both the 1973 and 1987 Philippine Constitutions. The goal of both Constitutions is the total national welfare. In the 1973 Constitution there is an emphasis on curbing growth and stabilizing population, while in the 1987 Constitution family planning appears within the context of total human development.

In the latter, the decision as to the number of children is left in the hands of the couple. Nevertheless, government efforts to promote the common good must take cognizance of population growth. In a country like the Philippines this calls for planning services which are provided by both public authorities and private groups like Church organizations. Bernas recognizes that in the wake of the Fifth Asian Meeting of Parliamentarians on Population and Development 'the search for a national policy will certainly intensify'.

Conclusion

There is one other important dimension to the family planning debate, since most of the Protestant Churches in the Philippines accept as moral some artificial methods of birth control. The 1987 Constitution acknowledges that there is a religious dimension to the issue, but this must be faced 'in the context not of a monolithic religious society, but in the context of a pluralistic society. 'Religious freedom is violated when there is an element of compulsion in state action. It is not violated when there is freedom of choice.' In a pluralistic society like the Philippines, lobbying by Catholic leaders to exclude from government-run family planning clinics methods of birth control which are forbidden by the Catholic Church is a violation of the freedom of choice of other religious groups.

The bottom line for Tablo and many other communities in most Third World countries is that populations will be controlled. There is a limit to the carrying capacity of particular bioregions. When that point has been reached, as it has in much of sub-Saharan Africa, the boom/bust syndrome takes over. The final straw is usually a prolonged drought which is itself caused by ecological damage to forests and soil. Then famine, starvation and death take over. There is a breakdown in social order and, finally, in peace and order. This is not a very pleasant scenario to contemplate, but it seems likely to occur unless the leaders and people begin to respond to the situation in the Philippines immediately.

The question which we have to face is not whether population growth will slow down or not, but whether we plan to use our intelligence to do it rationally and humanely through foresight and dynamic leadership. Should we try to avoid awful suffering and dislocation, or should we let the present growth rate continue unimpeded until we reach the point of disaster? Our future is in our own hands.

Chapter 3

When the trees are gone

The planet Earth is encircled by a sash of varying hues of green, comprising the tropical forests which are found in the Amazon region, Central America, West Africa and in Southeast Asia. These are not a single, undifferentiated mass of vegetation untouched by local conditions; biologists and experts on the tropical forest distinguish a number of diverse kinds of forests in tropical environments. These include the wet evergreen or rainforest, mangrove forests, moist deciduous forests, dry deciduous forests, open woodlands and pine and mossy forests.

The riches of the rainforest

As the pool of knowledge about tropical forests increases, biologists and other scientists marvel at the vast array of plants, animals, birds and insects that live together, especially in the community of the rainforest. At least half, and possibly as many as 80 per cent of the world's animal and plant species are found within the rainforests. If one adds insects, fungi, mosses and epiphytes, the species and genetic richness of the rainforest is enormous. Its bounty enriches the whole planet and is particularly valuable for our food, medical and other needs. The planet will be very much impoverished if this spectacular heritage is lost through ignorance, greed, and short-sighted economic policies.

The beneficence of the forest does not end at its boundaries. The rainforests are the lungs of the planet in that they produce much of the oxygen which we and every other oxygen-breathing creature depend on for life and energy. They also play an important role in regulating the climate and rainfall patterns both locally and around the planet. Over and over again in this book we will see that the impact of the living world of the rainforests reaches far beyond their boundaries and even those of the tropical region to affect the whole living fabric of the earth.

A poorly understood ecosystem

Despite their richness, beauty and colour, the rainforests have had a bad press. Few people ever visit a rainforest, even if they live in countries like the Philippines. They have never watched with delight and amusement the mimicry and camouflage which are common survival ploys among the creatures of the rainforest. They have little knowledge about the efficiency of the scavengers and micro-organisms of the forests that recycle dead matter back into the living tissue of the forest, or of how the layers of vegetative cover ensure that the torrential tropical rains do not pound the earth and wash away all the soil and its nutrients.

Little wonder, then, that the richness and splendour of the forest is not appreciated by many people. Sad to say, the majority of teachers and educators — even those who promote nationalism — fit into this category. They are ignorant about the forests and place little value on their preservation. Because of their lack of knowledge they are unable to communicate the wonders of this amazing world to their students or to the population at large. Except for the tribal people, who are at home there, and the handful of scientists who are deepening our knowledge of the rainforests, most people see them as dangerous, dark and forbidding places full of poisonous snakes and wild animals ready to pounce on human beings and devour them.

One reason for the bad press is the stereotype image of the rain-forest. Here man is pitted against nature. The hero is often portrayed as a Tarzan-like figure battling against the green hell of the jungle which is reaching out its clawing tendrils to encircle and defeat him. Anyone with the slightest knowledge of the rainforest knows that this image is totally false, yet it is deeply ingrained in modern western consciousness. Hollywood regularly shows us Rambo figures wreaking havoc on the forest. But even our everyday language betrays us: we speak of the 'law of the jungle' as if death and destruction were the primary realities there. On the contrary, the rainforest — like every other ecosystem — is made up of a complex web of co-operative and symbiotic relationships.

Why this senseless destruction?

This concept of man versus nature has played into the hands of the financial planners, entrepreneurs and politicians who see the rain-forest not as a rich tapestry of life which needs to be preserved, but as an unlimited commercial resource waiting to be exploited. In the recent past, the exploiters (especially the loggers) have exploited this myth. They have passed themselves off as knights in shining armour who are opening up this world of darkness to the bright light of the sun and making it available for human management, especially for agriculture; or as the shock troops of progress who are leading the other soldiers into the fray.

Some exploiters may be taken in by their own propaganda. The majority, it would seem, are motivated by more mundane and even selfish motives. Their eyes light up at the prospect of the handsome profit which can be reaped from exporting expensive tropical hardwoods or from clearing the forest for cattle ranching and tree farming. The urge to make a quick buck now, whatever the long-term consequences of their activity, blinds them to the fact that they are transforming the richest life-system on earth into wasteland, often in a period of less than ten years. Opening up the rainforest for agriculture, tree farming or cattle ranching is usually a recipe for disaster, since rainfall patterns, climatic conditions and soil structure ensure that none of these activities can be carried out in a sustainable way. The dreams of many an entrepreneur to transform the forest into plantations or agricultural holdings have turned to nightmares in the Amazon. Henry Ford's plans to double the world supply of rubber ended in disaster with a loss of $80 million, the equivalent of $1 billion today. In more recent times the US industrialist Daniel Ludwig also lost a fortune trying to establish jari farms and a wood-pulp export business.

A deadly mixture of ignorance, greed and induced poverty combine to destroy this indispensable living system. The destruction is taking place at an unprecedented rate: an area one-and-a-half times the size of Cuba is lost each year. The links in the greed chain bind industrial and developing countries together. People in First World countries are often unaware of the end result of their growing demand for tropical timber. They do not know, and often do not care, where the timber comes from, as long as they have new doors and furniture while their own forests are left untouched. Most First World countries play this beggar-my-neighbour game. The Japanese and Koreans are renowned for it in Asia. Strict laws protecting their own forests are stringently enforced, yet they are wreaking havoc on the forests of many Southeast Asian countries.

The demand for timber is readily met by lumber companies operating in tropical countries. These are often owned or funded by First World money. The profits which go into the pockets of a few rich people are staggering. The rules governing the business are loose. Moreover the tax man, the customs officer and the government agency entrusted with guarding the forest can be bypassed with a few well-placed presents or bribes.

Add to this the increase in population and the rising need for food and firewood, and all the factors which accelerate the destruction of the forest are in place. This is a cycle of death which is wasteful and short-sighted. The downward spiral which begins with the destruction of the forest inevitably leads to rivers drying up and arable land becoming barren. It is a tragedy that could be avoided with a little more thought, care and genuine concern for the needs of the forest and the needs of the poor.

Whatever the reasons may be, and they differ from country to country and region to region, the forests are being depleted at an alarming rate. The British biologist Norman Myers estimates that 20 million hectares of rainforests worldwide are destroyed or seriously depleted each year.[1] This destruction threatens the stability of all the other living systems of the earth. This perception is shared by the authors of *Global 2000 Report to the President, 1980* and more recently by the report of the World Commission on Environment and Development called *Our Common Future*. But this new understanding and feel for the forest will have to touch political and economic planners and ordinary citizens before a concerted effort of sufficient magnitude is launched to save the rainforest. The situation is so serious that the publishers of *The Ecologist* magazine have launched a campaign called 'Save the Forests: Save the Planet'. They are seeking one million signatures in order to request an extraordinary meeting of the United Nations to address this pressing problem.[2]

Rainforests of the Philippines

The tropical rainforest is the normal cover which nature has designed and perfected over millions of years to protect tropical lands. Originally, most of the 30 million hectares of the land surface comprising the Republic of the Philippines was covered with dense tropical rainforests. The dipterocarp forests are the most common in the Philippines. In areas where there is a distinct dry season, the molave forests are found. The narra and molave trees, which are found in these forests, are much sought after by furniture makers. Along the coast and in the estuaries, mangrove and beech forest once flourished and pine forests are still found on the higher slopes of the mountains.

All of these forests are currently under threat of extinction. The rate of destruction in the Philippines is alarming. Every three minutes the Philippines loses one hectare of its forest cover. The Haribon data sheet[3] on Philippine forest cover published in 1988 uses data from a Swedish Satellite to determine how much forest cover is left in the country. Its figures state that only 22.5 per cent of the total land area has forest cover. It is for this reason that the *1987 Yearbook* of the *Encyclopaedia Britannica* predicts that this 'may be the last generation of Filipinos to ever see a virgin tropical rainforest'. By the end of the century the Philippines will have lost all its primal rainforest. We have little more than a decade left. The main culprits are the logging companies, who supply the insatiable demand for tropical hardwood in First World countries. These are followed by the slash-and-burn farmers called *kaingineros* in many Philippine languages, who cultivate the steep slopes in the mountains, by people who collect and sell firewood for domestic use and by the cattle ranchers who produce meat for the growing fast-food industry.

The depletion of the Philippines forests was already under way during the three centuries of Spanish rule. Shifting cultivation, timber for ship-building, and the drive to open up land for large scale plantations of sugar, coconut and abaca had cut the forested area by half by the year 1910, according to the Bureau of Forestry figures. The population of the country rose steadily during the three centuries — from an estimated 500,000 when the Spanish arrived in 1521 to about 7 million when they left in 1898. Vast areas of forest were opened up in lowland areas in Luzon and the Visayas to meet the food and firewood needs of the growing population. The Spanish presence in Mindanao was sparse, so the forest there was not exploited for commercial purposes. The forests did, however, supply the needs of many tribal Filipino groups who lived either in the forests or close to them.

However, the really concerted attack on the forests began during the American period, which began in 1898 and continued until 1946. American logging companies with ties to some elite Filipino families took advantage of the colonial government's policies to exploit the natural resources of the islands. The build-up took some time to get under way. It was relatively slow in the years before World War II when only an average of 1.6 million cubic metres of logs were cut each year. After the war things changed drastically as the loggers moved in with a vengeance. Between 1945 and 1960 it was virtually a free-for-all. There was little effort to regulate the operations in any way. Logging companies usually went ahead of the settlers who arrived in Mindanao from the Visayas and Luzon. They were seen as an integral part of the settlement programme. The rich were happy on a number of counts: huge fortunes were amassed from the logging operations, with little or no monitoring by the government; the newly opened up land took the pressure off campaigns for land reform in both Luzon and the Visayas, so large plantations owned by a few rich families remained intact. There were some crumbs for the poor also. Some were given land in the settlement programmes. Others hoped that they would get their share too since the supply seemed limitless.

The volume of lumber cut shot up rapidly during these years. Through most of the 1950s and 1960s around 11.5 million cubic metres was cut each year. Foreign logging companies reaped the lion's share of the profits. Gradually, the local elite (who usually held political power) entered every facet of the operation, either alone or in co-operation with foreign companies or banks.

The logging companies showed little or no concern for the forest environment. The forest was a resource to be exploited in whatever way produced the fastest and highest profit. Harvesting methods which destroyed young trees, and clear-cutting, were regularly used. The philosophy was usually 'get in, get at it, get out' and move on elsewhere while the boom lasts. Few companies encouraged or funded any research into the forest. No major study of the forests was undertaken by either the government or the companies who were reaping huge profits. Reforestation and harvesting in a sustainable way was little more than a joke. Very few companies ever seriously attempted to replant trees. A few stands of exotic species along the roads and a well-placed contribution here and there could be expected to keep everyone happy. The researcher on Philippine forests Ooi Jin Bee[4] reports that during the heyday of the logging business only about 1 per cent of the area cut each year was reforested.

It is important to emphasize that, although rainforests are probably the most stable and resilient living system on earth in their natural state, when humans interfere with their functioning through logging, they are extremely fragile and easily damaged. Even so-called selective logging is destructive. In his book *The Primary Source: the Tropical Forests and our Future*, the tropical forester Norman Myers points out that 'repeated studies in Southeast Asia reveal that average logging leaves between one-third and two-thirds of the residual trees injured beyond repair'.[5] He quotes the cynical remark about selective logging: the corporation 'selects the forest and then logs it'.

Another important consideration has emerged in recent years to challenge the assertion that logging does not seriously damage the forest. Studies indicate that many of the life-forms in the rainforest live in the canopy. When the thinning exceeds 30 per cent, a rainforest ceases to operate as an integral ecosystem. Sunlight pierces through to the forest floor and disrupts the fragile ecosystem; the end result can mean a loss of up to 50 per cent of the species living there. The burning tropical sun bakes the laterite soil brick-hard during the dry season and the monsoon rains soon turn it into puddles of mud.

The Marcos legacy: felled forests and fat Swiss bank accounts

The destruction of forest by logging companies continued during the regime of the late President Marcos from 1965 to 1986. A new Forestry Code was introduced in 1974 (PD No. 389). This was eventually supposed to lead to a ban on the export of unprocessed logs. The idea behind this was good: it was meant to stimulate a local wood-processing industry. Like many other policies during the Marcos regime, it did not survive too long. It was only implemented for a short period; it seems that once it began to hit the pockets of Marcos's supporters, the ban was dropped.

But much of the rhetoric and tree-planting campaigns of the Marcos era were at best cosmetic and at worst hypocritical. The destruction of the forest continued unabated. In the late 1960s and 1970s NEDA (the National Economic and Development Agency of the Philippines) estimated that 170,000 hectares of forest were being destroyed annually. The actual figure was probably much higher. Large concessions were awarded to Marcos's relatives or supporters or to high-ranking military officers. Constitutional limits proved no barrier to Marcos. Even though the Constitution of the Philippines set a limit of 100,000 hectares for any single logging concession, Cellophil Resources Corporation (CRC), which was owned by Hermino Desini, a relative of Marcos, was awarded a 200,000 hectare concession in the ancestral territory of the Tingguian. Quite apart from flagrantly violating the Constitution, this fanned the flames of rebellion in the area.

Moreover, during the Marcos period high-ranking army officers got into the logging business. The usual practice was for the local commander to form an alliance with illegal loggers so that a good share of the profits went their way in return for military protection for the logging operation. Not to be outdone, the New People's Army (NPA) seem to be pursuing similar policies. In areas which they control in the Cordillera, Negros, Samar and Mindanao, they levy a tax on the concessionaire, subcontractor or even tabloneros (small-scale chainsaw operators who cut timber in the forests) for each log that is cut and shipped out. Unless the operators pay up, the NPA burn their lorries or logging equipment.

This taxation policy is still being pursued by the NPA and corrupt army officers under the Aquino government. It is reported that in Region 2 alone the NPA set out to collect between 18 and 20 million pesos on logging operations in 1987. Understandably it is difficult to verify these figures since some elements in the army spread NPA scare stories whenever it suits them. The *Manila Bulletin* of 10 December 1988 carried a story about the seizure of illegal logs in Mindanao. Tucked away at the end of the piece was a reference to a people's power picket which residents from the town of San Fernando in Bukidnon staged outside the DENR offices in the capital Malaybalay in order to call attention to the destructive impact of all logging in their area. The final paragraph contained the ridiculous claim by the military authorities that 'the picketers are being financed by the New People's Army'. Maybe these same military sources would like people to think that the bishops of the Philippines who praised an earlier initiative by picketers at San Fernando in their pastoral letter *What Is Happening To Our Beautiful Land?* (January 1988: see Appendix 2 below, pp. 207–16) are also financed by the NPA?

Anomalies during the Marcos period were not confined to doling out large concessions to relatives, supporters or returned rebels; figures for logs cut and logs shipped were also changed and falsified. For example, customs authorities reveal that in 1981 the export of logs of Japan amount to 364,441 cubic metres, while the *Japan Lumber Journal* records show that 1.4 million cubic metres were imported from the Philippines. Some of the excellent tropical timber exported to Japan ends up as disposable chopsticks, or as packaging or construction material.

The real extent of the pillage carried out during the 20 years of Marcos's rule is clear from recent satellite pictures on which the Haribon data sheet is based. They show an alarming situation as far as the Philippine tropical rainforests are concerned. Only a little over 20 per cent of the country has any forest cover at all. The primal forest cover has gone down from over 16 million hectares in 1945 to around 1 million hectares today. Agriculturalists, who are concerned for the long-term sustainability of lowland agriculture, are alarmed by the present lack of forest cover. As far back as the 1960s they pointed out that a tropical archipelago like the Philippines needs at least 50 per cent forest cover in order to ensure the long-term future of agriculture.

The Aquino presidency

That the plunder of the Philippine forests did not end with the ousting of President Marcos in February 1986 is clear from a report entitled 'The Politics of Plunder', which appeared in the *Far Eastern Economic Review* (November 1988). The authors, James Clad and Marites Vitug, say that the island of Palawan is, at present, being devastated by political families, backed by the military. Some of these families were cronies of Marcos, but changed sides in time to benefit from present largess of patronage under the Aquino administration.

Palawan is a remote and isolated island, set in the South China Sea to the west of most of the other islands in the Philippine archipelago. It is a place of outstanding natural beauty with forested mountains and coral-fringed coasts. In fact, it is one of the few remaining areas of the country which has an adequate forest cover. In 1986 the Department of Environment and Natural Resources (DENR) figures showed that Palawan had 54 per cent forest. This is not destined to last very long since large areas have already been carved up among logging concessionaires. James Clad writes:

> a glance at the maps in northern Palawan's Bureau of Forest
> Development (BFD) office is revealing. Overlapping
> concessions to prominent political families crisscross the
> BFD's 252,867 ha. territory out of Palawan's 780,000 ha.
> forest. Alvarez's [the ex-Marcos crony] concessions alone
> cover more than 50 per cent of the BFD's area and 25 per cent
> of Palawan's total forest area.[6]

The logging companies are cutting round the clock and the forest continues to dwindle as each month passes.

The Haribon Foundation of the Philippines, a non-government environmental organization, has campaigned for a log ban in Palawan in order to protect its unique habitat, the ancestral lands of tribal peoples like the Bataks, Tagbanuas and the Palau-ans and its potential as a tourist attraction. But in this struggle the conservationists are pitted against a powerful coalition of political, business and military interests. In the present political climate of patronage in the Philippines, James Clad thinks that the conservationists will lose.

Kaingineros, powerless and convenient scapegoats

Despite this saga of duplicity and venality by politicians and military, the destruction of the forest is laid at the door of kaingineros, the slash-and-burn farmers. Since they lack money and political clout they become a convenient target for the loggers and politicians when it comes to apportioning blame. Academics have also contributed to this myth. Ooi Jin Bee in his monograph *Depletion of the Forest Resources in the Philippines* describes the kaingineros in detail and castigates them for destroying the forest — while the role of loggers and corrupt politicians is hardly mentioned.

In some ways it is not hard to understand why the kaingineros receive a bad press. The loggers and government officials have continued to repeat their charges for almost 40 years without anyone really challenging them, so it is not surprising that the public is inclined to believe their version of events. Moreover kaingineros are not organized and have no access to the media, so they have no way of countering the charges made by loggers. It is also entirely consistent with the underlying philosophy of many economists, planners and politicians that the forest is seen primarily as a commercial resource which should be exploited in the most productive way. They are willing to overlook the saga of deceit and corruption presented above because of their bias towards the commercial utilization of the forest. They are convinced that business people do things more efficiently and profitably; in their world these are the sacred values. In the process, the exploiters earn foreign exchange through exporting the resource. The operation is seen to contribute to an increase in the Gross National Product (GNP), which also legitimizes it in the eyes of people who subscribe to this peculiar economic value system.

Yet it is this very fiction which has laid waste the forest during the past few decades. What is more, this myth has also destroyed the cultures and livelihood of the people who have lived within or close to the forest for thousands of years. Little thought has been given to the fact that, before the advent of large-scale logging, slash-and-burn farmers and, especially, tribal people, were farming the forests in a sustainable way often for over one thousand years. This is hardly ever mentioned because so-called 'development' people tend to look at the forest in economic terms and therefore miss the complex ecological and cultural reality which is staring them in the face. The simplistic economic view favours large-scale commercial exploitation and inevitably means the demise of the forest.

The people who have depended on the forest for generations lose on two counts. On the one hand they are presumed not to exist, since the forests are presented as uninhabited areas. Government officials or loggers pay scant attention to their needs and destroy their habitat, completely undermining their cultural and subsistence patterns. On the other hand, the kaingineros, because they do not fit into the planners' economic pigeonhole, are seen as unproductive and are blamed for depleting the forest.

It is not my intention to canonize the typical kainginero and paint him as a kind of latter-day noble savage. I have seen too many mountains ablaze and too much destruction to fall into that trap; but I do feel that the kaingineros are bearing the brunt of the blame, much of which should be laid at the door of the loggers and the economic planners who have contributed to grinding poverty in the rural tropics. As early as 1914, Dean Worcester, the Secretary of the Interior during the American occupation, foresaw the damage that unchecked logging would do. 'If adequate measures are not adopted for the conservation of the forests, we shall sooner or later be confronted with the danger of the devastation by the lumbermen.'[7] Forester Nestor Baguinon, in a paper written in 1987 entitled *Development and Conservation of Indigenous Non-Dipterocarp Trees and Shrub Species*,[8] looks back at the destruction of the Philippine forests in the 1960s and 1970s. He insists that the main culprits are the loggers not the kaingineros. He also casts a much more critical eye on other social and economic factors which have contributed to the destruction of the forest. These include a lack of appreciation of the forests which is fostered by cultural values, and the educational system; an alien concept of 'land ownership' and the support which banks and financial institutions give to those who are destroying the forest by bankrolling their operations, and the building of roads right into the heart of the forest.

For Baguinon, logging is the linchpin of the whole destructive process. He points out that 'the proliferation of logging roads into the forest hinterlands between 1950 and 1970 naturally made far-flung areas accessible to a swelling land hungry population, such that these roads were later to be called "the arteries of forest destruction" '. Kaingineros enter the forest along the logging roads. Many of them are people who have worked for the logging company, for instead of giving severance pay to its employees when the operation ceased, the company had often encouraged them to begin *kaingin* (slash-and-burn farming) in the concession area. Those who are not native to the area plant crops like corn, which are unsuitable for sloping and marginal land. A few croppings completely deplete the soil and begin the process of soil erosion and final degradation. Within a few short years, one of the richest life-systems on earth, with extraordinary potential if harvested in a sustainable way, is laid waste and ruined. Those responsible for issuing licences to concessionaires know that if logging permits are allowed to continue then, to quote Baguinon again, 'the remaining forests will suffer the same fate as their predecessors'. Each of the contributors to the 'Save the Forests: Save the Planet' issue of *The Ecologist* supports Baguinon's position.[9]

Baguinon does not overlook or exonerate the kaingineros, but he has a deeper understanding of the factors that force them into the mountains and sympathy for them, as many of them live below the poverty line. Three factors work together to push more and more people up into the rainforests. The first is poverty. People who have no money and no food will burn down the rainforest and try to till it. Mass rural poverty in many tropical countries is directly tied to the second social reality — the concentration of the best lands in the hands of a small local elite and of transnational agribusiness corporations. In South Cotabato, for example, much of the 250,000 hectares of arable land area is controlled by a few transnational corporations and a handful of Manila-based and local elite involved in logging, cattle ranching or cash-crop, export-oriented agriculture. The inequitable distribution of land is found nationwide, and the unwillingness of the political elite to carry out effective land reform makes it highly unlikely that this problem will be solved in the near future despite the Comprehensive Agrarian Reform Program (CARP) of Republic Act no. 6657.

Many of the same problems are found in Brazil. Local cattle ranchers and foreign companies are encouraged, through government subsidies, to produce beef for export. These hire poor, landless peasants to create new pastures by burning the rainforest each year. In 1988 alone around 80,000 square miles of the Amazon was burned. The switch in recent years to export-oriented cash crops has contributed to the destruction of the rainforest. In southern Brazil, much of the most fertile land is now devoted to soya bean production. Tenants who traditionally worked that land have been evicted. Rather than push through land reform legislation and incur the anger of the rich, the government has actively encouraged the displaced poor to migrate to the Amazon region and there to create new farmland.

In Brazil as in the Philippines, the destruction of the rainforest must be laid at the feet of the local elite. In a feature article in *The Weekend Guardian* (25–26 November 1989), Alexander Cockburn and Susanna Hecht write that the prime culprits for destroying the forest are to be found 'inside Brazil in the post war [World War II] alliance between the country's elite and military state'.

These, of course, did not act alone, but in tandem with transnational corporations, multilateral lending agencies like the World Bank, and US foreign policy strategists in Latin America.

Some consequences of forest destruction

The loss of our species and genetic storehouse

Scientists now maintain that the rainforests are the most important living system on earth. They are a precious gift to the whole planet and should be cherished. What accounts for their astonishing richness? First of all they are among the oldest living systems on earth, having evolved during the past 200 million years in an environment which was especially favourable. They are located within latitudes where there were no glacial interruptions during the planet's recent history. This means that the vegetative and animal life was not wiped out during the periodic ice ages, so evolutionary development has been continuous. The latitude also ensures a constant supply of rain and warm temperatures which are the conditions most suitable for optimum growth all the year round.

A combination of these two factors has produced an enormous variety of living species in the rainforest in comparison to other ecosystems. Even though they now cover only 6 per cent of the world's land surface, they are home to over half of the world's 10 million species. In the Amazon alone there are more than 1 million species of plants and animals and more than 2,000 species of fish. It is estimated that a single river in the Amazon may contain more species of fish than all the rivers in the United States.

This means that in the community of life which forms the rainforest we have a precious genetic treasure chest, far in excess of that found in the economically rich countries in the northern hemisphere. Biologists, for example, estimate that in roughly 6 hectares of rainforest there are more species of trees than in the whole of Britain. In the Philippines, the rainforests contain almost 20,000 species of plants and of the 13,000 species of flowering plants, 3,500 are found only in these. There are around 3,000 species of trees, most of which are members of the Dipterocarpaceae family. In addition to plants and trees there are untold species of mosses, fungi, epiphytes, algae and almost 900 species and sub-species of birds, including the famous Philippine eagle. There are many more unnamed species since the work of classifying species in the rainforest even now remains incomplete. This species and genetic diversity is surely a more meaningful measure of the wealth of a nation than the average income of its people. This wealth should not be squandered, abused or wantonly destroyed, merely to satisfy the greed of a few rich people.

In the ecosystem of the rainforest, one species is linked to a variety of other species through dynamic and interdependent relationships. Interrelations and connections are the key words. Life-forms depend on one another. There are co-operative, predator and symbiotic relationships. Studies show that the survival of each species is vital for the integrity of the rainforest. Furthermore, this species and genetic diversity is also very important for the human community. Our domestic food varieties need the species found in the forest to keep them resistant to disease. These plants have survived in the highly competitive environment of the forest and so have developed a high resistance to diseases and pests. Modern biological technology makes it possible to transfer these sturdy genes to domestic food crops and thus reduce the dependence of farmers on petrochemical fertilizers and pesticides. A species of wild maize found in a small patch of forest in Mexico contains genes which are resistant to many of the diseases which threaten domestic varieties of maize. A single gene from the Ethiopian barley saved the barley crop in California in recent years.

In addition, the plants, berries, nuts, fish and other creatures found in the rainforest are used as food by the tribal peoples who live there. Many of the 80,000 species of edible plants are highly nutritious and could easily be added to the larder of a much greater proportion of the human race. Humans have not begun to explore and use the bounty of nature. Today only around 200 plants are being cultivated in any extensive way, and even then we are heavily dependent on rice, wheat, maize and potatoes for the bulk of our diet. It is vital that we preserve the forests since new sources of food will be necessary to meet the nutritional needs of a rapidly growing population in the decades ahead.

Plants and animals from the rainforest are also very important in maintaining and improving our health care. Almost half the drugs which we find in a pharmacy are derived from plants which grow in the tropical rainforest. Medicines for many of the major diseases are derived from the rainforest. Probably the best known is quinine which has been used for the past three centuries in the treatment of malaria. The word is derived from the Indian name *quinaquina* which means 'bark of barks'. The story of how Jesuit missionaries in Latin America discovered Indians treating those suffering from malaria with this bark, and how they brought this knowledge back to Europe, is an extraordinary one, full of prejudice and intrigue. According to Catherine Caufield, Oliver Cromwell preferred to die of malaria rather than use what had become known as the Jesuit bark. In the eighteenth century the Dutch and English funded expeditions to smuggle seeds of the famed cinchona tree out of Latin America and plant them in their own tropical colonies. Little came of these efforts as the varieties which were brought contained little quinine.[10] But quinine is not the only forest-based drug which is used in the treatment of common illnesses. Ipecac is employed in the treatment of amoebic dysentery. Reserpine is often prescribed for those suffering from hypertension, whilst heart patients are often given strophanthin. Wild yams provided vital material in the development of the contraceptive pill.

In recent years the survival rate of children with lymphatic leukaemia has been greatly enhanced by a drug which is derived from rose periwinkle — a plant native to the rainforests of Madagascar. In the early 1960s four out of every five children suffering from leukaemia died. Today three out of five survive because of drugs derived from this plant. But scientists are keenly aware that what is already in use represents only the tip of the iceberg. Less than 10 per cent of rainforest plants have been studied for their medicinal properties. Scientists at the National Cancer Institute in the USA estimate that 70 per cent of drugs which show promise in cancer treatment come from the rainforest.

In his 'Requiem for the Philippine forests', Jun Terra lists a number of Philippine medicinal plants and their common use. *Talungpunay (Datura alba)* is used for asthma attacks; *duhat (Eugenia jambolana)* for treating diabetes; *acapulco (Cassia alata)* for skin infections; *yerba buena (Mentha cordifolia)* for arthritis and rheumatism; *sambong (Bluema balsamifera)* for high blood pressure; *madre de kakaw (Gliricidia sepium)* for scabies; and *bolon* fruit and *dudua* seeds to cure tuberculosis.[11]

Even from this brief overview, it should be clear that the destruction of the rainforest means that we are depriving ourselves of this rich resource, in many cases even before we are able to recognize its true potential.

Extinction

The death of the forest means the extinction of many of these valuable species. This is an appalling disaster for the fabric of life on earth. It should evoke an immediate response from every person, but especially from religious people who should respect and value life wherever it is found. The rate of slaughter is so extensive that some biologists estimate that over 25 per cent of all living species will become extinct in the next 30 years. Nothing comparable has happened since at least the end of the Mesozoic era, when the dinosaurs were wiped out, over 60 million years ago, and probably since the first flicker of life appeared on earth 3.5 billion years ago. Seeing that each extinction can in time lead to the extinction of around twenty other living forms, biologists worry about the domino effect of this wholesale slaughter. Each strand pulled from the closely knit fabric of life endangers the survival of other species, including human beings. Even if humankind survives this slaughter, it will still be much diminished in its beauty, vigour and fruitfulness.

Finally, extinction will also affect the long list of industrial products which are derived from the rainforests. Leaving aside commercial timber, the list of uses for rainforest products is surprisingly extensive. Canes and fibres are used in the furniture and clothing industries. Oils derived from the tropical forests are found in beverages and deodorants. Edible oils are used in manufacturing detergents, emollients and lubricants, especially for high-speed engines. When we shampoo our hair, play golf or tennis, fly from city to city or simply dress in an expensive shirt, we are using products which have come ultimately from the rainforests. Yet we have only just begun to see the value of less than 10 per cent of the plant species of the forest and much less of the animal life in the forest. This extraordinarily rich source for enhancing life in the future is now in peril. Spurred on by greed for quick profits, the proprietors of a few exploitative operations are killing the goose that lays the golden egg.

While all of us are familiar with the death of individual members of particular species, the extinction of entire species touches very few of our lives so we find it hard really to understand and respond in an appropriate way. We also find the scale of the destruction and the numbers involved hard to imagine so we tend not to grasp its full import. But it is imperative that we try to study this phenomenon seriously and understand its significance before we lose a third, or maybe even half, of all life on earth.

The first thing that must be appreciated is that extinction is not like the death of a single organism. With death, individuals die but the species continues. With extinction, the species disappears for ever. Nothing can ever retrieve it again, despite our much-vaunted discoveries in biotechnology. Large-scale extinction sterilizes the planet and makes it inhospitable for life for all time.

Many species of plants, insects, birds and animals are at present on the brink of extinction in the Philippines. Some of the better known ones are the mouse deer, the calamian deer and the Philippine eagle. Scientists working with the Philippine Eagle Conservation Programme in Davao estimate that originally the country supported over 11,000 pairs of eagles. Today this majestic bird is on the brink of extinction, with only about 100 pairs now, found mainly in Mindanao. The primary cause of extinction in most cases is the destruction of habitat.

From a religious perspective, extinction means that the integrity of creation is seriously compromised. It is also an injustice to future generations to pass on to them a sterile and barren planet. Religious people's concern for life must challenge them to do everything possible to preserve these endangered species. In practice this means making sure they have sufficient territory on which to survive and campaigning to stop activities which encroach on their habitat and degrade it.

A cartoon in the *Philippine Star* on 19 March 1988 aptly illustrates what extinction and ecological degradation means. On the previous morning there had been a total eclipse of the sun, visible in the southeastern tip of Mindanao. The cartoon shows a viewer looking at the moon blocking out the sun. Every now and then the viewer looks back at the earth on which he is standing. He realizes that it is gradually taking on the barren, lifeless features of the moon. This is the face of eternal death.

Throughout this presentation I have underscored the value of the rainforest for people living today and for future generations. The argument is simple: in the rainforests we have an extraordinary world which is providing valuable products for human beings. Rather than treating it as a renewable resource, we are destroying it irreversibly in the space of a few decades. From a medium- or long-term perspective this is sheer madness, even in the narrow economic view.

While it is important to emphasize the instrumental value for people of the rainforests and other entities in the living world, it is more important to realize that they have an intrinsic value and a right to exist. Any discussion of extinction must face the moral right which other species and habitats have to exist on the planet. In recent centuries religious traditions have focused their moral precepts on interpersonal behaviour because the ecological dimension did not seem so important. Now they must broaden their perspective and include the relationship between human beings and other species.

In the light of the accelerated destruction of species, the Christian tradition needs to emphasize the broad base of the Covenant which God made with Noah and 'with your descendants after you; also with every living creature to be found with you, birds, cattle and every wild beast with you; everything that came out of the ark, everything that lives on the earth' (Gen 9:8–10). This right of other species to exist is recognized in the World Charter for Nature which was adopted by the United Nations in 1984. The drafters of this document and similar ones (like the proposed Philippine Charter for Nature) would like to see this principle enshrined in national and international legal codes.

Soil erosion

Many of the negative effects of forest destruction illustrate what is often called the first law of ecology: everything is connected to everything else. Contrary to popular perception, most of the soils of the tropical rainforest are not rich. All of the nutrients are stored in the vegetation rather than in the soil. When there is no human interference these nutrients are quickly recycled because the system works so well. But when powerful machinery removes the cover, there is little left to nourish plants and the host of other life forms which live together in the forest. Burning the vegetation will only provide one or two good harvests for the kaingineros. After that, the soil is either washed away or becomes unproductive.

Once the trees are removed, any topsoil is quickly eroded by torrential rain and carried down into the streams and rivers. Studies in Central America have demonstrated that a single tropical storm can dislodge up to 150,000 kilogrammes of soil from one hectare of hillside which has been stripped of trees. The comparable figure from the same area of forested hillside is a mere 44 kilogrammes per year. Because so much of the Philippines is now bare, the Bureau of Soil estimates that the equivalent of 100,000 hectares of soil one metre thick is lost each year through erosion. This in turn silts up riverbeds, irrigation canals and estuaries, rendering useless expensive irrigation projects, destroying rich agricultural lands and causing a drop in the water table.

The forest also supplies water to agricultural land, through streams and irrigation canals. This is crucial during the dry season. Double cropping helps the farmer financially and increases the supply of food for the population at large. When the forest is cut, the vegetation and soil no longer act as a sponge to absorb the water and gradually secrete it through river systems. Instead it quickly runs off, to cause flash floods and silt up the rivers. In recent years in the Philippines the life-span of irrigation projects has been cut drastically. At this moment, forest destruction is endangering the countrywide network of irrigation projects and many water sources for towns and cities. Finally, the silt is carried out to sea where it chokes and eventually kills the delicate coral polyps, thus destroying rich fishing grounds. Even in the early 1960s the loss of forest cover and the extensive cultivation of corn significantly increased the rate of erosion on the island of Cebu.[12]

It is easy to see how the destruction of the forest casts a long shadow over the long-term future of agriculture in a tropical environment when the rains that cause floods are followed almost immediately by severe droughts. In Southeast Asia, for example, millions of people live in the heavily farmed, rich alluvial plains that depend on the forest watershed for a constant supply of water. If, through flash floods, erosion and long droughts, these lands are rendered unsuitable for agriculture, millions of people will starve. The final act in the drama of destruction is the appearance of deserts. These are now spreading in Ilocos Norte and Ilocos Sur where the rainforest has been destroyed through burning wood for firewood and tobacco curing. Deserts are also beginning to appear in the once fertile lands of the Visayas and Mindanao.

Flash floods

A denuded watershed leads to widespread and severe flash flooding during the heavy monsoons and typhoons. Typhoons like Unsang and Yoling in October 1988 took an enormous toll on human life, crops, roads, bridges, schools and houses. Public authorities spend enormous sums of money building diversion canals on roads and embankments on rivers, but neglect the more basic cause of the problem — the denudation of the hills through logging and slash-and-burn agriculture. When particularly devastating flash floods follow in the wake of a typhoon an outcry goes up from the press, public officials and perhaps religious leaders. But it is soon forgotten. The public rage subsides and the exploiters, after donating a few sacks of rice to the victims, go back to work. In South Cotabato a particularly important bridge near General Santos city was undermined by flash floods in 1987. The local congressman campaigned to have a temporary structure built and a sign was erected giving him credit for this. What was forgotten is that this man and his family had, over the years, been one of the biggest loggers in the province.

Flash floods are not the only problem. Deforestation also leads to prolonged periods of drought. The water crisis which Manila and the surrounding provinces experienced in 1986 was a direct result of the destruction of the forest in the Angat watershed reservation. More severe crises can be expected in the years ahead as the remaining forest cover is removed. In Mindanao the future of the Agus river hydroelectric project is endangered by the drop in the level of Lake Lanao. The primary cause of this is logging operations in the watershed area.

The rainforests stabilize our climate

The rainforest also plays a role in stabilizing climates. 60 per cent of the rain that falls in the forest is absorbed by the vegetation and transpired back into the atmosphere. In this way the rainforest cleans and filters the fresh water so that it is recycled many times before it finally makes it way down through the river systems into the sea. An extensive forest cover also minimizes the impact of large-scale droughts caused by such external phenomena as El Niño.[13] If much of the rain is locally generated the area is not subjected to droughts when major meteorological changes like the suspension of the monsoons or the appearance of El Niño occur. Twice in the 1980s this phenomenon has brought severe drought and consequent loss of crops to millions of Filipinos. There is every reason to believe that an adequate forest cover would have significantly lessened the impact of the drought.

Another way in which the forest stabilizes the global climate is by locking up billions of tons of carbon in the vegetation. When the forests are destroyed and the trees are burned this releases millions of tons of carbon dioxide into the atmosphere and adds to the condition known as the 'greenhouse effect'. The increased destruction of the Amazon in the 1980s may be responsible for pumping anything between 3 and 6 billion tonnes of carbon into the air each year.[14] The carbon traps solar heat in the lower atmosphere. This, in turn, raises the global temperature. Scientists estimate that the level of carbon in the air has increased 40 per cent since the 1850s. As a result the polar icecaps are beginning to melt. If the condition persists, these same scientists predict that the level of the oceans may rise by between 2 and 5 metres during the next 40 years. That would mean severe flooding in many coastal cities worldwide, including Manila, Cebu and Davao.

The destruction of tribal cultures

Laying waste the forest also sounds the death-knell for numerous tribal cultures worldwide. The Brazilian forests are home to 220,000 Indians from 170 different tribes. These people, in common with tribal peoples in other parts of South and Southeast Asia, have depended on the forest for centuries for their food, clothing and medicine. Their hunting, farming, fishing and gathering has been carried out in such a way as not to deplete the forest. The survival of these cultures is directly threatened by timber concessionaires, mining companies and by cattle ranches. This is very obvious to me living among the T'boli people of South Cotabato. Scores of tribal cultures in Mindanao face extinction as integral cultures in the next few decades if the devastation of their habitat continues.

For this reason tribal people in the Amazon area, in Sarawak and in Mindanao have, in the past few years, begun to place human barricades across logging roads. The Penans and the Dayaks of Sarawak began barricading logging roads in 1987 in an effort to stop the logging which was wreaking havoc on their forests and destroying their culture and way of life. In a letter to the government in Kuala Lumpur they stated in somewhat faltering English that:

> We see with sorrow the logging companies entering our country. In these areas where timber is extracted there is no life for us nomadic people. Our natural resources, like wild fruit trees, sago palms, wood trees for blowpipe, dart poison and other need will fall. Animals like wild boar, our daily food, and deer will flee. Rivers will be polluted and quickly overfished.

> So, we now declare our wood reserved. We don't sell the lands of our fathers. Please you our Sarawak government and you Timber Companies, respect our origin rights.[15]

In their protests they have been supported by international organizations like Survival International. Locally, however, they have faced the armed henchmen of the exploiters and also local army and paramilitary personnel who are often bought off by loggers and miners. Time is also running out for the Penans and their forest. Between January and April 1989 the volume of timber exported rose by 44 per cent. At this rate much of the area will be destroyed within 18 months.[16] Like those who were picketing in San Fernando, Bukidnon, the Penans and their supporters are often labelled as communists or subversives; then they become fair game for anyone who wishes to exterminate them.

Extinction impoverishes the community of the living earth. In much the same way, the human community is impoverished by the disappearance of tribal cultures. These cultures that have lived lightly on the earth have much to teach our Western earth-consuming culture if we are to evolve more sustainable ways of living on this planet. In an article 'Vanishing tribals' which appeared in *Newsweek* (21 September 1981) a spokesperson for Survival International lamented the demise of tribal cultures. The destruction of a single culture was likened to ravaging a complete library with no chance of ever recovering the information. A range of cultures enriches the whole human family; 'if we get rid of these people we are effectively destroying ourselves'.

The plight of tribal peoples seldom makes front page news, even in their own countries. They live on the bottom rung of the political and economic ladder so they have little political clout and few agencies to champion their cause. Their interests are seldom taken into account by government planners or multinational lending agencies that provide the foreign loans which are used to rape their lands. Any comprehensive study of tribal people in Mindanao will show that the extinction of tribal cultures is, in fact, taking place right before our eyes. Because tribal people are not highly visible, lowland Filipino communities tend to ignore their desperate situation or else look the other way.

What can be done

Individuals

Each and every one of us should try to respect all living beings. Given the threat to the forests, those who own land can plant and care for trees and join together with other members of the community in campaigning for reforestation programmes. As Christians who believe that the God who created this world is reflected in each creature and particularly in each species, we are called to live in a much simpler way. In the present context, we should try to use firewood sparingly as a way to conserve our forest; indeed we should plant trees for that specific purpose. More efficient stoves would minimize energy losses. Local inventors and technical schools could exercise their creativity and come up with a cheap, fuel-efficient stove.

Schools

Education is primarily about communicating values to the next generation. The value-formation programmes currently in use in the schools should inculcate a respect for the earth. From the earliest years students should be taught about the beauty and fruitfulness of the forest and the need to conserve and protect this life-system. Well-designed ecology courses are essential at high school and college level. Colleges and universities, especially in areas where forests exist, should set up or strengthen forestry departments. These should help foster a much more detailed study of the forest environment. Often in the past these departments were simple training grounds for foresters who went on to work with logging companies. Forestry departments should now reject that exploitative mentality and set out instead to nurture men and women who will become forest conservers and who will strive to extend our knowledge of the forest, and conserve it for the future.

The forest environment is still very poorly understood. A glance at any bibliography on Philippine forests shows that the standard works (like Merrill's three-volume *An Enumeration of Philippine Flowering Plants* and Brown's work on Philippine vegetation) were produced early in this century. Nothing comparable in scope has been produced in recent years. These works badly need updating and are difficult to obtain. There is an urgent need for extensive interdisciplinary studies on the forest environment which could be undertaken by a consortium of colleges and universities with active government financial and logistical support. Literature on Philippine flora and fauna is needed for elementary school, high school and college level in order to communicate knowledge about the forests to teachers and students. The *Guide to Philippine Flora and Fauna* published in 1986 by the DENR and the University of the Philippines is a step in the right direction.

Research is needed into problems faced by re-forestation programmes. A single example will illustrate how little research is being done in either the private or government sectors. In 1986 the giant ipil-ipil was attacked by jumping lice. This tree is regarded very highly for a number of reasons. It grows quickly, provides animal feed and, as a legume, it is used as a breakline in the sloping land agricultural technology (SALT). It is an easily recognized tree and was planted along roads and highways, so the impact of the disease was evident to everyone: strand after strand of bare trees lined the roads. Yet it seems little research was conducted on the infestation itself and on appropriate ways of combating it. And whatever research was carried out in academic circles, little of what was learned was communicated to the ordinary person through the media.

Extensive tree-planting programmes must form a vital part of any school programme. In this way, practical skills of preparing small nurseries, growing trees and caring for them could be communicated to the students. This practical work would also help generate income for the students to help them subsidize their education. Schemes worked out between the Department of Education, Culture and Sports (DECS) and the Department of the Environment and Natural Resources (DENR) could, within a few years, have a major impact on the landscape of much of the rural Philippines.

Environmental groups

Non-government environmental organizations can play a variety of roles in the campaign to protect the forest and encourage reforestation. Some can help fund the studies proposed above. Others may prefer to work at disseminating this knowledge among the public, especially through the media. In 1988, Haribon used the media to call attention to the destruction that is presently taking place in Palawan. In urban areas like Manila public opinion needs to be mobilized so that people really appreciate how central the forests are to the survival of the country.

Networking with international conservation agencies is also essential. International pressure can be quickly brought to bear on government agencies when particular ecosystems are under threat. These international agencies have the resources and the know-how to put pressure on commercial banks and multilateral lending agencies which often provide the loans for projects which destroy the environment. The World Bank has recently adopted a more sensitive approach to environmental issues. These will remain at the level of rhetoric unless they are implemented.

First World environment agencies can lobby to ban tropical timber imports into their countries from areas where timber production is not carried out in a sustainable and just way. This can be quite effective. In response to pressure from environmentalists, Senator Graham Richardson, Federal Minister for the Environment in Australia, announced at a meeting in Sydney on 29 April 1989 that he was awaiting a report on rainforest logging. 'Once I've got the information', he said, 'I hope to come out with a submission that will enable us to stop importing rainforest timber absolutely.'[17] Similar moves are under way in Europe. The effectivness of these proposed bans can be gauged from the response of the logging industry. The *Sydney Morning Herald* reported that representatives of logging companies in Brazil and the Philippines, including the current president of the Philippine Wood Products Association, visited Australia in July 1989 to lobby against such bans.[18]

The green movement in First World countries is beginning to recognize the power of consumer pressure. Some First World non-government organizations (NGOs), like the Rainforest Information Centre at Lismore in Australia, have published two lists, one to help the timber-using industry and consumer to identify wood products which come from tropical rainforests, and a second to help them choose an alternative timber or non-timber material, especially for formwork ply. They are also in the process of drawing up a good wood guide, which will grade timber-using businesses according to whether they use or trade in rainforest products. Consumers are encouraged to ask their furniture supplier whether the timber used comes from rainforest or plantation timber. The Centre recommends recycling wood, particularly the timber used in old buildings and timber crates, and other ways of cutting down the use of timber are also recommended.

Other non-government organizations either in the Philippines or in First World countries may have a different focus. Some may devote their energies to monitoring the remaining forest areas and protecting the wildlife which inhabits the forest. NGOs with a political focus can lobby for better legislation and help organize people's power movements to protect the forest wherever it is threatened through logging or kaingineros. Others may decide to undertake the planting of trees and caring for them.

Church groups

The Church should mobilize people at every level to protect and conserve the forests. Catechetical literature and liturgical celebrations, like tree-planting liturgies or harvest festivals, can touch people's hearts and raise their consciousness about what is happening to the world around them. Liturgies woven around the life experience of farming and fishing communities would help these communities to appreciate more deeply the privilege and awesome responsibility that is theirs as God's co-workers and caretakers of planet Earth.

Church authorities must scrupulously avoid any collusion with loggers. They should resist the temptation to accept donations of logs for church buildings. In order to deflect criticism many logging operators donate timber to Church and school authorities. In the context of the reciprocal relationships which are so important in Philippine culture, this is one of the most effective ways to silence criticism. The prophetic voice of the Church on this issue will be undermined if priests, bishops and religious continue to fall into this trap.

In many religious traditions the bird is the symbol of the human striving for transcendence. With the death of the forest the habitat of many birds is being irreversibly destroyed. Hunting and preying on birds is also taking its toll. It is not uncommon to see boys four or five years old lurking behind bushes with sling or catapult in hand, ready to kill any bird that might appear. The sad fact is that today birds are being systematically eliminated from the Philippine environment and so few people seem to notice or care. The elimination of bird life is an ecological and spiritual disaster. The Church should combat this by systematic moral teaching about biocide (the destruction of species) and by bird liturgies which energize the human spirit.

It should be very easy to tailor reforestation programmes to the needs of the thousands of basic Christian communities which have sprung up all over the rural Philippines in recent years. These are communities of common prayer and mutual support which have been formed and nurtured by poor people themselves. The logistics of working with these communities should not be too difficult as they are normally linked together through parish and diocesan structures. In this way, they provide an excellent channel through which the government or private institutions can respond in a very concrete and economical way both to the ecological needs of an area and the social and economic needs of poor rural people. Small projects designed and executed in conjunction with local people can be very successful, especially when the local people see that they too will benefit in a variety of ways from the reforestation scheme. These reforested areas could also become bird sanctuaries.

Example, of course, is better than a thousand sermons. This should stimulate priests, bishops and communities of religious men and women to establish tree nurseries on Church property in order to make seedlings more readily available to the public. Lands surrounding churches and schools should, where possible, be planted with trees, rather than be cultivated as lawns.

Government

The role of government will be crucial if the remaining forests of the Philippines are to survive. There is a dire need for commitment, honesty and integrity among people staffing government agencies responsible for the forest, especially the Bureau of Forest Management. This was admitted by Secretary Factoran in an interview with jamil Maidan̄ Flores of *Panorama* magazine in Manila (6 December 1987). 'I am now making certain', he said, 'that our people understand that should they be involved in any illegal logging activity, they will be transferred, replaced, terminated.' The interviewer interjected that 'it will not be easy changing the culture of an entire bureaucracy'.

The new policies in the Department of Environment and Natural Resources (DENR) must reflect a concern for the preservation of the remaining forest and a willingness to facilitate and speed up reforestation programmes. In the above interview, Secretary Factoran highlighted the importance of the human factor in ensuring the success of the Department's work. Strict selection procedures are called for in choosing the staff to run these agencies. The success of the conservation programme depends on integrity, competence and the provision of adequate tools to perform the job well. Salaries commensurate with the task are also essential. In the absence of adequate salaries, government personnel are more prone to accept bribes.

Need for a moratorium on logging

A nationwide moratorium on logging is essential until the real condition of the remaining forest is clarified through *independent* research. It makes little sense to spend millions of dollars reforesting denuded hills while allowing primary and secondary forests to be denuded. The need for research is vitally important. This calls for maps and surveys in regions and provinces. These studies must be made available to the public, especially groups that are committed to monitoring the forests. At present it is almost impossible to get hold of maps: one can spend days 'to-ing and fro-ing' between civil and military authorities in a futile search for maps, getting blank stares and apologies from department officials or homilies on national security from military people. This means in practice that it is almost impossible to get accurate information on logging concessions.

Accurate estimates must be drawn up by independent researchers to determine what forest cover is left and how many square kilometres of forest must be left intact in a particular area to ensure the sustainability of the forest ecosystem. This will also help generate a new realism in the public consciousness regarding how little land remaining in the so-called public domain is suitable for agriculture. Research is necessary also to establish the acceptable ratio between forest ecosystems and agro-ecosystems in the country as a whole and in local bioregions. The policies which one might expect from this approach could help protect the forest from loggers and kaingineros who are continually chipping away at it to the point of no return.

A comprehensive land-use policy is essential. One immediate benefit of this would be to speed up the bureaucratic procedures involved in land classification. The present situation is very confused and often bizarre. President Marcos's decree, PD 705, was an example of the latter. It lumped together as squatters everyone who was living on land of 18 per cent gradient slope or above, whether they were newly arrived lowland Filipino peasants or tribal people who have been living on their lands for over a thousand years. Tribal peoples all over the Philippines bitterly resented being called squatters on their own land. A previous decree, PD 410, outlined a process whereby tribal people could gain titles to their lands, but it was so cumbersome and complicated that no tribal people could avail themselves of the opportunity.

Every effort must be made to improve the enforcement of legislation designed to protect the forest from further encroachment and to reforest areas above 18 per cent gradient slopes. In this way, farm lands and mini-forest can exist side by side with the farmers benefiting from the regenerated forests in the area. This, in turn, would encourage the farmers to protect the forest. Very often today the Bureau of Forest Development (BFD) reforestation projects are burned down by the farmers who are unaware of the benefits of the forests and feel that the reforestation programmes of the government are actually encroaching on their farm lands, particularly when the title issue is contested or vague. A much more co-operative relationship could exist between government agencies and the citizens if the agencies took non-government and people's organizations more seriously.

When the comprehensive survey has been completed, all forms of logging and kaingin should be prohibited in areas where the forest cover is less than 30 per cent. In other areas logging could be carried out on a small scale, primarily to supply the needs of the domestic market. If this kind of policy is implemented one can presume that it will raise a hue and cry from the loggers. Many logging company owners and executives will raise the excuse of the plight of their poor workers. They will need to be reminded that unless stringent measures are introduced immediately to save the forest, nothing will be left in a decade and their workers and their children and their children's children will be in a much more pitiful state.

Commercial operations could easily be carried out by small co-operatives of people who live close to the forest. These operations could be monitored by representatives of the Department of Energy and Natural Resources (DENR) and in conjunction with local environmental groups. If large-scale operations aimed at the export market are allowed to continue then the forest has no future. In an interview in *Panorama* magazine (6 December 1987) Secretary Factoran seemed to favour small-scale local operators. 'Instead of timber licensing agreements owned by very few people with a lot of money, we will now have entire communities allowed to extract the trees, using carabaos, using very small motor vehicles and extracting lumber for the immediate needs of the community.'

One year later the secretary had to back off from this commitment. Priscilla Arias, writing in the *Manila Bulletin* (11 December 1988) in a report headed 'Timber concessions open for public bidding', quoted Secretary Factoran as saying that the government will allow private groups or community organizations to bid for timber concessions of up to 40,000 hectares. One cannot help wondering whether the inclusion of community organizations is merely a sop to public opinion. One could place a bet (without fear of losing) that only a very small percentage of such licences will be offered to small-scale community groups, as Secretary Factoran seemed to envisage in his 1987 interview. Later in the report, a give-away line reveals the true direction of the programme. It says that the DENR is in consultation with the leaders of the wood industry, particularly the Philippine Wood Products Association, in developing guidelines for timber licence agreements. No mention was made of the government consulting bona fide ecological groups like Haribon or Lingkod Tao who might question the whole programme on ecological grounds. After all, there is only a little over 20 per cent forest cover remaining, which is completely inadequate for a country like the Philippines. Surely at this stage of denudation the preservers should be heard from as well as the exploiters?

There is a certain irony in all of this. In 1988 Secretary Factoran and Undersecretary Celso Roque responded to the Catholic Bishops' Conference of the Philippines (CBCP) pastoral letter on the deteriorating environment, *What Is Happening to Our Beautiful Land?* Their open letter praised the bishops for their concern and saw the pastoral letter as a milestone in generating interest in environmental problems. At one point the authors of the letter took issue with the bishops' suggestion that 'the government group together into an independent Department all the agencies which deal at present with ecological issues'. They point to the 'popular misconception that DENR's primary concern is the exploitation of our natural resources'. In their letter they insist that the 'basic mandate of the DENR articulated in EO 192 is to assure the availability and sustainability of the country's natural resources as its principal function'. Yet in practice, as the above example illustrates and as we will see again below, most of the DENR's energies are involved with those who are exploiting rather than conserving the environment.

Call to reforest

To repair the damage which has already been done to the forest, wildlife, rivers, soil, and marine ecosystems of the country, the government must give top priority to reforestation programmes. There is need for careful planning; otherwise the schemes might end up by destroying instead of conserving the forest and undermining further the social and economic life of the people who live within or on the edge of the forest. As far as possible these programmes should be implemented through non-government agencies. Researcher Ooi Jin Bee estimates that a total of 5.1 million hectares of forest lands need to be reforested immediately. 1.4 million hectares of this area is located within critical watershed areas. These figures probably err on the conservative side. They do, however, give some idea regarding the extent of the task which confronts the country if the forest area is to be preserved and regenerated and thus become a sustainable resource.

Plantations are not forests

Before rushing out to plant trees it is important to understand what reforestation means in the Philippines. It does not refer to planting one or two species of tree all over the country. This could be disastrous, as the experience with ipil-ipil has shown. A single disease or infestation could wipe out the whole project. True reforestation should attempt to replicate as closely as humanly possible the tropical rainforest which has existed here for millions of years. As we have seen throughout this chapter, diversity, interdependence and symbiotic relationships between trees, plants, birds, animals and insects are the hallmark of the forest.

In this mix of trees, pride of place must be given to indigenous trees. At the moment there is a danger that in the rush to reforest, the native dipterocarp species will be forgotten. In fact it seems that the Bureau of Forest Development (now the Forest Management Bureau) favours exotic species like *Albizzia falcatara* (falcata), *Gemelina arborea* (gemelina) and *Leucaena leucocephala* (ipil-ipil). In

1984, exotic species accounted for 84 per cent of the 52.5 million seedlings produced by the BFD in its various nurseries. Many people, including Ooi Jin Bee, favour this reliance on commercially saleable species and shun any tree with a 30-year or more cycle. He baldly states that 'of the many reforestation programmes the industrial tree plantation is the most important in terms of resource replacement'.

Nestor Baguinon, on the other hand, urges that 'ecological compatibility and not economic value' should be the main criterion in designing a reforestation programme. There is enough experience gleaned from other countries to make us wary of single-species tree farming. *The Ecologist* carried an article on 'The Failure of Social Forestry in Karnataka' (India), arguing that:

> Karnataka's social forestry programme was intended to
> increase the availability of food, fodder, fertiliser and fuel for
> the rural poor through a massive reafforestation scheme. It has
> done none of these things. The bulk of the trees have gone for
> pulp and rayon manufacture. The ecological costs of the
> project have been ruinous.[19]

The same criticism is levelled at PICOP by Catherine Caufield in *In the Rainforest*. She quotes a local priest who acknowledges that PICOP is one of the best companies in the Philippines in terms of how they treat their workers, yet 'the tree-farming scheme has failed in two of its three aims — helping poor people and reclaiming wasteland'.[20] The DENR Memorandum No. 11 specifies the rules and regulations governing contract reforestation. In discussing the choice of species it comes down in favour of 'species that are considered to be useful and desirable with marketing and processing potential'. Yet even in terms of growth potential some of the local species are as good as, if not better than, the exotic species. In the remaining forests around Lake Sebu, a tree which the T'boli call *nabul* (*Biscofia javanica*) compares favourably with the falcata tree. This is being used extensively in the Santa Cruz Mission reforestation programme for the Allah Valley watershed area. Indigenous species have the added advantage of being locally available and therefore cheaper. When the remaining forest is conserved, planting materials can be obtained from the forest. Planting indigenous species will tend to coax back the primary forest together with its wildlife, on to the denuded areas.

One reason why commercial operators prefer tree plantations to harvesting the rainforest is that it holds out an even higher level of profitability in the short term. Despite the richness of the rainforest, very few of the trees have commercial value. Yet for the ten or twenty mature trees which can be harvested per hectare, the logger must build roads in order to bring in heavy equipment and bring out the logs. Most loggers would prefer to set up their own timber plantations with two or three fast growing species and thus be assured of a steady income after ten years when they can begin to harvest the lumber. The loggers and many other planners are impatient with the slow processes of nature. Some of the finest trees of the Philippine rain-forests take between 50 and 70 years to mature, whereas they can harvest falcata after ten years. 70 years is an unacceptably long period for people who are brought up on reaping profits as quickly as possible. If nature seems recalcitrant, there is an urge to tear it down and replace it with man-controlled entities which, in our hubris, we think are bigger and better. As people are finding out all over the tropics wherever these schemes are being pursued, they in fact fail to address the needs of poor rural people and they promote ecological disaster.

Indigenous species are more suited to the soil and climate and are resistant to pest infestation. The cost of reforestation can also be reduced since there is less need for expensive foreign seeds and consul-tants: seeds are readily available from the remaining forests. Setting up small-scale nurseries of indigenous species is much cheaper than working with imported exotic ones. With a little technical help local people can be encouraged to set up backyard nurseries so that the seedlings are prepared in the vicinity of the area to be reforested. This saves hauling costs and also gives local people an income from the reforestation project. Even with these costs, the price will compare favourably with exotic species. The price for some of the exotic seeds range from $75 to $200 per kilogramme. This centralized buying of foreign species is in itself a temptation to some personnel of the Forest Management Bureau (FMB) to cream off some money from the whole operation. Anything that helps to remove this kind of temp-tation should be encouraged.

This does not mean that there is no place for fast-growing exotic species. In any major programme a certain percentage of the land area can be planted with a mix of exotic species. This area can be harvested within a period of 10 to 15 years by the community and thus provide an income for the inhabitants. The projected shortage of timber within 10 years will make this a very lucrative investment. Primary consideration must be given to rehabilitating the Philippines tropical rainforests, and even in areas where exotic species are planted, mono-cropping should be avoided at all costs.

The Santa Cruz Mission has reforested 410 hectares from private sources and is now in the process of reforesting an additional 1,250 hectares in 1989 with ADB money made available through the DENR. Our experience to date confirms the importance of community-based programmes. A major component in this is a well-conceived educational programme which will help the local com-munity recognize the value of the forest for sustainable agriculture and the economic value which will accrue from agroforestry and, eventually, small-scale timber operations. This raised consciousness creates the incentive for the community to protect the forest.

Need for government support

It goes without saying that community reforestation programmes need government financial support and back-up services. Extensive research and experimentation is necessary to determine which species are suitable for different soils and altitudes in a particular province. What species go well together? What are the first species to return to a particular area — the so-called pioneer species? Obviously these are the ones that should be propagated first. Which species initially shade other trees and effectively nurse them until they can cope with direct sunlight? Which species control cogon grass or other weeds most effectively? In the economics of reforestation, cutting cogon grass or 'brushing' can represent over 10 per cent of the costs of the operation. In the Santa Cruz Mission reforestation programme, which has been in operation for four years, we have discovered that a traditional tree which the T'boli call *lemenge* (*Macaranga tanarius*) helps to suppress cogon grass. Communicating current research on the best approaches to fire prevention is also essential. Many government foresters will admit that this is the number one enemy of government reforestation programmes.

Every forester knows that controlling fires is more than a technical problem. It is primarily an educational problem and points again to the importance of a massive educational campaign, involving the schools, civic groups, churches and the media. The government, Church and environmental agencies working together have far-reaching networks which, if properly tapped, could disseminate the message of reforestation to every part of the country. Without an effective educational campaign it will be impossible to generate public support to enforce the legislation which is designed to protect the forest from further encroachment by either loggers, cattle ranchers, kaingineros or firewood gatherers.

Banks and NGOs

Extensive resources will need to be allocated to reforest the Philippines. The multilateral banking agencies have an important role to play. The *Manila Bulletin* for 20 January 1987 reported that the Philippine government was about to receive a loan of $120 million from the Asian Development Bank (ADB) for reforestation purposes.

The multilateral funding agencies and banks involved in making such loans available must also be challenged to look seriously at the likely impact of the kinds of programmes they are funding. During the past 20 years they have made hundreds of millions of dollars available to Third World governments, even though they must have known that the money is often not used to improve the living conditions of the vast majority of the population. Much of the money has been used for large-scale projects like dams, mines and steel mills which often destroy or pollute the environment. The consequent huge debts are now a terrible burden to Third World countries, causing poverty, social disintegration and ecological destruction.

In recent years, multilateral lending agencies have begun to look at how they might begin to work more closely with non-government organizations in developing countries. A meeting to accelerate this process attended by representatives of NGOs, banks and governments took place in Tokyo on 6 October 1986. The meeting recognized that people in Third World countries are 'entitled to expect that each group take the others into account when designing, planning or carrying out development projects'.[21] The meeting also recognized that 'NGOs are an effective way for development to reach the grassroots — the landless, the rural populations, the marginal urban groups — in a word the neediest'.[22]

'Compared with governments and international organizations, NGOs were considered better suited to provide such assistance because they are flexible, cost-effective and able to respond to the needs of the poor in developing countries fairly quickly.'[23] People working with NGOs now feel that it is time for lending institutions to move beyond these laudatory statements and insist that, when they are lending money to governments for livelihood and environmental projects, NGOs be included in every facet of the development process instead of being left out in the cold as they obviously have been in the programme under discussion. Involving NGOs will necessitate making available to them resources which will enable them to increase their effectiveness by developing technical and managerial skills. Designing a reforestation programme should provide an ideal opportunity for developing co-operative links between banks, governments and environmental and tribal NGOs. Only if this kind of co-operation is forthcoming can one confidently predict that the interests of the environment and the poor will be served.

Ironically, a loan designed to enhance the environment may actually have the opposite effect. It seems probable, based on the experience of previous reforestation programmes undertaken by the Bureau of Forest Management, that only a fraction of the 350,000 hectares targeted in the latest Philippines reforestation programme will actually be reforested. Where, for example, will the people who live in the 500-hectare plot awarded to a corporation for reforestation find food? In all probability they will move back into the remaining 1 million hectares of rainforest and continue to destroy that.

At the World Bank–IMF meeting in Berlin in September 1988, the World Bank, under pressure from a number of environmental NGOs, promised to review its policies so that they might be more sensitive to the environmental impact of their projects. In this regard, World Bank officials must know that there is a growing literature which questions the wisdom of giving priority to commercial rather than ecological and social factors in designing reforestation programmes. Paul Simons, writing in *The Guardian* (4 December 1988), states the case succinctly. 'Without the co-operation of local people, projects to save tropical forests are not worth the glossy paper they are written on.' The relevant literature, especially studies done in India, assert that when pride of place is given to commercial interests, reforestation programmes often worsen the ecological situation instead of improving it.

Conclusion

Ooi Jin Bee ends his monograph with the comment that 'it is difficult to escape the conclusion that the forests of the Philippines are under a state of siege, and are unlikely to survive beyond this century'. This judgement is certainly accurate if the present policies and activities continue unchecked. If this happens the Philippines will be forever impoverished and everyone — exploiters, government officials, Church personnel and ordinary people — will share some of the blame; the exploiters because they raped the land, the government officials because they allowed it to happen, and the rest of us because we refused to raise our voices and do something about it.

Appendix

Letter to President Corazon Aquino from the 1988 annual conference of the Episcopal Commission for Tribal Filipinos

December 1, 1988

Dear President Aquino,

We, the Episcopal Commission for Tribal Filipinos (ECTF), Commission Bishops, Tribal Filipino Apostolate Coordinators, and Church workers from the various dioceses in the Philippines met for our 10th Annual National Convention in Calapan, Oriental Mindoro from November 28 to December 1, 1988.

Following the leadership given by our own bishops in their Pastoral letter, 'What Is Happening to Our Beautiful Land?' we took as our theme 'Promoting Ecological Balance As A Way Towards Integral Development of Tribal Filipinos'.

During our convention we were informed about the Contract Reforestation Programme (CRP) which the DENR is about to launch. While we share the overall goal of the programme to promote widespread reforestation, we have grave reservations about it.

First of all, the programme was conceived without adequate consultation with the Non-government Organizations (NGOs) who are working with tribal Filipinos.

The programme is heavily biased in favor of commercial interests. Based on many years' experience of working with tribal Filipinos, we know that the entry of large scale commercial interests into their lands will inevitably lead to violence and the further escalation of insurgency.

Everyone agrees that the tribal Filipinos have been dispossessed of their ancestral domain and that their interests have been disregarded. How sad that this programme will actually undermine tribal communities and trample on their rights.

We know that unless local communities are actively involved in planning reforestation and are seen as partners in development, instead of being merely a source of labour for corporations, they will not protect the trees. We assure you that without the support of tribal Filipinos, the project will not succeed and billions of pesos will be wasted.

We are also concerned that the programme will allow unprecedented opportunities for graft and corruption. It is ironic that many of the commercial interests which were involved in destroying the forest will benefit from the programme in which tribal Filipinos and their lands will suffer.

In the light of the above criticisms, we feel that, based on our present knowledge, the programme is poorly conceived. We ask you to direct the Secretary of the DENR to hold it in abeyance pending more extensive consultation with tribal Filipino communities and NGOs who are working with tribal communitites.

We thank you for your kind consideration of our request.

Sincerely yours in Christ,

All the delegates including the Chairman Bishop Generoso Camina and Bishop Vicente Manuel, signed the letter.

PART TWO

Creation in Scripture and Tradition

And God saw that it was good

A theology of creation

What kind of God do we believe in?

Part One of this book looked at concrete ecological and development problems — the debt burden, population pressures and the destruction of rainforests. It is clear that these pressures are devastating many Third World environments. Quite simply, these are survival issues which must challenge all human beings, especially religious people. They are called to reflect on these issues in the light of their own cultural and religious tradition, in order to understand what is happening, and to be energized to turn back the tide of death. Needless to say, any theological reflection on creation today, if it is to remain relevant, must not lose sight of the pain of the earth, or forget the forces which are destroying it, by flying off into an abstract discussion on creation and creaturehood. At the same time, a theology of creation would be useless for believers if it did not situate a 'state of the earth today' discussion within a broader context.

It must begin by enquiring about the way people today understand God, the gods or the creative spirits whom they consider responsible for creating the universe. In truth this is the crucial question; our beliefs about the earth and a human's proper relationship with it rest on the bedrock of our attitude towards the creator of the earth. Any search for answers to the question as to whether a particular people respect the earth as sacred or see it merely as something to be used by them, must begin by focusing on their assumptions about God, the gods or the supernatural creative spirit(s). These in large measure determine how people view the Divine, themselves and the world of nature.

It is vitally important to understand this backdrop against which people view reality in order to appreciate fully a people's perspective on creation. The fact of being religious does not automatically mean having a positive and holistic approach to creation. There are numerous historical examples of deeply religious people who do not, for example, see humans as part of a much larger and older life process, and see no religious value in embracing an attitude of intimacy with the natural world. In fact, they may see this world as hostile, needing to be mastered, tamed and domesticated. Francis

Bacon, René Descartes and Isaac Newton were religious men, yet their scientific discoveries in the seventeenth century succeeded in undermining the organic, holistic, though static and often erroneous, view of the world which had prevailed in the Western world for the previous thousand years. For the earth-centred and static universe they substituted an undoubtedly more scientific view of nature. However, because it failed to take into account a holistic view of all the living world, it contributed significantly to the development of the modern scientific and technological paradigm which regards the world as complex and intricate, but ultimately a lifeless machine. In recent decades the technologies which have resulted from this reductionist science and machine metaphor itself have contributed enormously to the devastation of many of the vital ecosystems of the earth.[1]

Creation myths

Creation myths give us a glimpse of how traditional societies view God, themselves and the world. These myths are very powerful; they survive from one generation to the next and as they are passed on they help shape a people's experience and guide the important choices about how to live and regulate their personal and collective lives. Over the centuries the wisdom encapsulated in these myths protects a society and ensures that it persists. Most creation myths reflect the values which a people have developed in creative interaction with their environment. For example, many creation myths of the North American Indians emphasize the unity and interconnectedness of all creation in a way which is surprisingly compatible with our modern understanding of how the universe and the earth emerged. The creation myth of the Cheyenne of the Great Lakes is a good example of this:

> With his power, Maheo [the all Spirit] created the great water, like a lake, but salty. Out of this salty water, Maheo knew he could bring all life that ever was to be. The lake itself was life if Maheo so commanded it. In the darkness of nothingness, Maheo could feel the coolness of the water and taste on his lips the tang of the salt.

> 'There should be water beings', Maheo told his Power. And so it was. First the fish, swimming in the deep water and then the mussels and snails and crawfish lying on the sand and mud Maheo had formed so his lake should have a bottom . . .

> 'Our grandmother Earth is like a woman; she should be fruitful. Let her begin to bear life. Help me, my Power.'

When Maheo said that, trees and grass sprang up to become
the grandmother's hair. The flowers became her bright
ornaments, and the fruits and seeds were the gifts that Earth
offered back to Maheo.[2]

This is a holistic view of reality. It does not attempt to shut out
either the divine or the human from the natural world. In the words
attributed to Chief Seattle of the Duwamish Indians, 'the rivers are
our brothers, they quench our thirst . . . the air is precious to the red
man, for all things share the same breath — the beast, the tree and the
human . . . '[3] Bruce Chatwin in his book *Songlines* writes 'that the
aboriginals [of Australia] had an earthbound philosophy. The earth
gave life to man; gave him food, language and intelligence; and the
earth took him back when he died. A man's own country, even an
empty stretch of spinifex, was itself a sacred ikon that must remain
unscarred.'[4]

In this perspective nature is not seen as valueless, raw material to
be kneaded and shaped into whatever configuration humans desire,
or merely as the stage on which the human drama takes place. Nature
has its own meaning and purpose irrespective of its value to humans.
Christianity and some of the other great religions, especially Islam,
have much to learn from this approach to the natural world.

It is also true that in many tribal societies the Divine is not seen in
personal, individual terms but rather as a pervasive spirit-presence
diffused throughout the cosmos and the earth. This presence may be
particularly active in specific natural phenomena. Among the T'boli
people of South Cotabato in the Philippines, for example, each river,
tree or mountain has its own spirit. Much of the religious ritual is
geared to attracting benign spirits or repelling malign ones. The
believer tends to avoid any activity which might be construed as
displeasing to the spirits; before cutting down a tree an appropriate
offering must be made to the spirits in order to avoid any punishment
for interfering with the habitat of the spirit. In the same way the
prudent farmer who wishes to secure a bountiful harvest will make an
offering to the spirits. After the crops are harvested he will also offer
something by way of thanksgiving to the spirits for co-operating with
him.

God — as primary cause

The rise of the great religious and cultural traditions signalled an
important change in the way many cultures viewed the divine, the
world and human beings. In Greece, for example, religious cult
emerged from the traditional animistic religion and elements
borrowed from other cultures. The development of philosophical

thought raised questions about both the character and multitude of the gods which appeared to reside in the Greek pantheon. The philosophical tradition under the influence of people like Plato and later Aristotle no longer emphasized the primordial unity of all reality. Their differentiation between levels of reality introduced diverse forms of dualism into human consciousness. In this perspective the divine element and human consciousness were disengaged from the rest of creation. Reality was seen as hierarchical: God, or the gods, occupied the pinnacle of the hierarchy, spirits came next, followed by human beings, then the animals and finally crass matter. In this schema spiritual and intellectual realities had priority over matter, which often was not valued very highly. In fact, it was often seen as a prison which shackled and constrained the more noble spiritual element. Intellectual pursuits and spiritual exercises were directed towards liberating the spirit from these constraints.

Futhermore, nature was stripped of all spirit presence. The God or the spirits were seen to transcend the world of phenomena. A number of factors gave rise to this shift. An important one was their understanding of perfection and change. Perfection meant that a being already existed in an unchanging manner. Change then had to be seen negatively. It stemmed from decay or corruption. If perfection was the main attribute of the Divine it was important to uncouple the Divine from any intimate involvement with a world which was obviously subject to change and decay. This cleavage between heaven and earth led to a further dualism which cut the human off from the rest of the earth community. The hierarchical principle was once again applied. Man, which in practice meant free citizens of the city states, was placed at the top of the hierarchy of earthly beings. He was viewed as rational and free, and his life had value and purpose. Below him came women, minors and slaves. A huge chasm separated humans from nature which was often seen as inert and lacking any inherent purpose.

This perception shatters important links in the chain which connects all reality. The break was further stretched by the mechanistic assumptions which have crept into Western culture's understanding of God, of human beings and the rest of creation during the past few centuries since the rise of modern science and technology. In the view of Isaac Newton (1642–1727), the universe, in all its interrelated parts, functioned like a giant clock. A God who had created the system lived outside it: he was viewed as the omnipotent clock-maker who had fashioned the cosmic clock in a wonderful way. Once he had finished his work he wound up the clock, set it in motion and more or less abandoned it to its own devices. This view of God, known as deism, is a static and distant one. He is seen as an omnipotent being who lives in his own perfection and is not touched in any real way by what is happening either to human beings or the rest of the creation.

Israel came to birth in a harsh and hostile land

The Greek understanding of God and its subsequent transformation under the impetus of the modern scientific and industrial revolution has shaped Western Christian understanding of God. The second source from which Western Christianity draws its knowledge about God is, of course, the biblical tradition. In contrast to tribal religion which stressed the continuity between the natural world and the world of the spirit, the Bible is anxious to differentiate between all three. According to Phyllis Bird, the most basic assertion in Gen 1:27 — 'God created man in his own image, in the image of God he created him' — is that God and human beings are distinguished from the rest of creation.[5] In the first account of creation (Gen 1:1 – 2:4a), Yahweh does not use any instrument or intermediate reality in creating the world. There is no potter's clay like that found in the second account of creation (Gen 2:4a – 3:22).

Before looking at the biblical creation accounts in more detail it is worth calling attention to the thesis of Frederick Turner. In his book *Beyond Geography*, he insists that environmental factors must be taken into account in any attempt to understand the biblical perspective on the natural world.[6] In the barren, inhospitable environment of the Middle East, both the pastoralists and the early settlers felt the need to separate the Divine and human beings from the natural world. In order to survive in the sparse mountains, barren deserts, steppes and narrow plains, human beings had to channel all their efforts into dominating, controlling and taming the natural world. In the Fertile Crescent, countless generations wrestled with nature by draining swamps, designing irrigation canals and terracing hillsides. This was absolutely essential so that the natural world might be productive and support the growing population and emerging civilizations. When compared with the lush, abundant vegetation of the tropics, or even the temperate lands of Europe, much of the land in the Middle East is barren, difficult to work and not very fruitful.

Besides the drudgery of work there was also a need for constant vigilance. Unless human beings continued to do battle against the elements the wilderness might, in a very short period of time, overrun what man had accomplished so laboriously. Vestiges of this need constantly to keep the wilderness or chaos at bay are present in the drive to separate the light from the darkness and the waters above from the waters below in Gen 1:3–8. Only through the constant toil of building and clearing the irrigation ditches, planting vineyards, and rotating crops and pasture lands could the wilderness be kept in check (cf. Ps 104:5–9, Job 3:8–11). This is reflected in the punishment which God meted out to Adam in Gen 3:17–19.

Accursed shall be the soil because of you!

Painfully will you get your food from it
as long as you live.
It will yield you brambles and thistles,
as you eat the produce of the land.
By the sweat of your face
you will earn your food,
until you return to the ground. (NJB)[7]

The text acknowledges that the earth is the source of life; however, it is not a benign and abundant mother earth. There is nothing like the bounty of a tropical environment, of the T'boli hills for example, where a minimal human effort can provide sufficient food for a person's basic needs. In the above text the world takes the role of an adversary. A person has to plan, organize and almost use military tactics to break the earth with the plough and transform it by the sweat of human labour in order to make it fruitful and responsive to human needs.

This need for constant watchfulness and a marked preference for nature transformed by human hands can be seen in a very concrete way in the cities which grew up in the Middle East during the second and first millennia BC. Three elements of the culture symbolized this — the wall, the garden and the granary. The thick, sturdy wall insulated those lucky enough to be living inside from the buffeting and uncertainties of nature and the attacks of enemies. Inside the wall, people felt secure and able to design their own world in whatever way they chose. The garden was a place of refreshment and repose removed from the unpredictable and dangerous world of the wilderness which began outside the walls. Even Yahweh enjoyed 'walking in the garden in the cool of the day' (Gen 3:8). Nevertheless, no matter how much effort might be expended, human beings could never hope to control and domesticate the wilderness completely. They had always to be alert and vigilant. Nature could never be fully trusted; a storm, a flash flood, a prolonged drought, or a plague of locusts could overwhelm them when they least expected it.

In gardens — those cultivated spaces within the city wall — humans could achieve their goal of dominating nature completely. Here people could take delight in nature in the full knowledge that they were the masters and that nature had been shorn of its fearful, awesome and unpredictable aspects. Snakes and other creatures considered hostile to humans were banished from this humanized space. The garden image is very much to the fore in the second account of creation in Gen 2:4a – 3:22.

Finally, the communal granary provided the necessary food security for the population. Given the vagaries of the weather and the ever-present possibility of crop failure through disease or locust attack, the granary was essential for survival. It also distanced humans from an immediate, day-to-day dependency on the whims of nature. Instead they could use their rational processes to plan and organize themselves even in the face of a harvest failure or a drought.

A unique history also formed the people of Israel

The human environment also played a central role in shaping the biblical understanding of the divine, the human and the rest of creation. The contours of the biblical message were worked out in Israel in opposition to the fertility cults which were practised by the Canaanite inhabitants of the land. The constant railing of the prophets against going up 'to the high places' is a powerful testimony to the seductive power which these fertility rituals had for the ordinary Israelite farmer.

The Canaanite religion had much in common with other tribal religions. The Divine revealed itself primarily in the rhythms of the natural world, especially in the mystery of fertility and sexuality. Male and female dimensions were considered to be present with the divine reality itself. The mating of the gods and goddesses was vitally important in order to guarantee the fertility of the crops, the fruit trees, the flocks and even the human community. Temple prostitution provided the ritual mechanism through which this vital union could be achieved. The suppliant farmer went up to the Canaanite temples or 'high places' and engaged in ritual intercourse with the temple prostitutes. This in turn precipitated the mating of the gods and goddesses, thus assuring the farmer of blessings, peace and an abundant harvest.

The trust which many Israelite farmers placed in the gods of the Canaanites was anathema to the prophets of Israel. For them it was a denial of Yahweh's power over creation and so it was tantamount to blasphemy. Worship of the Baals as a rejection of Yahweh is a theme which is worked out in a particularly poignant way in the Book of Hosea. The prophet compares his own marriage to his adulterous wife Gomer to Israel's unfaithful relationship with Israel. Gomer had played the prostitute but so had Israel, constantly deserting Yahweh (Hos 4:12).

It is important to remember that while Canaan and other nations experienced the Divine in the cycles of fertility, Israel experienced God in concrete historical events. Yahweh was not seen so much as the One who created the world or particular elements in creation like rivers, mountains or lakes; rather he was perceived as the God who had liberated Israel from slavery in Egypt and who identified completely with his people (Ex 3:6–12, 19:4–6; Deut 6:4–15, 20–24). The earliest creed of Israel (Deut 26:5–9) recalled the historical events of the Exodus out of which Israel emerged as a people. The Exodus became the central historical event of Israelite history; a kind of fulcrum on which everything turned and to which the prophets and latter writers would return over and over again to revivify the faith and give it contemporary relevance.

This liberation which embodied the gift of a new land was sealed in a once-for-all covenant which linked God and the people of Israel in an unbreakable bond (Ex 24:3–8). This covenant was celebrated each year in the feast of the Passover (Ex 12:1–28). It is worth noting that the Passover and the feast of Unleavened Bread were originally agricultural feasts. In the light of the overwhelming experience of the Exodus, however, they were transformed into feasts which celebrated Yahweh's intervention in time on behalf of his people.

All of the above means that the experience of Yahweh as saviour was of prior and paramount importance; belief in Yahweh as creator did not emerge until a latter period. Even then it was often seen as an extension of Yahweh's saving role, rather than as the primary revelation of the Divine.

In the milieu in which Israel was born, then, the Divine presence in historical events took precedence over the experience of God in nature. In wrestling with its environment and the historical challenges that it faced, Israel articulated its understanding of the Divine as personal, monotheistic, transcendent, yet intimately involved in the events of human history. The gains from this rich interplay were vital to Israel's survival as a nation as it attempted to set down roots in the land of Canaan and adjust to the turbulent political and social realities of the ancient Near East. It fixed a profound sense of the Divine which encouraged a special, intimate relationship between humans and God and it also challenged humans to accept responsibility for their behaviour towards each other. It inspired Israel to weld together a community where peace and justice might reign. In a very profound way the whole human community is indebted to Israel for shaping this vision of the Divine.

Still, there are losses with every gain. The dominant vision of the Divine which Israel developed is so focused on the Divine–human relationship that it can dull people's sensibilities to the natural world. People shaped by this powerful religious tradition tend to be less sensitive to the presence of the Divine in the sky, the sun, the moon, the stars, the blossoms of wild flowers or the spider weaving its web. In defence of this tradition, it must be said that it was shaped at a time when there was little danger to the continued fruitfulness of the natural world. In the latter part of the twentieth century with the attack on the ozone layer, the 'greenhouse effect', the poisoning of water by toxic waste, the rape of the forests and massive erosion of soils, our dulled sensitivity to the presence of God in the natural world can have tragic, devastating and irreversible consequences.

Before looking at some specific biblical texts it is important to note that the biblical tradition is not a monolithic one. It encompasses many cultures, spans many centuries and cherishes many different perspectives. Given our present ecological crisis it behoves us to search out those insights which cherish all of the living world and build on them a theology of creation which is faithful to the biblical tradition and relevant to the problems facing us today.[8]

Genesis 1:1 – 2:4a

The first line of the Bible affirms that the world is created by a loving, personal God. 'In the beginning God created the heavens and the earth.' The world is good in itself; God contemplates what he has done and found that 'it was good' (Gen 1:10, 13, 18, 21, 26). This statement is very important. Israel grew up cheek by jowl with cultures which maintained that the spirit world was created by a God or a good spirit and that matter came from an evil spirit. The Genesis story rejects this radical dualism. There is no such unbridgeable dichotomy between spirit and matter; both are under God's dominion.

This first account of creation comes from what is called the Priestly source. Modern scriptural scholarship sees the early part of the Hebrew Bible as a composite of various traditions which were handed on orally. Four traditions are identified. The Yahwist (J) is a historical epic which emerged as a result of the optimism engendered by the territorial expansion and cultural flowering during the reign of David and Solomon. The Elohist (E) tradition is more sober and rural and contains material which had been handed down among the northern tribes. After the fall of the northern kingdom this material was combined with the J account to form the JE epic. Later again before the fall of Jerusalem, the Deuteronomic material (D) was merged with the J and E traditions. It was inserted into the tradition before the account of the death of Moses to give its message added weight. Finally, the Priestly (P) tradition gathered together the tradition of cultic worship, especially that which had grown up around the Temple in Jerusalem. It was compiled and woven into the Pentateuch before or possibly during the exile. In this way the Priestly writers performed a sort of editorial function for the whole Pentateuch.

Genesis 1:1 – 2:4a comes from the Priestly source. The text has a ritual cadence and structure, finely tuned by decades of use in the temple worship. Even in translation one can sense the majesty and rhythm, 'God said, let there be light . . . God said, let there by a vault in the waters', building up to a climax in 2:3, 'God blessed the seventh day and made it holy, because on that day he had rested after all his work of creating'.

In reading the text or better still listening to it being read aloud, it is obvious that the author did not set out to give a scientific account of creation in either an ancient or modern sense. While it builds on the cosmology of the day, it was written to answer the more basic questions — who created the world and why? The answers were clear and emphatic. God created the world and sustains it by his power. If this power were withdrawn, the cosmos would immediately slip back into the primeval chaos from which it was drawn forth. In the Priestly tradition the Hebrew word *bara'* is only used for Yahweh's creative activity. This denotes that it is different from all other activity by either humans or animals. The human craftsman, for example, needs some material on which to work. By using a special word the author is insisting that Yahweh does not use some pre-existent matter, nor does he fashion the world out of the Divine being itself.[9] The Fathers of the Church later use the Latin phrase *creatio ex nihilo* to capture this unique meaning.

Moreover, the Bible is adamant that the God who creates the universe is self-sustaining and transcends the universe. Nevertheless, God's creative power is orderly and extends to all reality. There is nothing hidden from his domain. God's creative outpouring reaches its zenith in the creation of man and woman.

'Let us make man in our own image, in the likeness of ourselves and let them be masters of the fish of the sea, the birds of heaven, the cattle, all the wild beasts and the reptiles that crawl upon the earth.' God created man in the image of himself, in the image of God he created him, male and female he created them.

God blessed them, saying to them, 'Be fruitful, multiply, fill the earth and *conquer it*. Be masters of the fish of the sea, the birds of heaven and all living animals on the earth.' (Gen 1:26–28) (JB)

Psalm 8:3–8 echoes the same view.

When I look at thy heavens, the work of thy fingers,
the moon and the stars which thou hast established;
what is man that thou art mindful of him,
and the son of man that thou dost care for him?
Yet thou hast made him little less than God,
and dost crown him with glory and honour.
Thou hast given him *dominion* over the works of thy hands,
and hast put all things under his feet,
all sheep and oxen, and also the beasts of the field,
the birds of the air, and the fish of the sea,
and whatever passes along the paths of the sea. (RSV)

The repercussions of this command 'to fill the earth and conquer it' has had a profound impact on the way Jews and Christians have related to the natural world. The New Jerusalem Bible uses the phrase 'subdue it'; others render it 'have dominion over it'. All carry a strong overtone of actively shaping the natural world. Some people, like the American historian Lynn White, maintain that our modern ecological problems stem from 'the orthodox Christian arrogance towards nature'.[10]

But does the Genesis text support such human arrogance towards nature? First of all the injunction makes sense in the light of the earlier discussion on the urge within many Middle Eastern cultures to control the chaos and wilderness. Notwithstanding this need to control the elements, many modern biblical scholars insist that the Divine command cannot be interpreted as a licence for humans to change and transform the natural world according to any human whim or fancy. Ted F. Peters writes that originally the commission was, in fact, a challenge to human beings to imitate God's loving kindness and faithfulness and act as his viceroy in relationship with the non-human component of the earth. This, he argues, is the original meaning of the Hebrew word *radah* used in the text. Like viceroys of the king, men and women are expected to be just, honest and render real service. They were forbidden to exploit the people or the earth.[11] The virtues of the righteous king are portrayed in Ps 72:4–6. He will combine defence of the poor — 'may he defend the cause of the poor', verse 4 — with concern for the fertility of the land — 'may he be like rain that falls on the mown grass, like showers that water the earth', verse 6. The leadership role of people in relationship to the rest of creation is not unlike that of the good shepherd who cares for his flock (Ezek 34).

Humans are called to be stewards of God's creation. In the biblical view, as we will see in many texts, this visualizes people standing before God in a posture of worship and joyfully accepting responsibility for the management of human affairs and the well-being of creation. Even though in the biblical view men and women are somewhat segregated from the non-human components of the earth, there is recognition that they are totally dependent on the natural world, and that this is an interrelated and interdependent world with its own laws which reflect the will of the Creator. God rules creation and humans are challenged to understand these laws and respect God's designs (Gen 1:29–30). Finally, at the dawn of creation humans were expected to be vegetarian; plants are the only food permitted to both animals and humans (Gen 1:29).

This call to be vegetarian takes on added significance in our modern world when we realize that cattle ranching is one of the great destroyers of the rainforest — the most diverse ecosystem on earth. This pressure is particularly strong in both Central and South

America. There huge tracts of forest are burnt down and cattle are driven in to graze among the blackened stumps. When the tree cover is removed the land quickly degrades, so the original ranch must be abandoned and a fresh section of forest burned. The scale of the destruction is mind-boggling. In 1988 in Brazil, 40,000 square miles of tropical forest, an area the size of England, Scotland and Wales, were burned down. The beef produced through this plunder is exported to North America where it is snapped up by the fast-food companies. Thus the hamburger connection is one of the causes of extinction of species in today's world. Despite rhetoric about saving the rainforests, the scale of destruction is rising each year as the expanding fast-food chains establish outlets in the Third World itself. It may come as a shock to many people to realize that something as innocent as treating the family to a Sunday meal at a fast-food outlet may contribute in a very real way to the despoliation of the earth. In the interconnected world in which we live, believers are challenged to be more cognizant of the repercussions of our activities or omissions.

Exegetes today remind us that the first account does not end at Gen 1:31 with the creation of humans. It ends rather in Gen 2:3 with the sabbath rest of God. The sabbath was a very important institution for the Priestly author. He knew that during the exile Israel survived as a unique culture and religion because it had distinctive institutions like the sabbath and synagogue worship. During the sabbath worship the story of Yahweh's love for and involvement with Israel was retold in a way that strengthened the faith of the community. By placing this particular account of creation at the beginning of the Pentateuch, the author wished to assert that the sabbath was not merely a celebration which emerged from the Mosaic law; rather it was there from the very beginning, since Yahweh himself rested after his work and blessed his creation with the institution of the sabbath.

Reflecting on this final note of the first account, Jürgen Moltmann argues that the ultimate goal of God's creative activity is not homocentric, but rather theocentric. In *God in Creation* he writes that:

> the crown of creation is not the human being; it is the sabbath.
> It is true that, as the image of God, the human being has his
> special position in creation. But he stands together with all
> other earthly and heavenly beings in the same hymn of praise
> of God's glory, and in the enjoyment of God's sabbath pleasure
> over creation, as he saw that it was good.[12]

Before moving on to look at the second account of creation it is worth recalling that while Moltmann and other modern biblical scholars are correct in insisting that the first account of creation is not totally homocentric and that it is much less contemptuous of the natural world than was formerly thought, this is not how the text was interpreted in the past. Keith Thomas in his book *Man and the Natural World* writes that during the sixteenth century, Western literature, theology and popular preaching ascribed no intrinsic value to the natural world. According to the many divines and preachers from the Tudor period onwards, humans were unique among all species of the earth. Animals were inert and lacked any spiritual or emotional dimension. Humans stood to animals as did heaven to earth, soul to body. There was a total qualitative difference between man and the brute. The logic of domination embedded in this hierarchical perspective gives those on the top a divine right over whatever they consider inferior to them. Humans judged that they had ascendancy over plants and animals. These had no intrinsic right and no other purpose apart from their role in serving human needs. These claims that humans had the right to subjugate the natural world were promoted by theologians by constantly referring to the Genesis texts — Gen 1:28 and 9:2–8.[13]

Genesis 2:4 – 3:24

The second account of creation comes from the Yahwist tradition (Gen 2:4 – 3:24). This is a much older story; it predates the Priestly account by a few hundred years. In this story the Yahwist set out to situate this history of God's saving activity on behalf of Israel within the broader parameters of human and cosmic history. For the Yahwist the same God who brought Israel out of Egypt and bestowed on her the land was the One who had created the world and all human cultures. In telling this story the Yahwist felt free to borrow myths from other cultures. He did, however, change them and infuse them with a thoroughly Yahwist perspective on God and history. In his creation story he deals with themes which were common among cultures of the Near East and are found, for example, in the famous *Gilgamesh* epic. These included the creation of the world, an initial state of paradise, the origins of tribes, institutions such as marriage, and universal questions like the origin and meaning of suffering, evil and death. Given Israel's unique experience of Yahweh, the reality of evil demanded a special answer. Israel knew from experience that Yahweh is full of loving kindness and compassion and that he had rescued them from oppression in Egypt. Yet evil is an ever-present reality in the world around them and even in their own collective and personal lives. The question arose, how can one explain the emergence of evil if God is good? It could not originate from a rival spirit co-equal with Yahweh; therefore it had to have come from some primordial disobedience by humans themselves.

In comparing the two accounts of creation, the first thing that strikes one about the Yahwist account is that it is more earthy. Humans are created from the earth, *'adamah*, which is a play on the word '*adam*.[14] 'God formed man of dust from the ground and breathed into his nostrils the breath of life; and man became a living being.' The image employed here is one of a master potter carefully moulding his creation (Gen 2:7). But there is another determining element. Man is more than the earth from which he is fashioned. Humans come alive because Yahweh breathes a living spirit into them.

Yahweh's involvement with humans does not end with creating and setting them loose to do as they please. Immediately 'the Lord God planted a garden in Eden, in the east and there he put the man he had formed' (Gen 2:8). In Gen 2:15 God 'took man and put him in the garden of Eden to till it and keep it. And the Lord God commanded the man, saying "you may eat of every tree of the garden; but the tree of knowledge of good and evil you shall not eat, for in the day that you eat of it you will die".' Human activity was circumscribed by God's command to 'till and keep'. The Hebrew words used here are *abad* and *shamar*. *Abad* means 'work' or 'till', but it also has overtones of service, while *shamar* means 'keep', with overtones of preserving and defending from harm. This account cautions about the limits of the earth, with the command not to eat the fruit of the tree of knowledge of good and evil. In *Sollicitudo Rei Socialis*, no. 34, Pope John Paul II interprets this text in this way. He writes of 'the limitation imposed from the beginning by the Creator himself'.

Genesis, chapter 3 goes on to recount how Adam and Eve transgressed God's command and ate of the fruit of the tree. In their pride and arrogance they wished to take complete control of their own destiny and be 'like God, knowing good and evil' (Gen 3:5). These fantasies were quickly dashed. Their act of disobedience severed their intimate friendship with God (Gen 3:8) and transformed their human situation. Pain, suffering and death entered into the human condition (Gen 3:16, 19b). Moreover the Fall also ruptured their relationship with nature. It was no longer the bountiful and fruitful garden (Gen 2:9), but it became antagonistic and inhospitable:

> Cursed is the ground because of you;
> Painfully will you get your food from it
> as long as you live.
> It will yield brambles and thistles.
> as you eat the produce of the land.
> By the sweat of your face
> you shall eat your food,
> until you return to the ground,
> as you were taken from it;
> you are dust and to dust you shall return. (Gen 3:17b–19)

Other Genesis creation myths

The Yahwist account continues with a story about the spread of evil to Cain and Abel (Gen 4:1–16). Like a rock thrown into a still pool, original sin sends ripples out in all direction. Very soon a jealous Cain murdered his brother Abel; discord and sin thereby entered the very heart of the human family. Cain's punishment also involves the earth. 'Now be cursed and banned from the ground that has opened its mouth to receive your brother's blood at your hands. When you till the ground, it shall no longer yield its strength to you. A restless wanderer you will be on earth' (Gen 4:11–12). The text continues to record important moments in the human saga, the development of the arts and metallurgy (Gen 4:21–22). Despite such progress, evil continued to grow, culminating in the unusual story of the union of the sons of God with the daughters of the earth (Gen 6:1–4). 'Yahweh regretted having made human beings on earth and was grieved at heart' (Gen 6:6), and decided to punish them by flooding the earth (Gen 6:6 – 8:14). This connection between human sin and ecological disaster which is first made in Genesis is repeated many times in the Bible (Lev 18:25; Deut 29:22–25; Amos 4:7; Rev 8:10–11).

'And all living things that stirred on earth perished; birds, cattle, wild animals, all the creatures swarming over the earth and all human beings. Everything with the least breath of life in its nostrils, everything on dry land, died' (Gen 7:21–22). 'Only Noah was left, and those that were with him in the ark' (Gen 7:23b).

Noah

The Noah story (Gen 6:11 – 9:17) has a profound message for the modern world where so many creatures are facing extinction as we saw in Chapter 3, p. 87. God commanded Noah to conserve nature, 'From all living creatures, from all living things, you must take two of every kind aboard into the ark, to save their lives with yours; they must be a male and a female' (Gen 6:19). In the late 1980s, biologists like Norman Myers tell us that we are now losing many species each day and that within another decade the number will rise to several species per hour. Over the next few decades we could lose 20 or even 50 per cent of all the species on earth. The impact of this mega-extinction will be devastating for the web of life on earth. Myers also has a sobering thought for modern man. We are rightly proud of the achievements of modern science. Nevertheless, we are still at a kindergarten level as regards accurate knowledge of the creatures who share this 'ark' with us. We have identified 1.7 million species, but recent studies in the rainforest estimate that there may be 10 or 20 or conceivably 30 million species. If the rainforests are destroyed many of these will be lost for ever.[15]

In the wake of the flood Yahweh renews the command of Gen 1:28. This time the covenant is entered into not merely with humans but with all creation (Gen 9:8–17):

> God spoke to Noah and to his sons. 'I am now establishing my covenant with you and with your descendants to come, *and with every living creature that was with you*; birds, cattle and every wild animal with you; everything that came out of the ark . . .'

> 'And this', God said, 'is the sign of the covenant which I now make between myself and you and every living creature with you for all ages to come. I now set my bow in the clouds and it will be a sign of the covenant between *me and the earth*.' (Gen 9:8–14) (NJB)

The biblical scholar Bernard Anderson sees many striking linguistic and thematic parallels between Genesis, chapters 1 and 9. Both are moments of origin: the beginning of the cosmos and the new beginnings after the flood. He sees a radical expansion of the covenant community. In chapter 1 it is confined to humans, while in chapter 9 it is expanded to encompass all living reality.

Before we turn to other parts of the Bible it might be worthwhile summarizing what Genesis tells us about God, the human and creation. Genesis is absolutely clear about the central fact that the world, the human and all the creatures of the earth were created by God for his glory. It recognizes that humans have a special place in God's creation; they are created 'in his image and likeness', not to lord it over creation and despoil it, but rather to be stewards of God's creation — to 'till the garden and keep it' (Gen 2:15). But while humans might be special, Genesis is adamant that they are earthlings. They are created from the earth (Gen 2:7) and so they are organically connected with the rest of creation.

Yahweh, the creator, is also the saviour of Israel. Therefore he is not a remote prime mover, uninvolved in the world. Yahweh is a caring God; he practises good husbandry and looks after all his creatures by 'giving them their food in due season' (Ps 104:27). It recalls that 'You visit the earth and make it fruitful, you fill it with riches; the river of God brims over with water, you provide the grain' (Ps 65:9). He is also a God who is faithful both to the human community and to all creation (Gen 8:22; 9:9–13). The seasons, dawn and dusk, planting and harvesting are experienced by the believer as expressions of Yahweh's commitment to the community of Israel, the community of humankind and all the earth.

Genesis insists that creation is good (Gen 1:12). God created it and has blessed it with the sabbath rest. Yet Genesis avoids any starry-eyed romanticism. Evil, pain, suffering and death are part of this world. Humans who are called to 'be each other's keepers' (Gen 4:9) and stewards of creation often fail and sin. Their sins poison human relationships and also bring about ecological destruction. Human goodness, on the other hand, like that of Noah, brings hope and healing not to human relationships alone but to the whole earth as well.

Chapter 5

The covenant tradition

The community of Israel was not born out of a common language or a common cultural experience. The Hebrews did not win freedom by their own actions (Deut 8:17–18). Rather, Yahweh chose as his people a group of oppressed slaves; he liberated them and bound them to himself by covenant relationship (Ex 19:3–9; 24:3–8). For this reason the covenant and its renewal was to play a dominant role in the history of Israel down through the ages. At crucial moments in its history, such as when it entered the land of Israel, the community renewed the covenant (Jos 24:1–28). Later, in the brief period of reform before the exile in Babylon, a formal covenant renewal service was held (2 Kings 23:1–3). Prophets like Amos, Hosea, Isaiah, Jeremiah and Ezekiel reminded the people that they had been unfaithful to the covenant and challenged them to return to its spirit. Gradually Israel began to realize that their unfaithfulness had left the covenant in shreds; yet Yahweh, the faithful God, was willing to enter into a new covenant with Israel (Jer 31:31; Ezek 36:26–32).

The covenant ceremony was modelled on agreements made by kings and vassals in the ancient Middle East. These agreements began by recalling what one party had done for the other. This memory or retelling (*anamnēsis* in Greek) of the graciousness and goodness of the king was the bedrock on which the covenant rested. Ex 19:4, 'you have seen for yourselves what I did to the Egyptians, and how I carried you on eagle's wings and brought you to me', merely summed up all that Yahweh had done for his people as recounted in the previous 18 chapters of the book.

This recalling is followed by the demands of the Law of Yahweh. 'So now, if you are really prepared to obey me and keep my covenant, you, out of all peoples, shall be my personal possession, for the whole world is mine' (Ex 19:5). The Law covered not just religious observance and moral behaviour but every aspect of life. Some of its more prominent stipulations are set out in Ex 20:1–17.

> I am Yahweh your God, who brought you out of Egypt,
> where you lived as slaves,
> You shall have no other gods to rival me.

You shall not make yourself a carved image. . . .

You shall not misuse the name of Yahweh your God,
for Yahweh will not leave unpunished anyone who
misuses his name.

Remember the sabbath day and keep it holy . . .

Honour your father and your mother . . .

You shall not kill.

You shall not commit adultery.

You shall not steal.

You shall not give false evidence against your neighbour.

You shall not set your heart on your neighbour's house.

You shall not set your heart on your neighbour's spouse, or
servant, man or woman, or ox, or donkey, or any of your
neighbour's possessions. (NJB)

Much of the Law, or Torah, deals with Israel's relationship with
God, with fellow Israelites and with outsiders; its attention is focused
on humans' relationship with God and with one another. Nonetheless
the demand for stewardship and respect for animals is not completely
lacking. This care was rooted in the fact that Israel did not win the
land by its own effort; it received the land as a gift from God. Israel
was simply the caretaker and therefore 'the land shall not be sold in
perpetuity, for the land is mine; for you are only strangers and so-
journers with me' (Lev 25:23). In 1 Kings 21 King Ahaz compounds
the sin of murder with the sin of usurping the rights to Naboth's land.
Even though Ahaz promised Naboth a more productive vineyard,
Naboth's reply, 'The Lord forbid that I should give you the in-
heritance of my fathers' (1 Kings 21:3), proclaims the faith of Israel.

Respect for Yahweh's sovereignty, care for the earth, concern for
the poor, sensitivity to the needs of both wild and farm animals, all
come together in Ex 23:10–12, which decrees that:

For six years you shall sow your land and gather in its yield;
but the seventh year you shall let it rest and lie fallow, that the
poor of your people may eat; and what they leave the wild
beasts may eat. You shall do likewise with your vineyards, and
your olive orchard.

Six days you shall do your work, but on the seventh day you
shall rest; that your ox and your ass may have rest, and the son
of your bondmaid, and the alien, may be refreshed. (RSV)

The same message is repeated once again in Lev 25:4–7.

> But in the seventh year there shall be a sabbath of solemn rest
> for the land, a sabbath of the Lord; you shall not sow your field
> or prune your vineyard. What grows of itself in your harvest
> you shall not reap, and the grapes of your undressed vines you
> shall not gather; it shall be a year of solemn rest for the land.
> The sabbath of the land shall provide food for you, for yourself
> and for your male and female slaves and for your hired
> servants and the sojourner who lives with you; for your cattle
> also and for the beasts that are in your land all its yield shall be
> for food. (RSV)

The people cannot disregard the law without serious consequence
for the community. Only when these commands of God are obeyed
will the people live in security and abundance in the land. Lev
25:18–22 is directed to silencing the murmurs of the greedy and nig-
gardly people who would like to abandon these laws which they find
restrictive. In their selfishness and shortsightedness they wish to work
the land each year even though this may exhaust the soil and leave it
useless. They rationalize their greed by saying that it was necessary to
ensure a constant food supply. The text contends that:

> Therefore you shall do my statutes, and keep my ordinances,
> and perform them; so you will dwell in the land securely. The
> land will yield its fruit, and you will eat your fill, and dwell in it
> securely. And if you say 'What shall we eat in the seventh year,
> if we may not sow or gather in our crops?' I will command my
> blessing upon you in the sixth year, so that it will bring forth
> fruit for three years. When you sow in the eighth year, you will
> be eating old produce; until the ninth year, when its produce
> comes in, you shall eat the old. (RSV)

If, however, the people refuse to obey this sabbath of the land they
will be punished. The people will be exiled and the land will be
devastated. This joins together the familiar theme of Yahweh's chas-
tisement touching the people and the land. The author of Lev
26:32–35 insists that the land will be ruined in order that it might
enjoy the sabbath which the people in their avariciousness refused to
give it.

> And I will devastate the land, so that your enemies who settle
> in it shall be astonished at it. And I will scatter you among the
> nations, and I will unsheathe the sword after you; and your
> land shall be a desolation, and your cities shall be a waste.
> Then, the land shall enjoy its sabbath as long as it lies
> desolate, while you are in your enemies' land; then the land
> shall rest, and enjoy its sabbath. As long as it lies desolate it
> shall have rest, the rest which it had not in your sabbaths,
> when you dwelt upon it. (RSV)

Many ecologists insist that modern agriculture should attempt to recapture this sensitivity to the land. Industrial agriculture is completely tied into the money economy and only respects economic considerations — not ecological ones. Land may be taken out of production because of an over-supply of a particular commodity in the market; it is not allowed to lie fallow so that it might regain its fertility. In many Third World countries cash crops are given precedence over food crops. In the Sahel region in the 1970s and 1980s, many farmers, under pressure from private interests and the French government, shifted away from staples like millet and sorghum and planted a cash crop — peanuts. This undermined their traditional mechanisms for coping with drought, as most of the marginal land had been brought into production in response to a fall in the price of peanuts in Europe. When drought struck in the 1970s and 1980s, hundreds and thousands of people died. At the same time the soil was being depleted by monocropping peanuts. In line with the biblical perspective, both the land and the people suffered together.

Industrial agriculture is leading to massive soil erosion in many First World as well as Third World countries. In the USA one-third of the cropland is now seriously eroded. For every bushel of corn which a US farmer in Iowa harvests, two bushels of soil are lost through erosion. This adds up to a loss of 4,000 million tonnes of topsoil each year. In the Philippines, 100,000 hectares of soil one metre deep is lost each year through deforestation, plantation agriculture and inappropriate agricultural methods. The modern world would do well to heed the warnings sounded by the biblical authors. Otherwise what Wendell Berry calls the 'side-effects' of modern agriculture might endanger the future of agriculture in every country in the world.[1]

Respect for birds and domestic and wild animals was also enjoined in the Law. 'You must not muzzle an ox when it treads out the grain' (Deut 25:4). This thoughtful and respectful attitude is extended further to include all wildlife:

> If you chance to come upon a bird's nest, in any tree or on the ground, with young ones or eggs and the mother sitting upon the young or upon the eggs, you shall not take the mother with the young; you shall let the mother go, but the young you may take to yourself: that it may go well with you, and that you may live long. (Deut 22:6–7) (RSV)

The same ecological wisdom worked out over the centuries is embodied in the prohibition on cutting down fruit trees. Not even the besieging of an enemy city was considered a valid excuse: 'When you besiege a city for a long time, making war against it in order to take it, you shall not destroy its trees by wielding an axe against them; for you may eat of them, but you shall not cut them down' (Deut 20:19) (RSV)

Both of the above prohibitions show that the Torah was aware of the consequences of damaging the creative impulses of the natural world. Providing food for the individual and the community is important, but it must not come at the expense of the breeding stock or the seed grain. If it does, each succeeding generation will suffer. Modern agriculture, because of its success with agrochemicals and hybrid seeds, has abandoned this wisdom. Our pride in human ability to manipulate the natural world, most recently boosted by some of the fanciful predictions about genetic engineering, may prove catastrophic in the long term.

Despite what I have written above, some commentators stress that the Jewish tradition gives more prominence to human–divine and inter-human relationships. There is no denying this; the insights emerged at a time when the impact of human agency on the natural world was nowhere as noticeable or destructive as it is today. Nonetheless it is worth remembering that the Jewish tradition is flexible and adaptable. Many of the stipulations of the law, especially the conditional ones, are found in legal collections, e.g. the Code of Hammurabi. This covenant tradition, which stands on the side of life and justice, would have little difficulty incorporating modern prescriptions which respect ecological laws.

Personal choices to conserve and save planet Earth

In First World countries there is much that people can do as individuals in their homes, gardens and work places and as members of environmental groups. As we will see in the section on eco-justice, major institutional transformations are called for to alleviate world poverty and to redesign technology so that it serves the needs of all humanity without destroying the living systems of the earth. Nevertheless, people must be encouraged to take personal responsibility for their lives and to reduce their consumption and avoid the use of toxic substances.

Energy

Energy conservation is an important way to reduce our use of fossil fuels. This will help conserve limited resources and reduce the 'greenhouse gases' (carbon dioxide, chlorofluorocarbons or CFCs, and nitrous oxide). One good way of conserving fuel and saving money is to insulate buildings more efficiently and to wear warmer clothing rather than turning up the heating when the weather gets cold. Where possible, people should consider using solar heating systems and support initiatives that aim at producing electricity from renewable sources, such as solar, hydroelectric or wind power, or power derived from biomass. Using electricity more efficiently means turning off

lights, using low-watt light bulbs and high-efficiency electrical app-
liances, especially for cooking.

Transport is a major feature of Western life and, unfortunately,
public transport in many areas is poor or non-existent. Nevertheless,
people should attempt to reduce car use or make it more efficient by
arranging car pools with friends. Obviously one should buy or use
cars which are more energy efficient. For short journeys it is more
healthy and more enjoyable to walk or cycle. Citizens' groups can
encourage the use of bicycles in towns and cities. This will mean
providing cycle lanes and parking facilities at stations. Where possible people should use public transport and support political initiatives which aim to make it more extensive and efficient.

Conserve and recycle

We live in an extremely wasteful society. Christians should reduce
waste as much as possible and be in the forefront of recycling activities. If there are no recycling facilities in the area, they should try
to interest civic and religious organizations in providing such services. Where possible people should use paper products sparingly and
show a preference for recycled paper. Cups and mugs are preferable
to paper or Styrofoam cups; cloth towels and nappies are more
environmentally friendly than paper ones. Disposable goods should
be avoided. Shoppers should aim to buy things that are reliable, can
be repaired or refilled.

There is much talk today about the power consumers have to put
pressure on manufacturers and suppliers. People should avoid buying
products like plastics which are non-biodegradable or goods wrapped
in packaging which contains chlorofluorocarbons (CFCs). Consumers should be encouraged not to buy timber products from rainforests unless it is clear that the wood has been produced in a sustainable way. This is difficult to determine, although environmental
groups are encouraging furniture manufacturers to mark tropical
hardwoods. Use a basket when shopping, to minimize the use of
plastic bags.

Avoid toxic substances

The use of insect sprays, pesticides, detergents, toilet disinfectants
and toilet paper that contain toxic substances, and tobacco should be
avoided. Oil, paint products or other toxic substances should not be
flushed down the sink. Citizen groups should make sure that companies in their area minimize the use of toxic chemicals and do not
dispose of chemicals by shipping them to Third World countries. Buy
phosphate-free biodegradable soaps and detergents and encourage
the local shop or supermarket to stock such items. Unprocessed food
free of chemical additives is usually much more nutritious and healthy. Support local shops and co-operatives that supply organically
grown food.

Owners of gardens or farms can plant trees, especially deciduous species. If possible, grow one's own food organically. Do not burn organic matter unnecessarily; compost it for use in the vegetable garden. Encourage family and friends to develop an appreciation of the environment by joining environmental organizations or bird-watching clubs. Support programmes that protect wildlife and work to establish wildlife sanctuaries. Surplus money should be invested in 'ethical investments'. These socially responsible investments have a twofold aim: one, to avoid investing in companies that pursue objectionable practices — armaments, nuclear power, exploitation of animals, alcohol and tobacco, and pollute the environment, and two, to support companies who act in a caring manner towards society and the environment. Voters should write to politicians, and to civic and religious leaders about local and global environmental problems. At election time they should vote for candidates who are concerned about these issues and willing to work to preserve the environment.

Some attempts have been made to incorporate many of these ethical choices into a new religious framework not unlike the Decalogue or Ten Commandments. Marshall Massey, in an address to Quakers at Mount View, Denver, Colorado, offers one such attempt to integrate modern ecological thinking within the framework, ethos and language of the Decalogue. The text of this new challenge which Massey puts on Yahweh's lips is found in Appendix 1 (pp. 204–6).

All the Christian Churches would do well to raise believers' consciousness about what is happening to the earth, and challenge them with ethical demands arising from the depths of religious tradition as it confronts the unique problems of our time. A truly life-centred ethic would attempt to include heightening the awareness of believers of the interdependence of all reality, and would point out how this is intimately connected to the relational thinking at the heart of the Torah. This would provide the only valid parameters within which to criticize our modern industrial society. Only such a wide-angled perspective can challenge our modern industrial and economic enterprises to respect the basic ecological laws of the earth. As we will see below, our industrial, consumer, throw-away society is acting like a parasite on the rest of the living world, consuming it and often damaging it in ways that are irreversible.

Is our technological society just and sustainable?

From the dawn of human history until about 150 years ago, humans lived close to nature. They were surrounded by and dependent on plants, animals and birds. With the emergence of agriculture and the domestication of animals they grew their own food while animals supplied the main source of energy. This closeness to nature has, in large measure, been severed since the emergence of an industrial civilization in Western Europe 200 years ago and its subsequent spread during the past five decades to almost every part of the globe. Nowadays a growing percentage of the human population lives in cities. For the most part people do not grow their own food. Industrial farming produces, processes and transports food to the local supermarket where consumers buy it if they have the money. City dwellers are dependent on technology to carry them to the supermarket, take them to work or move around the large urban sprawls. Even human interaction is now mediated by technology through TV, radio or the telephone. While some of this technology has brought comforts and ease to a segment of humanity, many people have been impoverished by it and the earth has suffered grievously.

In the 1980s the technosphere is still expanding through the new microchip phase of industrialization. This is rapidly making itself felt in manufacturing and commerce and even in education. With the growth of ecological consciousness in many First World countries, a number of people have now become more aware that the growth in technology or the expansion of the technosphere is directly connected with the contraction and impoverishment of the biosphere. This is taking place through the extinction of species, the degradation of habitat and the deleterious impact of industrial processes, 'greenhouse' gases, and acid rain on vital systems like the ozone layer, the forests, land and the oceans. Anyone looking at the impact of this recent industrial phase against the backdrop of the history of humanity and the planet itself, would have to agree that industrialization has primarily served the needs of the rich — transnational corporations, the military and First World consumers — and that it has not yet established any sustainable way of living with the rest of the planet.

People in Third World countries remind Westerners that from the outset industrial economies operated in an unjust way. They siphoned off primary commodities from their colonies in order to supply them cheaply to Western industrial enterprises. Those who worked to supply this raw material were inevitably paid poor wages; monopolies and single-crop economies worked together to keep down the prices of these raw materials. This in turn, ensured that the colonies would remain dependent on the parent economy. Through the nineteenth and twentieth centuries these colonial economies undermined traditional subsistence and craft economies in many parts of the Third World. In the process land was often accumulated by a few rich people in order to grow luxury cash crops for export. By 1979 it was noted that an estimated 110 million acres of Third World land was growing export-oriented crops.[2] In many of these countries 70 per cent of the population are suffering from some degree of malnutrition. Since the best land is taken by agribusiness, farmers are forced to till marginal lands and deplete the soil, causing erosion.

Technology promises a wonderworld

The Disney EPCOT Center near Orlando in Florida, USA is a robust statement of faith in the ability of modern technology to solve human and ecological problems. This message is repeated like a credal formula at every pavilion at EPCOT, beginning with the central pavilion, 'Spaceship Earth', where the visitor takes an imaginary journey through the various stages of human communications from rock painting to modern satellite technology, courtesy of AT&T.

The same evolutionary perspective is also present in the pavilion 'Listen to the Land'. Here the visitors take a boat trip through a selection of different environments and look at their potential for food production. They are introduced to plants, animals and fish in a tropical forest and desert environment. While some of the research on plants, fish culture and the biological control of pests is valuable, the underlying message, that science, technology and the agribusiness corporations can solve all our food needs, is misleading. There is no attempt to criticize modern chemical farming, to show for example that for every bushel of corn that a farmer in Iowa grows the land sheds at least two bushels of soil. Nor is the cumulative effect of chemicals faced honestly. In the late 1940s at the beginning of the move to chemical agriculture, American farmers used 15 million pounds of insecticides and lost about 7 per cent of their crops. In 1989 they used 125 million pounds of insecticides and lost 13 per cent of their crops.

Modern high-tech agriculture is presented as much more efficient than the agriculture of the T'boli farmers in South Cotabato in the Philippines. But when one looks more closely at what efficiency might mean, the T'boli farmer comes out on top. When the costs of transport costs and food processing are included, American farmers and consumers expend 10 calories of non-renewable energy for every calorie they consume. The T'boli farmers, on the other hand, expend less than a tenth of a calorie for each calorie they consume.

'Listen to the Land', which is presented by Kraft Inc., overlooks the fact that the food shortage in the world today does not stem primarily from lack of scientific research into the properties of various plants and trees, but from the fact that much of the most productive land in the world is owned or controlled by agribusiness corporations and big farmers who grow crops for export, not in order to provide food for local people. Land reform, adequate prices for agricultural commodities, access to markets and capital at reasonable interest rates are much more important for farmers worldwide than more sophisticated farm technologies. New technologies may in fact, further undermine the livelihood of small farmers and force them to sell out their lands to large corporations.

EPCOT is silent on these political, economic and social implications of technology. It sees all our problems as technical rather than as social and political and so would like people to believe that the micro-chip will solve all our problems. It readily endorses the claims of Alexander King of the Club of Rome that:

> the promise of the microprocessor is that through its ubiquitous applications in the automation of industry and the tertiary sector, it is capable of increasing productivity to the extent that it should be possible to provide all the resources required by a country, including those of defence, health, education, nourishment and welfare, to provide a reasonably high material standard of living for everyone, without depleting or degrading the resources of the planet, with only a fraction of the physical work expended today . . . This could lead to the virtual abolition of poverty and the tyranny of work. In fact the microprocessor could be the key to Utopia.[3]

This quotation is blind to the current impact of technology on the biosphere; moreover it fails to recognize that the cutting edge of tech-nological innovation in today's world is at the service of the military. A huge proportion of earth's resources and human creativity is wasted under the ruse of providing a more secure and stable society. In reality each leap in arms technology is only inducing a greater level of insecurity and creating a climate in which weapons, which are supposedly designed for security reasons, will be used to destroy all life on earth.

But it is not just the arms industry which holds out false, and possibly lethal, promises. The nuclear power industry was launched in the 1950s under the misleading slogan of 'cheap power for everyone'. Its supporters insisted that it was clean and safe. This has proved to be far from the truth. Nuclear waste is toxic and some of the by products are radioactive for hundreds of thousands of years. No safe way has yet been found to dispose of this waste. Scientists are only gradually uncovering the full devastation of the chemical accident at the Chernobyl nuclear plant 1986. As the reserves of fossil fuel diminish it would be sheer folly for the human community to depend on this highly dangerous technology to meet our projected energy needs.

Garbage mountains grow worldwide

Many items manufactured by the industrial, throw-away society are not necessary for human well-being and end up in rubbish dumps. *Newsweek* (27 November 1989) saw the industrial world being 'buried alive' in garbage. Each consumer in the industrial world accumulates 3.5 pounds of garbage each day. This is now cluttering up landfills, polluting the atmosphere when burned and leaching into ground water. Apart from consuming and destroying the natural world, where to put all this rubbish is becoming a major national and inter-national problem. More than two-thirds of the landfills in the USA have been closed since the late 1970s. Trains and trucks loaded with garbage criss-cross the USA, and ships full of toxic waste have dumped their cargoes on unsuspecting Third World countries. Recycling paper, aluminium and glass can reduce the volume of waste, but many throw-away items like plastics or Styrofoam cups will continue to pollute landfills for decades and centuries to come.

In addition to this, thousands of man-made chemicals which may have long-term toxic or mutagenic effects are now used in agriculture, food and industry. These long-lived pollutants, like chlorofluorocar-bons, used as a propellant in aerosol cans, as a refrigerant and in the production of insulation for the packaging industry, are depleting the ozone layer in the upper atmosphere and thus subjecting all living creatures on earth to harmful solar radiation. The fossil fuel energy used to drive our industrial society is responsible for releasing the 'greenhouse' gases. These are changing the world's atmosphere and threaten to raise the global temperature worldwide within the next few decades. It is impossible even to predict all the negative con-sequences of such a rapid change. It is sure to involve freak storms, droughts, the inundation of prime cropland and cities and an unprecedented stress on the world's ecosystems as plants and animals attempt to adapt to the new environment.

Like the Israelites who went up to 'the high places' in search of security and fertility, many people, primarily in Western countries, have been seduced by gadgets which are mass produced. These machines hold out a promise of ease and comfort for the user. Often they do, but their cumulative effect on the planet is easily forgotten. Take the family car as an example. Given a good car, an uncluttered country road and somewhere to go, a car is a real boon. But thousands of cars competing for space on clogged-up roads are a major health hazard in many cities today. Furthermore, the emissions from car exhausts contribute to the 'greenhouse' effect and to the increase in acid rain which is destroying forests, soil and freshwater lakes in many parts of the world.

This is not intended as a blanket criticism of all technologies, but intended to heighten our awareness of the shadow side of modern technology; it is written as a corrective to the positive, pro-technology current in Western thought in recent decades, irrespective of whether the technologies are in the long run harmful to the fabric of life on earth. We often forget that many of our technologies were probably learned from the natural world. Spiders spun webs before humans wove cloth, swallows built nests before architects designed houses, bats used sonar before we did.

Appropriate technology

Appropriate technology has played an important role in human history. Humankind emerged through the creative use of stone implements. However, there is a vast difference between technologies which are sustainable and technologies which oppress people and destroy the fabric of creation. Geoff Lacey defines the former technologies as being 'grounded in an ecological matrix and deeply attuned to it'.[4] He feels that 'conviviality', a term coined by Ivan Illich, should also characterize technology. 'A convivial technology is one that people themselves engage in and manage, individually or collectively. They may use it to provide for their needs, to create a culture, to learn, to explore, or for enjoyment.'[5]

This discussion assumes that Christian social teaching must not focus exclusively on activities which directly oppress and exploit people, like militarization, inequitable distribution of the earth's resources, offences against human rights, starvation wages and the like. Today it must also champion the rights of every other creature and entire ecosystems. It must emphasize the importance of safeguarding the integrity of creation. A moral–religious code similar to the one enunciated by Marshall Massey in Appendix 1 below could become a modern-day Decalogue or Ten Commandments and promote positive action to secure justice for all creatures. Such a code, and similar ones like the *World Charter for Nature*,[6] challenge humans to live in conformity with the law which Yahweh has written at the heart of his creation and which operates at every level of life. It means recognizing that there are geophysical and biological limits on earth and that we must not be deluded by the false promise that technology will allow us to circumvent these limits indefinitely without experiencing a catastrophic backlash.

Eco-justice

This attempt to link concern for justice with ecology is now often called working for *eco-justice*. The term was coined by Richard Jones after the first United Nations Conference on the Human Environment in Stockholm in 1972. At that meeting, some of the delegates from Third World countries were unsympathetic to the ecological concerns expressed by people from First World countries. They were particularly suspicious, and rightly so, of some expressions of the 'limits to growth' thesis which sought to freeze all economic growth at then current levels. Third World countries rightly pointed out that, in effect, that would mean perpetuating for ever the present gap between First and Third World countries. Third World delegates argued that many First World countries could easily aim at overall negative economic growth as they abandoned and discarded industries involved in producing totally unnecessary luxuries which consume scarce resources and energy. Third World countries, on the other hand, need growth, not in grandiose industrial projects which will encourage their elites to ape Western lifestyles, but to provide basic services like food, clothing and shelter for the majority of their population. Only by seeking such eco-justice can just and sustainable human societies be established on earth.

Eco-justice adds a new powerful dimension to the biblical notion of peace — *shalom*. In the Old Testament the various covenants promoted peace between warring factions. In Gen 26:26–31 Isaac enters into a covenant relationship with the Philistines that 'you will do us no harm, just as we have not touched you and have done to you nothing but good and have sent you away in peace'. *Shalom* implies more than the absence of war; it involves a healthy creative relationship with God and other humans, and it must now include the well-being of all creation.

War and militarization create ecological disasters

Even before the invention of gunpowder, war always had a deleterious effect on the environment. The traditional damage is dwarfed by the capacity of modern nuclear, chemical and biological warfare to destroy the earth. The use of defoliants, including the dreaded dioxin, by the US forces affected between a quarter and a half of Vietnam in the course of the Vietnam War. The legacy of the herbicide known as 'Agent Orange' still lives on. The rate of birth defects in the area has risen by 50 per cent and there is also a marked increase in the rate of Down's syndrome babies.[7] It is now generally thought that humanity would not survive an all-out nuclear war, and all life on earth would be permanently damaged.

Even if the arsenals which are being built up in the various military blocs are never used, the continuous growth in military expenditure is diverting vital human and natural resources away from the much needed areas of development and ecological restoration. Lester Brown of the WorldWatch Institute in Washington DC has isolated some of the important ingredients in creating sustainable societies. These include adequate food stocks, basic health care, population planning, soil conservation, energy conservation and reforestation. According to Brown, the programmes which would necessary to achieve this would cost about $150 billion annually. This figure might seem exorbitant but it is merely a sixth of the total worldwide expenditure on arms. In 1985 the United Nations estimated that one trillion dollars was spent on arms; this exceeds the combined income of the poorer half of the earth's people.

This prodigious waste is not confined to rich countries. Many poor countries are spending on armaments money which is desperately needed for health care, education and environmental protection. The Philippines, for example, are debating a deal with the Italian government which would allow the Philippine airforce to buy military training jets at a cost of $70 million. The military hardware will not be paid for in hard cash but in prawns (*Malaya*, 16 March 1989). The Philippines has expanded its prawn exports in recent years from 5,000 metric tons in 1983 to 20,000 metric tons in 1988. But this rapid expansion is already creating ecological problems in many parts of the country. Negros Occidental, the heartland of prawn production, is experiencing major problems with ground water which can only get worse as the industry expands. The massive pumping of water to feed the prawn beds is depleting the ground watertable and allowing salt intrusions into the aquifer. This, in time, will affect everyone including the prawn-producers. Coral reefs and mangroves — breeding grounds for most fish species — are also suffering from the growth of the prawn industry. This kind of long-term and irreparable ecological destruction will increase dramatically as prawn production is expanded to meet the military bill for planes that are not needed.

But there are ironies in First World countries also; Norman Myers estimates that if the money which the United States spends on its Rapid Deployment Force in the Persian Gulf were diverted for a single year to weather-proofing buildings in the United States, this would virtually have eliminated the need for the US to import oil, thus making the Rapid Deployment Force redundant.[8] The wastefulness of the modern military apparatus can be gauged from the fact that the fuel consumed by the Pentagon in a single year would run the entire public transport system of the US for 22 years.[9]

Already the day-to-day operations of many armies have a negative impact on the environment. Jonathan King in his book *Troubled Waters* lists some of these:

> The combined United States Forces generate 1 billion pounds of hazardous material each year. The navy alone generates 19 million gallons of liquid hazardous waste and 35 million pounds of hazardous waste solids.

> Many of the 400 waste handling facilities of the military in the US are poorly managed. Leakage from one such site in California threatens the drinking water supply of 500,000 people.[10]

More and more it is becoming clear today that the world cannot have guns and butter. Disarmament, sustainable development, a marked improvement in the fulfilment of basic needs, procurement of basic services, and environmental protection and restoration must begin to take place simultaneously. Ted Trainer in *Developed to Death* is insistent that true peace depends on First World people living more simply. 'What most people in rich countries fail to grasp is that their living standards, their empire, involve and require extensive violence on the part of regimes which force their people to adhere to economic strategies which deprive them and enrich us.'[11] The need is for First World countries to live more simply. All of these roads converge on and lead to the only path to *shalom* or that cosmic peace which the angels proclaimed at the birth of Jesus, 'Glory to God in the highest heaven, and on earth peace for those he favours' (Luke 2:14).

Sealing the covenant with a ritual meal

Covenants in Israel and elsewhere in the ancient Middle East were sealed by ritual activity. Gen 31:44–55 recounts how a covenant between Jacob and Laban was solemnized in a common banquet. In Exodus 24 the covenant between Yahweh and his people was sealed through the sacrifice of oxen, the sprinkling of blood (3–8) and finally a meal (9–11). The same urge to seal the covenant with a meal spills over into the New Testament. Before his sacrifice Jesus breaks bread and shares the cup (Mark 14:17–25; Matt 26:20-29; Luke 22:14–23; 1 Cor 11:23–33). The early Church continued to recall the death and resurrection of Jesus 'by breaking bread' (Acts 2:46). Down through the ages members of the Christian community have brought to the Eucharist the fruits of the earth transformed by human labour. As with the ancient covenants in Israel, the Eucharist calls to mind the graciousness of God in creating and redeeming his people. In the Eucharist the Christian community is recreated by recalling the mighty deed of God. Like the father who in answer to his son's query — what does this ritual mean? (Ex 12:26) — recounts the *haggadah* or story of liberation, the Christian community in celebrating the Eucharist recalls the story of God's faithfulness and loving kindness in creating our world and redeeming his people.

Unfortunately, in the present Roman Missal the focus on creation is often hurried and perfunctory. Eucharistic Prayer II is a good example. We glide over the stupendous reality of creation in a single line — 'He is the Word through whom you made the universe'. The Preface of Sundays in Ordinary Time V is more sensitive:

> All things are of your making, all times and seasons obey your laws, but you chose to create men and women in your own image, setting them over the whole world in all its wonder.
> You made them the stewards of creation, to praise you day by day for the marvels of your wisdom and power through Christ our Lord.

One of the finest expressions of the creation theme to date is found in a preface composed by the International Commission on English in the

Liturgy (ICEL). The text has a poetic ring to it as it attempts to capture the beauty and majesty of the reality of creation. It reads as follows:

Blessed are you, strong and faithful God.
All your works, the height and the depth,
echo the silent music of your praise.

In the beginning your Word summoned light;
night withdrew, and creation dawned.
As ages passed unseen,
waters gathered on the face of the earth
and life appeared.

When the times had at last grown full
and the earth had ripened in abundance,
you created in your own image humankind,
the crown of all creation.

You gave us breath and speech,
that all the living
might find a voice to sing your praise.
So now, with all the powers of heaven and earth,
we chant the ageless hymn to your glory . . .

It is obvious that the creation theme offers extraordinary opportunities for Christian communities in different parts of the world to praise God from the depths of their own experience of nature and in the most appropriate idiom of their culture. Here too each region, or more accurately each bioregion, will celebrate a different dimension of creation in their eucharistic celebration. People living in mountain regions will obviously incorporate that experience with all the creatures that live with them in the mountain into their hymn of praise. Those living on the sea-shore in tropical regions can incorporate the world of wonder, beauty, symmetry and abundance that is revealed in the coral reefs and the mangrove forests. The bishops of the Philippines, in their pastoral letter *What Is Happening to Our Beautiful Land?* on the environmental challenges facing their country, call attention to this grounding of creation theology in the rocks, trees and creatures of the earth. 'There is a great need for a Filipino theology of creation which will be sensitive to our unique living world, our diverse cultures and our religious heritage.'[12]

In recalling God's graciousness in the context of the life, death and resurrection of the Lord, our gifts are transformed into his body and blood. Christians believe that as members of a community we share the gifts of Christ's body and blood. But this breaking of the bread and pouring out of the cup reminds us of Christ's sacrifice — that his life was poured out for others to bring salvation, wholeness and peace to humanity and the earth.

In 1 Cor 11:27–31, Paul challenges the community to participate in the Eucharist in a worthy manner. He insists that there is no place for bickering, lack of concern or social inequality 'because there is one bread, we who are many are one body, for we all partake of the one bread' (1 Cor 10:17). Today we are more and more aware that this one body encompasses the body of all created reality.

There are undoubtedly many other strands in the New Testament's understanding of the Eucharist. Many exegetes, however, argue that the earliest understanding linked it directly to Jesus' action of feeding the multitude (John 6:5–15; Matt 14:13–21; Mark 6:32–44; Luke 9:10–17). In this event the disciples were intimately involved in sharing the bread and gathering up the left-overs: 'pick up the pieces left over so that nothing gets wasted' (John 6:12). In today's world, wherever the Eucharist is celebrated the disciples of the Lord are challenged to share their bread with the poor and needy. This involves, among other things, challenging economic and political structures which persist in keeping a large segment of humanity hungry. It must also mean working to ensure that the creative powers of God's creation are not permanently impaired through agrochemicals, soil erosion of the elimination of traditional varieties of food plants.

Any discussion of food and drink, which are at the heart of our Eucharistic celebration, raises questions about who controls seeds. Many Third World countries are located in a tropical or semi-tropical environment which is 'gene-rich'. It is estimated that 90 per cent of the genetic material for our food plants originated in Third World countries. Most of this is now in gene banks in First World countries, leading to what some call 'genetic imperialism'. The genetic material was used by research institutes like the International Rice Research Institute (IRRI) in Los Banos, Philippines, to develop high-yielding seed varieties (HYVs) for cereals. The HYVs initially produced higher yields than the traditional seeds which over the centuries had adapted to the particular climate and environment, but they were dependent on a mix of chemical fertilizers, pesticides and irrigation. Farmers need money to buy the seeds and the package that goes with them. This works to the detriment of poor farmers who lack capital to invest. If poor farmers lose a crop because of bad weather or pest infestation it may well wipe them out altogether.

It is no coincidence that, over the years, petrochemicals become deeply involved in seed production. Royal Dutch Shell in recent decades bought up many small-scale seed-growing companies. By 1983 it had become the largest corporate seed owner in the world and in 1989 it controlled 34 per cent of the varieties of spring barley and 55 per cent of winter barley. Not content with gobbling up smaller seed-producing companies, transnational companies have successfully lobbied many governments to protect their rights by passing seed-patenting legislation which gives the holder the right to specific plant reproductive material for decades.[13] This monopoly of seed control in the hands of a few transnational corporations is extremely worrying. A friend of mine, known for his humour, underlines the seriousness and religious dimension of this trend by saying that within 20 years, instead of asking our heavenly Father to 'give us this day our daily bread', we will have to direct the prayer to the management of Shell Oil, because they will effectively control all the seeds we use!

Discussion of the politics of seeds now has a new aspect, that of genetic engineering. Many Christians can see benefits from genetic engineering in the field of medicine and agriculture. Nevertheless there is profound disquiet at what might be unleashed into the environment, and at the kind of arrogance that underlies the claim that some human being can lay an exclusive claim to a living entity. Dr F. Rajotte of the World Council of Churches writes that:

> the very word creation implies that there is no owner of the planet, with all that lives on it, except the living God. To claim the patent of a life form is a direct and total denial of God as creator, sustainer, breath of life and immanent spirit in the within of all beings.[14]

Patenting works to the disadvantage of the poor and Third World people. First World corporate seed companies can pillage the genetic resources of Third World countries, develop new varieties of seeds, sell them back to Third World countries and in the process make huge profits. The Christian Churches should lobby to ensure that this kind of power over the living world is not concentrated in the hands of a few. They should also insist that all aspects of genetic engineeering be debated within an ethical and religious context and that whatever emerges from it by way of techniques or knowledge must belong to the public domain and must not be used to disadvantage the poor further.

It might seem that this discussion has moved a long way from the altar or communion rail. Yet it deals with the future of the control and availability of food. In partaking of the Eucharist we are challenged to live not merely justly but also in a way that will not injure the fruitfulness of the earth and impair the lives of other creatures for all time. The Eucharistic dimension reminds us that in caring for the earth we must act as a community. Individual conversion and changes of life style are undoubtedly called for, but the problems facing the earth are so gigantic and often so intractable that it will take massive community action to stem the tide of destruction and heal the damage which has already been done. A retreat into the kind of private religion which has been so prevalent in the West since the beginning of the industrial revolution will not help very much.

Prophets of Israel, the Psalms and wisdom literature

Prophets

The prophets in Israel were not seers who gazed into a crystal ball to foretell the future, but men who were called by Yahweh to remind Israel, often in blunt and uncompromising language, to be faithful to the covenant. The aim of the prophet was to help people see the designs and call of God in the present moment. They challenged, cajoled and inspired Israel with hope when the sky was full of black clouds and no bright dawn seemed to be spreading from the horizon.

The prophets were very much aware of the fact that the earth will also punish those who by their extravagant consumption oppress the poor and destroy the earth (Joel 1:4).

> Is not the food cut off
> before our eyes,
> joy and gladness
> from the house of our God?
>
> The seed shrivels under the clods,
> the store houses are desolate;
> the granaries are ruined
> because the grain has failed.
> How the beasts groan!
> The herds of cattle are perplexed
> because there is no pasture for them;
> even the flocks of sheep are dismayed. (Joel 1:16–18) (RSV)

The contemporary equivalent of the characters of *Dallas* and other such television programmes are upbraided by the prophet Isaiah. These people live in a lavish manner while so many live in poverty and squalor. Isaiah declares:

> Woe to those who join house to house, who add field to field,
> until there is no more room, and you are made to dwell alone
> in the midst of the land. The Lord of hosts has sworn in my

hearing: 'surely many houses shall be desolate, large and beautiful houses, without inhabitant. For ten acres of vineyard shall yield but one bath, and a homer of seed shall yield but an ephah.' (Is 5:8–10) (RSV)

Prophets often challenged the political and religious leadership of their time. For this reason they were often not made welcome by people caught up with institutions like kings or priests. Amos was seen as a troublemaker (Amos 7:10–14). The prophets considered that those who are called to lead had a special obligation to be sensitive to the 'signs of the times' and not to miss or overlook dangers which the community was facing. Ezekiel stresses the responsibility of the watchman to alert the community in the time of danger.

But if the watchman sees the sword coming and does not blow the trumpet, so that the people are not warned, and the sword comes, and takes any one of them; that man is taken away in his iniquity, but his blood I will require of the watchman's hand. (Ezek 33:6) (RSV)

Unfortunately, the various institutional watchmen, including religious leaders, have failed to understand the magnitude of the ecological crisis that was unfolding during the past 40 years. Prophets like Rachel Carson, Barry Commoner, E. F. Schumacher, for example, were largely ignored. Only in the late 1980s have politicians and religious leaders begun to wake up to what is happening. Yet even at this late stage they have little positive guidance to offer beyond vague generalities. How different from the concrete options laid out before the people by the prophets.

An important dimension of the prophetic literature which should not be overlooked is the sense of hope that it engendered in Israel. Israel knew that, left to its own devices, it would continue sliding down the slope towards destruction. But Israel could call on other resources. Yahweh's power and strength was always available to help Israel build a new life. Isaiah, speaking on God's behalf, reminds the people of Yahweh's saving power which Israel had experienced in the past and which is a source of hope for them as they attempt to live in a new way:

Remember not the former things,
nor consider the things of old.
Behold, I am doing a new thing;
now it springs forth, do you not perceive it?
I will make a way in the wilderness
and rivers in the desert. (Is 43:18–19) (RSV)

Hope and new undreamed-of possibilities are also found in the resurrection scene which the prophet Ezekiel paints in chapter 37. At the word of Yahweh, the dry bones knit together, grow flesh and eventually begin to breath and live again. Yahweh promises the people to open graves and to 'resettle you on your own soil' (Ezek 37:14). This theme of new life will be given new significance in the resurrection of Jesus. This, as we shall see, opens up new possibilities which are sustained by God's grace and grounded in the earthly realities of soil and resurrected bodies.

Hope is so important in today's world. When one surveys the range of ecological problems facing particular regions of the earth, every ecosystem and the oceans and atmosphere, it is easy to become discouraged and to abandon hope. This often evokes a response like that of the Epicureans of old who counselled that one should live for today and forget tomorrow (*carpe diem* — seize the day). Such an outlook will inevitably increase the level of oppression which the poor and the weak are experiencing now, and it will escalate the plunder of the earth. Hope is essential in order to help humanity respond in a rational and constructive way to the problems facing the earth. Otherwise vast amounts of human energies will be dissipated and compound the problem rather than solve it. Religious traditions can provide a significant service for the human and non-human components of the earth by helping to lay the groundwork on which genuine hope can be based.

Yahweh's power to heal, transform and redeem touches not just the hearts of the stubborn Israelites. Redemption restores community well-being as well as the harmony, balance and fruitfulness of creation which was present at the dawn of creation before humans had sinned (Gen 1:28–30). The harmony will be so complete that it will heal predatory relationships in nature.

> The wolf shall dwell with the lamb,
> and the leopard shall lie down with the kid,
> and the calf and the lion and fatling together,
> and a child shall lead them.
> The cow and the bear shall feed;
> their young shall lie down together;
> and the lion shall eat straw like the ox.
> The sucking child shall play over the hole of the asp,
> and the weaned child shall put his hand on the adder's den.
> They shall not hurt or destroy in all my holy mountain;
> for the earth shall be full of the knowledge of the Lord
> as the waters cover the sea. (Is 11:6–9) (RSV)

In the First Book of Kings we find a theme which is common among many tribal religions. Animals are often seen to be helpmates of religious persons, especially of the shaman or healer, who is often called on to undertake an arduous journey in order to seek a cure for individuals or to rid them of malign spirits. During a long drought the prophet Elijah was fed by ravens 'and the ravens brought him bread and meat in the morning, and bread and meat in the evening' (1 Kings 17:1–6). The theme that the non-human world is particularly kind to holy people recurs repeatedly in stories about the Fathers of the Church, Celtic saints and, of course St Francis of Assisi.

Psalms

In its prayers and hymns we capture Israel's deepest aspirations and feelings as it responds to Yahweh's manifestation of himself in its history. These outpourings of praise, thanksgiving and supplication afford us a unique insight into the living faith of Israel, especially as the community joined together for common worship. In worship Israel celebrated in song its deepest faith in who Yahweh was and how he related to Israel as a people and to the world which he created. Israel did not champion a private religion which visualized God as a primary cause of the universe with little to do with the day-to-day shaping of the world and human history. Rather Israel glorified a God who was active in the world and who, through his mighty deeds, redeemed them from slavery and who continued to walk with them in good times and bad. In the Psalms, however, the motif of praising God as creator is almost as common as praising God as saviour of his people. In fact both themes are often blended together in the same psalm as in the well-known invitatory psalm.

Come, let us cry out to the Lord;
acclaim the rock of our salvation.
Let us come into his presence with thanksgiving,
acclaim him with music.

For Yahweh is a great God,
a king greater than all gods.
In his power are the depths of the earth;
the peaks of the mountains are his;
The sea belongs to him, for he made it;
and the dry land, moulded by his hands. (Ps 95:1–5) (NJB)

The praise of God was not confined to humans alone. In Ps 148:1, 2-4, 7-12, the psalmist invites all creation, animate and inanimate, human and non-human, to praise God, conscious of the fact that without this vast symphony, fitting praise of God would be lacking. It is worth remembering this intuition when discussing the extinction of creatures. The praise which that particular creature renders to God is silence for ever and thus the chorus of creation is impoverished.

> Praise Yahweh from the heavens . . .
> Praise him, Sun and Moon,
> praise him, all shining stars!
> praise him, highest heavens
> praise him, waters above the heavens . . .

> Praise the Lord from the earth,
> sea-monsters and all the depths,
> fire and hail, snow and mist,
> storm-winds that obey his command!

> mountains and every hill,
> orchards and every cedar,
> wild animals and all cattle,
> reptiles and winged birds! (Ps 148:2–4, 7–10) (NJB)

Psalms 96:11–12; 97:6; 103:22; 145:10–11, 21; 150:6, and the canticle of the three young men who were thrown into the furnace in Dan 3:26–90 reiterate the theme of all creation praising God.

The close connection between work for justice and concern for the fruitfulness of creation, and especially the croplands on which the people depend for their food, is another thread running through some of the psalms. Psalm 145 prays:

> The Lord is good to all,
> and his compassion is over all
> that he has made.

> The Lord upholds all who are falling,
> and raises up all who are bowed down.
> The eyes of all look to thee,
> and thou givest them their food
> in due season.
> Thou openest thy hand,
> thou satisfiest the desire of every living thing.
> (Ps 145:9, 14–16) (RSV)

This concern of Yahweh for the fruitfulness of creation is very explicit in Psalm 65.

You visit the earth and make it fruitful,
you fill it with riches;
The river of God brims over with water,
you provide the grain.

The meadows are covered with flocks,
the valleys clothed with wheat;
they shout and sing for joy. (Ps 65:9, 13) (NJB)

Nowhere is Yahweh's concern for his creation and knowledge of its intimate working better expressed than in Psalm 104. The author begins with a picture of Yahweh working meticulously, like the careful tent maker, to create the heavens and the clouds and the winds. These become vehicles of God's purposes on earth.

Bless Yahweh, my soul,
Yahweh, my God, how great you are!
Clothed in majesty and splendour,
wearing the light as a robe!
You stretch out the heavens like a tent,
build your palace on the waters above,
making the clouds your chariot,
gliding on the wings of the wind,
appointing the winds your messengers,
flames of fire your servants. (Ps 104:1–4) (NJB)

Then the psalmist goes on (Ps 104:5–35) to describe the creation of the earth, mountains, water sources, birds, wild beasts, towering trees, domesticated plants and animals, fish and sea creatures. The author has an observant eye and shows an intimacy with the behaviour and habitat of the wild birds, the goats, the lions and the rock badgers. Creation is not a miserly world which only gives meagre sustenance to humans. No, there is sufficiency, and wine and oil for celebration.

One can hardly read verse 26 about the leviathan or whale without being appalled at the way the human community has slaughtered these extraordinary creatures until their very survival is threatened. In the heyday of whaling in the nineteenth century, whalers killed over 60,000 whales each year. Many species are now on the brink of extinction. The 100-ton blue whales of the Antarctic region are now estimated to be at only 1 per cent of their original level. The humpback stands at about 3 per cent and finwhales have been reduced to 20 per cent. One species which has not so far been decimated is the minke whale. In 1989, however, the Japanese planned to kill 800 such creatures, ostensibly in the name of 'science', but in fact to supply whale meat for their gourmet restaurants.[1] This mindless slaughter concretely illustrates verse 35 that there are sinners on earth. One can only hope that the judgement and curse placed on them — that they be 'consumed from the earth' — will not fall on the heedless generation that has condoned this and so much other destruction in God's world.

For Israel, creation is not a dumb, inert, lifeless thing; it is not crass matter which can be discarded since it lacks meaning in itself or the ability to point beyond itself to the God who created the world and all that it contains. For the psalmist, creation gives a resounding testimony to the goodness and power of its creator. Its testimony should move humans to lift up their minds and hearts to God in recognition and praise:

> The heavens declare the glory of God;
>
> the vault of heaven proclaims his handiwork,
>
> day discourses of it to day,
>
> night to night hands on the knowledge. (Ps 19:1–2) (NJB)

Psalm 97:6–7 repeats this motif. Creation demonstrates the goodness and righteousness of God. The psalmist adds that creation itself should convince people that only Yahweh reigns and that idols, which some find attractive, are in reality, useless and deceitful.

Wisdom

The preoccupation of the wisdom literature differs markedly from that of the other writings in the Bible which deal mainly with Israel's unique history. Wisdom does not deal with weighty historical questions centred on the covenant. Nor does it have the penchant for the absolutes of the prophetic tradition which resolutely attempts to usher Israel down the way of the Lord. The wisdom literature is more cosmopolitan; it moves beyond the borders of Israel and shares in a common tradition which is found in many other cultures in the ancient Middle East. Like its parallels in Egypt and Babylon, this literature was preoccupied with the universal questions which face every person and culture.

Walther Zimmerli claims that 'wisdom thinks resolutely with the framework of a theology of creation'.[2] It avoids abstractions and instead explores everyday life, paying minute attention to the experience of concrete living. Even when it deals with vital questions like good and evil, suffering, pain, injustice and death, as it does in the book of Job, it is often forced to admit that there may not be any definitive answers. What it sets out to do is to cultivate the art of proper living and thus bring peace and prosperity to the individual.

Like everything else which she absorbed into her world, Israel wrapped her own unique cloak around this literature. The absence of a continual focus on God does not mean that this is secular literature in a modern sense. All activity in the natural world and in human history takes place within the sphere of Yahweh's nurturing care and concern. Again and again it affirms that 'the fear of the Lord is the beginning of wisdom, and the knowledge of the Holy One is insight' (Prov 9:10; Job 28:28). The beauty and goodness of creation should lead a person to God. 'Yes, naturally stupid are all who are unaware of God and who, from good things seen, have not been able to discover him-who-is, or by studying the works, have not recognized the Artificer' (Wis 13:1) (NJB)

The creation focus receives an initial boost in the example of King Solomon who is held up as the model of the sage. His wisdom surpassed that of wise men in the surrounding countries in its breadth, depth and insight. He was particularly knowledgeable about the natural world and so 'he spoke of trees, from the cedar that is in Lebanon to the hyssop that grows out of the wall; he spoke of beasts, of birds, and of reptiles and of fish' (1 Kings 4:33). This was a knowledge of intimacy with the natural world which is expressed so beautifully in Psalm 104 above. It was quite different from the perspective of someone like Francis Bacon (1561–1626) who only valued the kind of knowledge that facilitated the domination and exploitation of the earth. The text does, however, state that people came from all parts to hear this wisdom.

A reading of the wisdom literature, especially the Book of Job, confirms the contention above (pp. 120–1) that the Genesis account of creation is not entirely anthropocentric. One of the best examples of this wider vision is the Book of Job, which deals with the predicament of a just man who is made to suffer. He vehemently rejects the glib orthodoxy so facilely expounded by his three friends — Eliphaz, Bildad, and Zophar — who in their efforts to comfort Job insist that he must have sinned, even secretly. Gradually Job's self-pity dissipates when he begins to realize that he is not suffering in isolation; others are victims of even worse injustice and oppression. Job begins to experience a solidarity with all who are faced with unmerited suffering.

But the insight of the book does not end there. It moves beyond this horizon; the speeches of Yahweh help Job to comprehend that the demands of justice must be located within the broader frontiers of God's freedom and his gratuitous love. The human factor is not the only one on the mind of Yahweh. God has wider concerns which are not known to human intelligence. Nowhere is this more forcibly stated that in the speeches of Yahweh in Job, chapters 38–41. The following quotations are a sample of the wider concerns of Yahweh. After listening to Job's protests, Yahweh challenges and chides his conceit and arrogance:

Where were you when I laid the foundation of the earth?
Tell me, if you have understanding.
Who determined its measurements — surely you know!
Or who stretched the line upon it?
On what were its bases sunk,
or who laid its cornerstone,
when the morning stars sang together,
and all the sons of God shouted for joy?

Or who shut in the sea with doors
when it burst forth from the womb;
when I made clouds its garment,
and thick darkness its swaddling band,
and prescribed bounds for it,
and set bars and doors,
and said, 'Thus far shall you come,
and no farther,
and here shall your proud waves be stayed'? (Job 38:4–11) (RSV)

Chapter 38 continues to deal not with the world of human history
but with the world of nature in its beginning and vital processes.
Yahweh demands to know whether the proud Job understands or can
account for all the natural phenomena in the world around him.
Yahweh asserts that not everything which he has created is meant for
human use. Other creatures have their legitimate needs and Yahweh,
as the creator of all, provides them with their unique habitat:

Who has cleft a channel for the torrents of rain,
and a way for the thunderbolt,
to bring rain on a land where no man is,
on the desert in which there is no man;
to satisfy the waste and desolate land,
and to make the ground put forth grass? (Job 38:25–27) (RSV)

Who has let the wild ass go free?
who has loosed the bonds of the swift ass,
to whom I have given the steppe for his home,
and the salt land for his dwelling place? (Job 39:5–6) (RSV)

In his book *On Job*, Gustavo Gutiérrez comments on these texts,
pointing out that:

God's speeches are a forceful rejection of a purely
anthropocentric view of creation. Not everything that exists
was made to be directly useful to human beings; therefore they
may not judge everything from their point of view. The world
of nature expresses the freedom and delight of God in creating.[3]

Job's progression from being fixated on his own pain to empathiz-
ing with fellow-sufferers broadens even further to encompass a much
more extensive appreciation of the totality of God's creation. Job's
journey, painful as it was, helped to transform him from a self-centred
person to one who was sensitive to others, especially the weak and
oppressed. He also developed a much deeper appreciation of who
God really is and how he relates in an ongoing way to all creation.
This transformation enriched Job's life immensely.

Many people in the 'developed world' must traverse this same
road during this decade. We must break out of the narrow anthropocentric cul-de-sac on which much of our economic, educational, social, political, technological and even religious activities are
based. People in the 'developed' world must remove the scales from
their eyes so that they can really see how their life style is impoverishing hundreds of millions of people in Third World countries.
But we must now move beyond that and empathize with the pain and
groanings of the body of the earth as it is sterilized and gradually
shorn of its life-forms.

Killing Gaia

The work of two scientists has helped us understand more fully what
might be involved in the massive geological and biological changes
which modern man has wrought in the biosphere. In recent years
Professors James Lovelock and Lynn Margulis have formulated what
they call the *Gaia* hypothesis. They argue that all life on earth is
intimately related and that, as life slowly emerged over the aeons, it
actually created and stabilized the conditions which are now necessary for the continuance of life on earth. They contend that Gaia
operates like a single organism in that it exhibits important properties
like the homeostatic features of living organisms. These work to keep
an organism healthy and functioning despite changes in the environment.

Lovelock writes in *GAIA* that the biosphere is 'a self-regulating
entity with the capacity to keep our planet healthy by controlling the
chemical and physical environment'.[4] According to this hypothesis
the mixture of gases in the atmosphere, for example, is just right to
maximize a number of crucial operations which are essential for life to
continue; they allow animals to breathe and be energized, and plants
to photosynthesize sugars, and they keep the earth's surface at

temperatures which facilitate life and growth. The homeostatic mechanism has the ability to adjust to changes which take place in the external environment. The luminosity of the sun, for example, is now 30 per cent more than it was when life first emerged 3.5 billion years ago, yet the Gaia mechanism has ensured that the temperature of the surface of the earth has remained more or less constant. There is a delicate interplay between the various elements and organisms which compose Gaia.

Many scientists feel that humans have been crudely disrupting these complex relationships in the space of a few short decades by destroying the tropical forests, draining and poisoning mud-flats and pumping huge quantities of carbon dioxide into the air. These changes could throw Gaia completely off course with dire consequences for humans and for all life forms. If this hypothesis is accurate, humans will have to begin to live within the parameters of Gaia. This major paradigm shift will involve considerable suffering for individuals and changes for many cultures, especially those that today promote acquisitiveness and a hostile attitude towards the non-human components of creation. Yet the changes are essential for survival of life in its present extent and grandeur. It is an illusion to hope that future technological inventions can undo the damage which our exploitative way of living is inflicting on Gaia.

Speaking of Gaia — a Greek word for the earth — reminds us of an important fact about the wisdom literature. Much of the literature of the Hebrew Bible and Christian scriptures reflects a patriarchal viewpoint on all reality including God. This patriarchal paradigm is extremely pervasive and has undergirded Western civilization for five thousand years. It has suppressed 'feminine' sensitivities and spontaneities and in an aggressive way has dominated people, especially women, and has plundered the earth. Fr Tom Berry identifies four contemporary institutions which embody the destructive drives of patriarchy: the classical empires, the ecclesiastical establishment, the nation-state and the modern corporation.[5] Deep-seated changes in Western culture are demanded if the feminine dimension of life is to be liberated to play its full nurturing role and if the ecological crisis is to be faced at its deepest manifestation. Rosemary Ruether in her book *New Woman/New Earth* writes that:

> women must see that there is no liberation for them and no
> solution to the ecological crisis within a society whose
> fundamental model of relationships continues to be one of
> domination. They must unite the demands of the women's
> movement with those of the ecological movement to envision a
> radical reshaping of the basic socioeconomic relations and the
> underlying values of this society.[6]

Ecofeminism

The term ecofeminism has been used to describe much of what is involved in women's struggle against the patriarchal forces which have enslaved women and the earth itself. The term was first used by the French writer Françoise d'Eaubonne in 1974 in her book *La feminisme ou la mort.*

A number of important threads run through ecofeminist literature. Holism is central to ecofeminism. Planet earth is experienced as a single, interacting ecosystem, composed of other dynamic ecosystems. One cannot pretend that what humans do will not affect other ecosystems, and ultimately the planet as a whole. This approach contrasts with the dominant scientific and technological paradigm of recent centuries which sought to break down reality into the smallest units in order to understand and manipulate it. On a practical level the holistic approach insists that no matter where toxic chemicals, for example, are disposed of, they will eventually affect other ecosystems and ultimately the living earth.

Interdependence is also at the heart of ecofeminism. People are part of the earth community, not above it or beyond it. We are dependent on the earth to sustain us through the air we breathe, the water we drink and the food we eat. We also depend on the ever-renewing cycles of nature to recycle our waste. This interdependence is the pathway of life for all the earth's creatures, since the dawn of life on earth. But when we mistreat the earth, our interdependence can also become a pathway of death. Chemicals we spray on our food or use freely in our industries may well be a major cause of human cancers.

The interdependence of all reality emphasizes the importance of each element in an ecosystem which has its own unique and irreplaceable function. This cannot be assumed by another element. This concern for every entity and the organism as a whole contrasts with a patriarchal, hierarchical approach which often only gives value to the being or person who occupies the topmost rank in the hierarchy. Furthermore, sharing, exchange and intimacy in a human community are deemed more important than 'masculine' characteristics like power and efficiency.

But ecofeminism is not just about ideas, its primary concern is to change a very pervasive system that has dominated much of the world's history for thousands of years. Whether it is the Chipko women in Uttar Pradesh in India, or the women of the Green Belt Movement in Kenya or women at large who are concerned for justice and the environment, ecofeminism is about empowering women to stand against oppression and violence and to nurture the earth. Ecofeminism recognizes that women and children are the ones most affected by all the mechanisms of oppression. A recent United Nations report summarizes this: 'women make up half of the world's population, work almost two-thirds of all man-hours [sic], receive a tenth of the world's income, and own less than a hundredth part of the world's wealth'.[7]

Today's particular twist in the cycle of poverty also takes a heavier toll on women than on men. Third World debt, for example, means that rural clinics are closed down, depriving women of even rudimentary health care. Often they do not have the money or opportunity to travel to towns if they fall sick. Girls are usually the first victims of educational cut-backs in Third World countries. Deforestation means that women have to walk further each day to collect firewood and fetch water. Soil erosion results in less food to eat, requiring mothers to eat less themselves so that their children and husbands have something to eat.

In a holistic perspective religion is seen as one of the most powerful forces available for this mammoth task of reshaping cultures. This is why the wisdom literature is so important for the Judaeo-Christian tradition. This biblical strand distinguishes itself by being more sensitive to the feminine dimension of the Divine.[8] Fr Yves Congar has written about this feminine dimension of wisdom. In some texts wisdom is courted like a bride (Wisdom 8:2; Sir 14:22–27); in others wisdom is like a warm and tender mother or as a farsighted and discerning wife (Sir 15:2–6). Hosea 11:1–11 contains a moving, tender maternal declaration of God's love despite the fact that Israel, like Hosea's own wife Gomer, had played the harlot in her relationship with Him. Nevertheless Yahweh's love remained steadfast and tender. 'Can a woman forget her sucking child, that she should have no compassion on the son of her womb? Even these may forget, yet I will never forget you' (Is 49:15). Exegetes points out that the language used here is decidely feminine. The Hebrew word for 'compassion', *raham*, is the plural form of the word for 'womb', *rehem*.

In the wisdom literature wisdom is seen as the source of creativity, joy and playfulness. God himself employed her in creating the world (Prov 8:22–31; Wis 8:6; 9:9).

> The Lord created me at the beginning of his work,
> the first of his acts of old.
> Ages ago I was set up,
> at the first, before the beginning of the earth.
> When there were no depths I was brought forth,
> when there was no springs abounding with water.
>
> When he marked out the foundations of the earth,
> then I was beside him, like a master workman;
> and I was daily his delight. (Prov 8:22–24, 29–30) (RSV)

The Book of Wisdom (8:1) introduces wisdom as the principle which is responsible for 'ordering all things'. It is important to stress that this ordering is not to be identified with the masculine urge to dominate, control or use. Instead it is much more interested in the creative dynamism existing between all creation. It sees life not as a hierarchy which allows those on the top to exploit those occupying the bottom rungs. Some traditional dichotomies between the divine and the human, men and women, and human and the rest of creation are replaced with a vision of life as an ongoing interconnected process whereby creatures are present to each other in a mutually enhancing way. Small-scale participatory activity takes precedence over large-scale bureaucracies which tend to remove power from ordinary people and concentrate it in the hands of a few people who manipulate everything from the centre.

A decision made in a New York boardroom to close a factory in South Wales can devastate the lives of hundreds of workers and effectively dismember their community. The directors, who make the decision using purely economic criteria, usually have no personal knowledge of the history or culture of the people whose lives are affected, nor have the workers any real way of challenging and reversing the directors' decision. Impersonal power mechanisms are not confined to the political and economic world. They operate when ecclesiastical authorities choose a bishop for a diocese without really consulting the local church and discerning whether the candidate is pastorally suitable for the office. The wisdom literature sets its face against any political or social system which allows a few people to manipulate the majority. Rather it promotes the kind of social interaction which empowers people and helps them take charge of their own lives and destinies. This small-scale, participative society is the 'fountain of life' (Prov 13:14), and the 'path which leads to life' (Prov 2:19).

In the New Testament, the wisdom theme becomes fused with that of the spirit of God who brings forth life. This spirit is central to the drama of the incarnation. The angel tells Mary that 'the Spirit will come upon you, and the power of the most high will overshadow you; therefore the child to be born will be called holy, the Son of God' (Luke 1:35) (RSV). The same spirit is present at the baptism of Jesus (Luke 3:22; Mark 1:10; Matt 3:16), preparing him for his mission and facilitating the dialogue between the Father and Son which is revealed at the baptism scene. The role of the spirit is decisive in raising Jesus from the dead (Rom 1:4). The same spirit who guided and moulded Jesus for his mission is active within the Church. There she is the source of life, unity, strength and creativity (Acts 2:1–13). She is the one who inspires all fruitfulness and creativity — which are the true signs of bonding and intimacy. From her comes the present-day urge to heal what is broken, re-unite what is separated and recreate the face of the earth.

Jesus – 'I have come that they may have life and have it to the full' (John 10:10)

A Christian theology of creation has much to learn from the attitude of respect which Jesus displayed towards the natural world. There is no support in the New Testament for a throw-away consumer society which destroys the natural world and produces mountains of non-biodegradable garbage or, worse still, produces toxic waste when, for example, plastics or Styrofoam cups which are used once are eventually destroyed. The disciples of Jesus are called upon to live lightly on the earth — 'take nothing for your journey, no staff, nor bag, nor bread, nor money; and do not have two tunics' (Luke 9:1–6). Jesus constantly warned about the dangers of attachment to wealth, possessions, or power. These in many ways are what is consuming the poor and the planet itself. 'How hard it is for those who have riches to enter the kingdom of God' (Mark 10:23; Luke 16:19–31; cf. Matt 19:23–24; Luke 18:18–23). 'Fool! This very night the demand will be made for your soul; and this hoard of yours, whose will it be then?' (Luke 12:16–21).

Jesus shows an intimacy and familiarity with a variety of God's creatures and the processes of nature. He is not driven by an urge to dominate and control the world of nature. Rather he displays an appreciative and contemplative attitude towards creation which is rooted in the Father's love for all that he has created, 'Think of the ravens. They do not sow or reap; they have no storehouses and no barns; yet God feeds them' (Luke 12:24) (NJB). We need not be constantly fretting about acquiring more goods. God will provide for our legitimate needs: 'are you not worth more than the birds?' (Luke 12:24).

The gospels tell us that nature played an important role in Jesus' life. At his birth, Luke tells us that 'he was laid in a manger, because there was no place for them in the inn' (Luke 2:7). Pious tradition has immortalized this in the crib which appears in many Christian homes and churches during the Christmas season. Mary, Joseph and the animals surround Jesus at his birth. He was first greeted by people who were 'keeping watch over their flocks by night' (Luke 2:8). Mark tells us that the spirit drove him into the wilderness. 'And he was in the wilderness forty days, tempted by Satan; and he was with the wild beasts; and the angels ministered to him' (Mark 1:13) (RSV).

The time Jesus spent in the desert was most formative for the messianic ministry he was about to embrace. In order to be fully open and receptive to his call, Jesus forsook the company of people. He regularly returned to the hills to pray and commune with the Father (Matt 17:1; Mark 6:46; Matt 14:23). He prayed on the hills before making important decisions like choosing the disciples (Luke 6:12). His ministry was not carried out just in synagogues or in the temple. In Matthew's gospel the beatitudes and subsequent teaching are delivered on a mountain (Matt 5:1 – 7:29). Much of his teaching and miracles took place on the shores of the Sea of Galilee (Matt 13:1–52; Mark 4:35–41; John 21:1–14). The miracle of the loaves occurred in a 'lonely place' (Matt 14:15–21; Luke 9:10–17; John 6:1–13).

Many of his parables centred on sowing seed (Matt 13:4–9, 18–23; Mark 4:3–9, 13–20; Luke 8:5–8, 11–15), vines (John 15:1–17; Mark 12:1–12; Matt 21:33–44; Luke 20:9–19), lost sheep (Luke 15:4–7; Matt 18:12–14), or shepherds (John 10:1–18). His teaching is regularly interspersed with references to the lilies of the field (Luke 12:27), the birds of the air (Matt 6:26), and the lair of foxes (Luke 9:58). He was Lord of creation and could calm the waves (Mark 4:35–41; Matt 8:23–27; Luke 8:22–25), or walk on the water (Mark 6:48–49), or when food was needed multiply the loaves (Matt 14:13–21; Mark 8:1–10; Luke 9:10–17; John 6:1–13). Like most great religious personalities he was a great healer. He cured the sick and restored them to health (Matt 12:9–14; Mark 3:1–6; Luke 6:6–11). His healing had a deeper significance than merely restoring an individual to full health. His miracles were a tangible sign that the kingdom of God and the messianic age had dawned.

In his preaching also Jesus identified himself with the natural elements of water (John 4:13–14), bread (John 6:48) and light (John 8:12). He presented himself as the good shepherd (John 10:11; Mark 6:30–44) who came that 'they may have life and have it abundantly' (John 10:10b). He rode into Jerusalem on a donkey (Matt 21:1b–5). In Mark's gospel (16:15) the disciples were called to take the gospel to *all creation*. Finally in and through his death, Jesus participated in the most radical way in one of the key processes of nature.

Healing was a very important dimension of Christ's ministry. He cured the paralytic (Mark 2:1–12), the man with a withered hand (Mark 3:1–6), the woman who had been stooped for many years (Luke 13:10–17), and the man who had been paralysed for 38 years (John 5:1–15), and restored sight to the man born blind (John 9:1–41). While individuals are restored to health in each act of healing, the healing ministry of Jesus was not confined to individuals. Each healing was a sign that challenged social or religious prejudices, and it also aimed at sowing the seeds of healing within the community itself as it opened itself to the transforming power of God's compassion and graciousness.

The ministry of Jesus was not confined to teaching, healing and reconciling humans and all creation with God. Paul tells us that he is the centre of all creation:

> He is the image of the invisible God, the first-born of all creation; for in him all things were created, in heaven and on earth, visible and invisible, whether thrones or dominions or principalities or authorities — all things were created through him and for him. He is before all things, and in him all things hold together. (Col 1:15–18) (RSV).

Jesus is the word and wisdom of God who existed with God from the beginning. In the prologue of John's gospel the birth and life of Jesus is framed within the widest context of cosmic history. He is active in bringing forth creation; through him the universe, the earth and all life was created (John 1:3–5). All the rich unfolding of the universe from the first moment of the fireball, through the formation of the stars, the moulding of planet Earth, the birth and flowering of life on earth and the emergence of human beings, is centred on Christ. Hence all of these crucial moments in the emergence of the universe have a Christic dimension.

In the man Jesus, God who was active from the beginning in bringing forth the universe 'became flesh' (John 1:14). Johannine scholars tell us that the Greek word which is used here (*sarx*) has a very earthy ring to it. They believe that the author consciously chose this word to attack the Gnostic teaching which was prevalent at the time. For the Gnostics, *sarx* was evil and could not in any way be co-mingled with the Divine. In the face of this the author of the Gospel of John insists that Jesus enters into every dimension of earthly reality. The redemption which he accomplishes does not come by way of discarding, denigrating or abandoning *sarx*, but by transforming *sarx* from within. In John 3:16, Jesus' incarnation is seen as an out-pouring of God's love for the world — 'for God so loved the world that he gave his only Son, that whoever believes in him should not perish but have eternal life' (RSV).

Christ's life of service involved a radical stance on the side of life, which necessitated his own suffering and death. He atoned for sins against life (Heb 9:12). Paul presents Jesus' incarnation in this light in Phil 2:5–7 and Col 1:15–20.

> Make your own the mind of Christ Jesus;
> Who, being in the form of God,
> did not count equality with God
> something to be grasped.

But he emptied himself,
taking the form of a slave,
becoming as human beings are. (Phil 2:5–7) (NJB)

The leadership which Jesus gives in the New Testament is always a leadership of service. When an argument broke out among the disciples as to which of them was the greatest, Jesus admonished them,

Among the gentiles it is the kings who lord it over them and
those who have authority over them are given the title
Benefactor. With you this must not happen. No; the greatest
among you must behave as if he were the youngest, the leader
as if he were the one who serves. (Luke 22:25–26) (NJB)

This leadership involved accepting death joyfully. Paul in Philippians goes on to say:

And being in every way like a human being,
he was humbler yet,
even to accepting death, death on a cross. (Phil 2:6–8) (NJB)

A service which involves emptying oneself and working for the good of others is at the very heart of the Christian vocation. The follower of Christ does not seek power and riches in order to manipulate other human beings and beggar the earth. Rather he hears the call, 'if anyone wants to be a follower of mine, let him renounce himself and take up his cross every day and follow me' (Luke 9:23). In the contemporary situation, Christian service must mean working for a more just world and preserving the earth. This call to serve all creation throws a new light on the Genesis call to 'be masters of the fish of the sea, the birds of heaven and all living creatures that move on earth' (Gen 1:26). In following Christ's example this 'dominion' includes a deep respect for the ecological laws which bind creation together, the kind of care that Noah displayed when he took the animals into the ark (Gen 6:19). Only in this way can people of this and future generations experience the abundant life which Jesus promised (John 10:10).

The passion and death of Christ call attention to the appalling reality of suffering which humans inflict on each other and on creation. By causing others to suffer we persecute the body of Christ. We are beginning to realize that the parameters of the body of Christ are expanding to include not just Christians or all humans, but the totality of creation. Paul was reminded on the road to Damascus that in persecuting the Christians he was persecuting Jesus (Acts 9:4–5). In today's world many see the passion of Christ being re-enacted in the injustices which are inflicted on the weak and the poor, in cruelty to animals and in the devastation which humans are wreaking on creation. This pain experienced by the total body of Christ is captured in a prayer from the Byzantine liturgy: 'The whole creation was altered by thy Passion; for all things suffered with thee, knowing, O Lord, that thou holdest all things in unity'.[1]

Jesus' life shows us how to live our own life to the full in the face of the mystery of death. By facing death he achieved glorification. Paul again confesses, 'therefore God highly exalted him and bestowed on him the name which is above every name, that at the name of Jesus every knee should bow, in heaven and on earth and under the earth, and every tongue confess that Jesus Christ is Lord, to the glory of God' (Phil 2:9–11, RSV). Many psychologists believe that the frenzied grasping for more and more possessions which lies at the root of our consumer society arises primarily out of our anxieties in the face of our own death. By surrounding ourselves with more and more things we hope to avoid the reality of death and gain some measure of immortality, at least, in the things that we own.[2]

The New Testament tells us that this resistance to death is a blind alley. The tragedy for ourselves, the human community and creation as a whole, is that in pursuing this illusion, individually and collectively, we are destroying irreversibly God's creation — the air, the water, the soil, the forests and the abundance of life-forms.

In seeking to avoid death, we are literally killing planet Earth. This is why Jesus' way of living his life into death, trusting completely in the love of his Father, must become the foundational reality in our lives. His death, and especially his resurrection, is the basis of our hope that we can turn back the tide of planetary death.

The resurrection of Christ is the beginning of the new creation (2 Cor 5:17–19). All the writers of the New Testament are at pains to affirm the visible, bodily nature of Christ's resurrection. They are not professing that an immortal spirit put on the guise of a human body in order to be present to his disciples and others. The Greeks would have found such a concept very acceptable — not folly. The evangelists are adamant that he rose in the flesh (Matt 28:1–8; Mark 16:1–8; Luke 24:1–10; John 20:1–10). This corporeal nature of Christ's resurrection came as a complete surprise for the disciples and the early Church, so the writers of the New Testament are at pains to stress the bodily dimension of his resurrection. They do this by recounting a variety of incidents where Jesus touched people (John 20:27) and ate with them (John 21:4–14). In his resurrection Jesus was transformed in his total person, which naturally affected his body also. His resurrected body is no longer confined by previous limitations. He can pass easily through solid substances and visit his disciples who because of their fear are huddled together in an upper room on the evening of the resurrection (John 20:19).

Through the reality of Christ's resurrection all visible created reality is touched, given a new significance and transformed. Paul states 'God was in Christ reconciling the world to himself' (2 Cor 5:19, cf. Col 1:20). In this text Paul is affirming that all reality is both interconnected, sequentially linked over time and ultimately grounded in God. The Preface of Easter IV in *The Roman Missal* echoes this belief: 'In him a new age has dawned, the long reign of sin is ended, a broken world has been renewed and man is once again made whole. The joy of the resurrection fills the whole world.'

The resurrection is the cosmic sign of hope. All creation is united in Christ and therefore everything has a future in God, through Christ.[3] This hope for wholeness or redemption is anchored in the presence in the world of the spirit, who despite past human failures and sins can bring forth new things (Is 43:19; Ezek 37). This grace allows the believer to look forward confidently to the future and not be mired in the past of either our own individual or our collective failures. This is a profoundly liberating experience for the believer and can release new energies to work to bring about a healing of creation.

The redemption wrought by Christ which is experienced primarily by people is also extended to all creation. The Greek word for reuniting (*anakephalaiōsis*) means recapitulating all reality or bringing it together in one point. Christ is the summit upon whom all created reality converges. Everything in heaven and earth comes together in him, as Paul writes in Ephesians:[4]

In him we have redemption through his blood, the forgiveness of our trespasses, according to the riches of his grace which he lavished upon us. For he has made known to us in all wisdom and insight the mystery of his will, according to his purpose which he set forth in Christ as a plan for the fulness of time, to unite all things in him, things in heaven and things on earth. (Eph 1:7–12) (RSV)

In the classic text of Romans 8:22–24, Paul likens the yearnings of creation for redemption with similar human desires. Within the plan of God realized in the resurrection of Christ, humans can help bring about this cosmic redemption. 'We know that the whole creation has been groaning in travail together until now; and not only the creation, but we ourselves, who have the first fruits of the Spirit, groan inwardly as we wait for adoption as sons, the redemption of our bodies.'

The pastoral letter of the Guatemalan Bishops' Conference comments on this text: 'this liberation begins for all creation when the goods of the earth cease to be instruments of human rivalry and exploitation in order to become a means of friendship and communion'.[5]

Gradually it is beginning to dawn on many people that alleviating poverty, healing nature and preserving the stability of the biosphere is the central task for those who follow in the footsteps of Jesus in today's world. Human creativity, inventiveness and technology have a central role to play in this healing, but it must heed the warning of Lewis Mumford:

> This benign transformation can happen on only one condition, and that is a hard one: namely that the life-negating ideals and methods of the power system be renounced, and that a conscious effort be made, at every level and in every kind of community, to live not for the sake of exalting power but for reclaiming this planet for life through mutual aid, loving association and bio-technic cultivation. Not the 'advancement of learning', or the advancement of power, but the advancement of life and mind is the goal.[6]

Only the spirit of God working in and through creation and, especially, through human agents, can bring about this kind of thorough-going transformation. Looked at from the fast track of our modern industrial society, the chances of its taking place look slim indeed. But looked at in the light of Christ's resurrection and of our baptism through which we share in Christ's resurrection and healing ministry, this new way of living becomes possible (1 Cor 6:12–20; Rom 6:8–14; 1 Thess 4:15–18). This hope also shines through the book of Revelation. While the horror of sin and evil is clearly visible in the physical despoiling of the earth, the work of human hands, particularly the city, is also a symbol of salvation under the influence of God's transforming power. 'I saw the holy city, the new Jerusalem, coming down out of heaven from God, prepared as a bride dressed for her husband' (Rev 21:2) (NJB). In this book there is no false dichotomy between the sacred and the secular. In line with the perspective of the seamless robe, human sin can destroy individuals, societies and creation itself. But God's salvific power triumphs over sin and brings wholeness to individuals, human communities and the totality of creation. It offers new possibilities. As Moltmann puts it, in response to the spirit 'the present time of believers is no longer determined by the past. It is called forth by the future.'[7]

Chapter 8

Christian witnesses through the ages

The Christian tradition is 2,000 years old and has taken root in a variety of cultures and shaped them in unique ways. Everyone recognizes that there are major differences between, for example, the ethos of Irish Catholicism and the Russian culture, shaped as it is by centuries of Orthodox Christianity. My purpose in this short chapter is not to examine how to examine how Christian traditions over the centuries, and in different circumstances, viewed creation and the role of the human in relation to the rest of creation. Nor do I intend to dwell on the anthropocentric bias of various Christian doctrines, e.g. incarnation, redemption, eschatology, in different Christian Churches. Theologians like Moltmann, Carroll and Fox, to name just a few, are pursuing this kind of theological investigation. My purpose is merely to point out that down through the centuries, even when the dominant Christian tradition focused almost exclusively on divine/human relations, there were always a few witnesses calling Christians to look beyond this dyad to the wider cosmic context.

The Fathers of the Church

The Fathers of the Church, beginning with the early 'Apologists' like Justin Martyr, Theophilus of Antioch and Tatian, developed a theology of creation. Very often, this was elaborated in opposition to the prevailing Gnostic dualism which depicted the created world as radically deficient and often insisted that the body was evil. The Fathers affirmed the goodness of creation since it was created by the one God. To distinguish the Christian understanding of creation from that current in some of the philosophical schools at the time, the Apologists stress that God did not create the world through the mediation of spirits or from pre-existent matter, but that the world was created out of nothing (*creatio ex nihilo*).

The Fathers did not neatly seal off natural theology from the doctrines about Christ (or christology). Following in the footsteps of St Paul they saw a christological dimension at the heart of creation. In much of the patristic literature Christ is portrayed as the ruler of all (*pantocratōr*) and the ruler of the universe (*cosmocratōr*). The theology of Irenaeus of Lyons is one of the best examples of the Fathers' setting

Christ at the centre-point and culmination of creation. The Irish theologian Fr Denis Carroll puts it this way:

> Irenaeus' presentation of salvation history speaks of the recapitulation of all things in Christ. He echoes Paul's notion of the summation of the whole cosmos in one person.
> According to J. N. D. Kelly, Irenaeus allows his thought to pan across history from protology to eschatology: 'Christ recapitulated in himself all the dispersed people dating back to Adam, all tongues and the whole race of mankind, along with Adam himself.' As Adam originated a humanity plunged into disobedience and death, Christ inaugurated a new humanity unto everlasting life.[1]

One of the most important features of the patristic period was the rise of monasticism. One could easily interpret the flight from the world as a radical rejection of every aspect of the created order and therefore argue that the patristic period had little to add to a theology or spirituality of creation. Rejection there is, but as Susan Bratton Power argues, the rejection is not as complete as Roderick Nash presents it in his seminal work *Wilderness and the American Mind*. She counters Nash's views with a much more nuanced treatment of the desert experience. There is no doubt that the 'athletes of God' were fleeing what they saw as the decadence especially of urban life.[2]

Yet the early monks or hermits sought out the wilderness where they felt that they could concentrate their entire attention on purifying themselves, unencumbered by the cares and clutter of city life and in the process encounter God in a profound way. In the simplicity of the desert the monks felt that they could confront head on, as it were, the crucial questions of life without being unduly deflected by the cares and seductions of the world.

In the wilderness the monk, free from other distractions, could do battle with the Evil One. Yet the wilderness also had an inherent capacity to reveal the presence of God. When St Anthony, the father of monasticism, was asked, 'How dost thou content thyself, Father, who art denied the comfort of books?' Anthony answered, 'My book, philosopher, is the nature of created things, and as often as I have a mind to read the words of God, it is at my hands'.[3]

Many legends tell how the monks also developed friendships with the animals, even predators like wolves and lions. The feeling of dread which a human might normally be expected to have towards a lion is often replaced by an attitude of mutual help and friendship. In *The Life of St Paul, the First Hermit*, St Jerome recounts how St Anthony when he went to visit Paul found a she-wolf at the mouth of the cave. Paul was providing drink for the parched animal. When Paul and Anthony were together a crow carried a loaf of bread and dropped it at the feet of the saints in order that they might have something to eat.[4] According to another story, the Abbot Gerasimus had developed such a friendship with a lion whose paw he had cured that, upon the death of the abbot, the lion lay down on the abbot's grave and roared in grief. So upset was he that he died lying on the monk's grave.

There is a profound moral and religious message in the fact that holy people were considered to have friendly relationships with wild animals, even lions. The authors of these stories may wish to call the attention of Christians to the fact that holiness of life can even be appreciated by the 'wildest' of creatures and that, in living out the life of the new Adam, the monks were recapturing the original friendly relationship, which existed between all the animals in Paradise prior to the fall. The Isaiah text (11:6–7) obviously helped spread this belief in the Judaeo-Christian tradition. This perception, as we saw earlier, is shared by many tribal societies. The healer or shaman is considered to have a close relationship with animals and birds. At important moments the shaman can take on the characteristics of animals or birds and they can assist him in his religious activity.

The sensitivity of the Greek Church to the created world can be seen in a prayer which is attributed to St Basil the Great (c.330–379):

O God, enlarge within us the sense of fellowship with all living things, our brothers, the animals, to whom thou gavest the earth as their home in common with us.

We remember with shame that in the past we have exercised the high dominion of man with ruthless cruelty, so that the voice of the earth, which should have gone up to thee in song, has been a groan of travail.

May we realize that they live not for us alone but for themselves and for thee and that they love the sweetness of life.[5]

Among the Western Fathers a more rational understanding of creation supplanted the mystical one of the Eastern Fathers. St Augustine devotes considerable space to understanding creation in his commentaries on scripture and his writings against the Manicheans. Creation is not eternal or semi-divine. Everything in the universe is created by God who is eternal. Creation takes place in time and is distinguished by being finite in contrast to the creator who is eternal and uncreated. St Augustine, in line with orthodox Christian doctrine, taught that creation was good. In some of his writings there is a certain pessimism about the world which owes much to the philosophical climate of the times. Augustine in fact saw a trinitarian dimension in all creation. All things are created by the Father through the Son and they reach their perfection in the Spirit. Christianity owes to Augustine the phrase *vestigium Trinitatis* ('marks or signs of the

Trinity') which are evident in all creation when looked at from the perspective of faith.[6]

Though Augustine's approach to creation is anthropocentric, rational and utilitarian, he teaches that creatures have an inherent purpose in themselves because they are created by God:

> Therefore it is in the nature of things, considered in itself, without regard to our convenience or inconvenience, that gives glory to the Creator . . . And so all nature's substances are good, because they exist and therefore have their own mode and kind of being, and, in their fashion, a peace and harmony among themselves.[7]

Celtic spirituality

Local Churches in Ireland, England, Scotland and Wales have much to learn from early Celtic spirituality which was very much aware of the presence of the Divine in the world of nature. This spirituality grew out a marriage between the pre-Christian and the Christian traditions. The latter, because it was overwhelmingly a monastic tradition, was most probably affected by the early monastic tradition discussed above. The theologian John Macquarrie draws attention to the presence of the divine in the natural world, a theme which was so central to Celtic spirituality.

> Although it [Celtic spirituality] belongs to a culture that has almost vanished it fulfils in many aspects the condition to which a contemporary spirituality would have to conform. At the very centre of this type of spirituality was an intense sense of presence. The Celt was very much a God-intoxicated man whose life was embraced on all sides by the Divine Being. But his presence was always mediated through some finite, this-world reality, so that it would be difficult to imagine a spirituality more down to earth than this one. This sense of God's immanence in His creation was so strong in Celtic spirituality as to amount sometimes to pantheism.[8]

The ritual of the pre-Christian religion in Ireland was centred on the heavenly bodies and the cycles of nature. *Imbolc*, which later evolved into St Brigid's feast day, was celebrated to mark the end of winter. The sun was seen to be growing stronger and climbing higher in the heavens and the shoots of winter corn were beginning to break through the earth that hitherto had been cold and lifeless. The next major festival, *Beltane* (May Day), was also associated with the sun. By May, the sun's rays had become warmer and the people invoked the sun god to bless their crops. *Lugnasad* (Lammas in England and parts of Northern Ireland) is a harvest festival which is celebrated in the middle of August. A good harvest was the product of a fruitful marriage between the sun god and the earth mother. The word *lugnasad* means the wedding feast of the sun god Lugh. This was a festival of great rejoicing and also an auspicious time for weddings. The last great feast, *Samhain*, also dealt with the natural elements of light and darkness. It was, in a sense, a closing-down of the year. All fires were quenched and then relit from a ritual fire so that warmth and light would not be extinguished by the cold, dead hand of winter.

The forces of nature were also revered in the pre-Christian Celtic world in England as in Europe. In recent decades archaeological remains have demonstrated how important the sources of rivers were. Many were associated with fertility goddesses and healing centres. This reverence for springs and water sources carried over into the tradition of pilgrimages to holy wells.[9]

As in the Eastern monastic tradition, friendship with animals marked the lives of holy people. St Columban was well known for the austerity of his monastic rule, yet was also known to be friendly to animals. Legends which grew up around him at Luxeuil picture squirrels and doves playing in the folds of his cowl. Birds also approached him and nestled in the palms of his hands and even wild animals obeyed his commands.

Similar stories are told of St Colmcille. One story tells of a crane which St Colmcille predicted would arrive from Ireland at Iona weary and exhausted. The saint asked a young monk to be on the look out for the bird and when it arrived 'you will take heed to lift it tenderly and carry it to the house nearby, and having taken it in as a guest there you will wait upon it for three days and nights, and feed it with anxious care'.[10]

Johannes Scotus Eriugena (ninth century) was the most important Irish medieval scholar. In his writing on nature, Scotus maintained that 'the whole created universe is to be understood as unfolding within the Trinity, at no stage is creation to be seen as an alienation or separation of things from God . . . Eriugena's God is not static but dynamic, manifesting, unfolding and explicating Himself in spirals of divine history.'[11] Scotus was often accused of being a pantheist. It is more likely that he espoused panentheism — which teaches that the Divine is present in the phenomenal world and the phenomenal world is present in the Divine. Scotus's position is pithly summed up in the following quotation:

> It follows that we ought not to understand God and the creatures as two things distinct from one another, but as one and the same. For both the creature, by subsisting, is in God; and God, by manifesting himself, in a marvellous and ineffable manner creates himself in creatures.[12]

This experience of God and his closeness and involvement in the ordinary everyday life of people continued to be a feature of Celtic religion right into the late nineteenth century in the Celtic-speaking regions of Ireland and Scotland. Numerous examples are found in Alexander Carmichael's work. There is a wealth of prayers and blessing in the two volumes, *New Moon of the Seasons* and *The Sun Dances*, which have been published in the Floris Classics series. 'The Consecration of the Seeds' is typical of the collection:

I will go out to sow the seed,
in the name of Him who gave it growth;
I will place my front in the wind,
and throw a gracious handful on high.
Should a grain fall on a bare rock,
It shall have no soil in which to grow;
As much as falls into the earth
The dew will make it to be full.[13]

The gospel warns about putting new wine into old wineskins. No traditional spirituality is totally apt for the challenges of a new era. Nevertheless the Celtic experience can help guide the Christian Churches in their search for an appropriate spirituality for the ecological age.

Other threads in the Christian tradition

At this point it might be worth looking briefly at some approaches to the natural world which are inspired by the biblical perspective and which, in varying degrees, have helped shape Christian consciousness through the centuries. The first two approaches emerge from the Benedictine monastic tradition and the experience of St Francis of Assisi. Many people are familiar with these visions of the natural world, because they have left an indelible stamp on Western European agricultural and aesthetic traditions. The third strand arises from the writings of Hildegard of Bingen. Her writings have only become well known in recent years; hence her impact, to date, is still very limited.

Benedictine care for the earth

From the seventh century onwards, a network of Benedictine monasteries was established in Western Europe. St Benedict of Nursia, the father of Western monasticism, decided that his monks should live together in a stable community. The rhythm of the monastic life written into his famous Rule included liturgical and other forms of prayer, manual work and study. This inclusion of manual work was in a sense a revolutionary departure. Greek and Roman scholars in general showed a disdain for manual work. They felt that it was degrading for the scholar to engage in such a lowly task. By combining work and prayer, Benedict ennobled all kinds of manual work. He also insisted that each monastery should be self-sufficent, so the range of manual work included domestic chores, crafts, garden work, tilling the soil and caring for domestic animals. The stability of the monastery meant that the monks had to learn to cultivate the soil in a renewable way.

They learned to care for the land so that the model of interaction with the natural world to emerge from this tradition might be called the *taming of the Earth*. It was very much an extension of the garden tradition of the Bible itself. The monks set about draining marshes, cutting forests and tilling the soil. Many of the technologies which the monks introduced into the tradition of European agriculture, far from depleting the soil, actually enhanced its fertility. The monks and the peasants who worked with them exemplify René Dubos's more hopeful thesis, elaborated in *Wooing the Earth*, that: 'The interaction between humanity and the Earth often generates more interesting and creative ecosystems than those occurring in the wilderness'.[14]

The Benedictine model of relating to the natural world was marked by gratitude for the good things of the earth and respect for the earth in order to ensure its continued fruitfulness for human beings. Humans were called to be faithful stewards of the world and not to abuse the earth. But the point of departure was always the human perspective. There was still a fear that 'raw' nature was unpredictable and capricious and could easily overpower human beings unless constant vigilance was maintained. So the drive to domesticate nature and to bring it under human control was very much at the centre of the Benedictine tradition.

Franciscan fellowship with all creation

Unlike St Benedict, St Francis of Assisi (1182–1226) was a nomad at heart. He and his friars, who were street preachers, were constantly on the move. They had no possessions and were expected to live lightly on the earth, a burden neither to the earth nor to those who met their subsistence needs. In opting for the nomadic life, Francis abandoned any *homo faber* (humans as artisans) role for the brothers. There was no urge to remake the world, not even in the garden tradition of the Benedictines. The natural world was not seen from a utilitarian perspective, as providing food, clothing and shelter for human beings. Rather there was a sense of joy, wonder, praise, and gratitude for the gift of all life. For Francis, every creature in the world was a mirror of God's presence and, if approached correctly, a step leading one to God. What emerges here might be called a *fellowship approach* to creatures. There was no will to dominate or to transform nature in

Francis's approach. In his 'Canticle of the Creatures' Francis showed
a kinship with, and deep insight into the heart of all creation —
animate and inanimate — which was probably unique in the whole
European experience.

The Canticle of Brother Sun

Most high, all powerful, all good Lord!
All praise is Yours,
   all glory, all honour and blessing.
To You, alone, Most High, do they belong.
No mortal lips are worthy
To pronounce Your name.
All praise be Yours, my Lord,
   through all that you have made,
And first my Lord Brother Sun,
Who brings the day;
   and light You give to us through him.
How beautiful is He,
   how radiant in all his splendour!
Of You, most high, he bears the likeness.
All praise be Yours, my Lord,
   through Sister Moon and Stars;
In the heavens You have made them, bright
   and precious and fair.
All praise be Yours, my Lord,
   through Brothers Wind and Air.
And fair and stormy, all the weather's moods,
By which You cherish all that You have made.
All praise be Yours, my Lord, through Sister Water,
So useful, lowly, precious and pure.
All praise be Yours, my Lord, through Brother Fire,
Through whom you brighten up the night.
How beautiful He is, how gay!
Full of power and strength.
All praise be Yours, my Lord,
   through Sister Earth, our mother,
Who feeds us in her sovereignty and produces
Various fruits with coloured flowers and herbs.[15]

Francis's language and thought, his 'Brother Sun' and 'Sister
Moon', his loving relationship with the wind and water, resemble

more closely the language of India, China or the North American Indian tradition than the usual European, Christian approach to the natural world. Yet he avoided identifying the Divine exclusively with nature and denying any transcendent dimension in God. He did this simply by expanding the Christian call to love God and neighbour to include all creation in a way that healed the split between God, the human and nature so characteristic of much of Christian literature before and since.

The memory of Francis in our world today is a healing, reconciling and creative one. It inspires many people to become pacifists, to build a true fraternity among people and to renounce war before it is too late for humanity and the earth. It also inspires naturalists and ecologists to preserve nature untamed by humans. The protection of wilderness areas in our world today is essential for many reasons. Endangered species need a habitat if they are not to become extinct. Experiencing the wilderness is an expanding and uplifting sensation for the human spirit. It draws us out beyond our selves. An untamed environment, untouched by human beings, whether it be a vast ocean, a rainforest or a desert, points to the ultimate mystery at the heart of the world which continually calls us to a deeper communion with the earth and with God. Francis, the saint for all seasons, is particularly important today and so is a happy choice as the patron of ecologists.

Hildegard of Bingen: the greening of the earth

The approach of Hildegard of Bingen (1098–1178) adds a unique dimension to those of both Benedict and Francis. Unfortunately, her writings are not widely known. Selections from her writings have only been published in English in the past few years. This remarkable woman — poet, musician, painter, visionary, botanist, herbalist, counsellor to Popes, princes and Councils of the Church — has a unique contribution to make to the Western Christian's appreciation of the natural world. Her approach to the earth delights in its 'greening'.

The Divine is present in the 'greening' of the earth in a way reminiscent of the fertility poetry of the pre-Christian Celtic religion of much of Europe. Hildegard captures and celebrates in her writings the uniquely feminine experience of the most intimate processes of the natural world. The taming, organizing skills of Benedict and even the fraternal solicitude for all creatures of Francis are valuable elements of a masculine approach to reality. But Hildegard celebrates the feminine, fertility dimension. Her poetry pulsates with a rapturous, sensuous love for the earth. It is full of ardour and passion. In the following poem she delights in the love of the Creator for his creation and does not feel constrained to shy away from explicitly sexual language. 'I compare the great love of Creator and creation to the same love and fidelity with which God binds man and woman together.

This is so that together they might be creatively fruitful.'

There is no ambiguity towards creation in Hildegard; no revulsion at the mention of earthly, bodily or inanimate nature. She does not see the world as evil or corrupting, to be subdued and tamed through ascetical practices. Unlike the writings of many Christian mystics before and since, the person seeking sanctity is not encouraged to run away from the natural world. Hildegard insists that 'holy persons draw to themselves all that is earthly'. For her, the natural world is not an area of chaos or wilderness which humans must either avoid or do battle with in order to conquer and domesticate. Nature evokes joy, wonder, praise, awe and especially love. She is so beautifully adorned that even her creator approaches her in the guise of a lover to embrace her with a kiss.

> As the Creator loves His creation
>   so creation loves the Creator.
> Creation, of course, was fashioned
>   to be adorned, to be showered,
>   to be gifted with the love of the Creator.
> The entire world has been embraced by this kiss.[16]

When her writings are better known, it is to be hoped that Hildegard will assume her rightful place in Christian spirituality. In her company we may be able to overcome the deep-seated fear and hostility for the natural world which is found so frequently in Christian spiritual guides, ancient and modern. With her we can leave aside the gloom, pessimism and guilt that commonly haunt Christian spirituality and joyfully recognize God's presence in the world around us.

Chapter 9

The environment in the modern Catholic Church

The Church has always taught

It is a fact of recent history that the Catholic Church has been slow to recognize the gravity of the ecological problems facing the earth. She has not been alone. Most of the institutions of society — schools, governments, the media, financial and industrial corporations — have also refused to see what is happening to the delicate fabric of the earth. They have been lulled into a false sense of security by some of the successes of modern technology and have failed to understand the urgent need to face the despoilment of creation. Unless they become aware quickly, human beings and the rest of the planet's community will be condemned to live amid the ruins of the natural world. At last the Church is beginning to wake up to what is at stake. *Sollicitudo Rei Socialis* no. 34 addresses the issue. But Church people should not claim that the Churches have been involved extensively with this issue for decades, when the facts are otherwise. Claiming credit for something which she has not done neither serves the interests of truth nor helps the Catholic Church to face this issue squarely and honestly.

Ecology and recent Church documents

It is not easy to find any reference to the environment among the mountains of documents that have come from Rome in recent decades. Apologists for the Church often begin by quoting no. 34 of *Gaudium et Spes* (the Constitution on the Church in the Modern World) from the Second Vatican Council. Most Catholics would see this document as a milestone in the history of the Church's stance towards the world. It embodies a positive, liberating vision of life which refuses to seal off the religious world from the rest of human affairs. It cannot, however, be argued that it is grounded on an ecological vision of all reality.

Though the doctrine of creation is mentioned in *Lumen Gentium* (the Dogmatic Constitution on the Church), no. 36 and *Dei Verbum* (the Dogmatic Constitution on Divine Revelation), no. 3, Vatican II subscribes to what is called a 'domination' theology: the natural world is there for mankind's exclusive use. 'For man, created to God's image, received a mandate to subject to himself the earth and all that it contains, and to govern the world with justice and holiness' (*Gaudium et Spes*, no. 34). No. 9 of the same document insists that 'meanwhile, the conviction grows that humanity can and should consolidate its control over creation, but even more, that it devolves on humanity to establish a political, social and economic order which will to an even better extent serve man'. The call for sensitive human institutions which will promote equity is admirable, but it is not accompanied by a recognition of the need to consider the fruitfulness of the natural world as well.

This anthropocentric bias is even more marked in no. 12 of *Gaudium et Spes*, which claims almost universal agreement for the teaching that 'according to the almost unanimous opinion of believers and unbelievers alike, all things on earth should be related to man as their centre and crown'. The cultures of tribal peoples and the great religions of the East, Hinduism and Buddhism, can scarcely be used to support this claim. The wisdom attributed to Chief Seattle is much more holistic: 'If all the beasts were gone, we would die from a great loneliness of the spirit, for whatever happens to the beasts happens also to us. All things are connected. Whatever befalls the Earth, befalls the children of the earth.'

In fact, recent Church teaching on the role of people *vis-à-vis* the rest of creation has failed to take into account an important strand within biblical literature, found for example, in the Book of Job, especially chapters 38 and 39. This, too, rejects an exclusively human-centred view of creation (cf. pp. 151–3 above).

Despite its great achievement in helping bring the Catholic Church into the modern world, Vatican II did not pick up on this issue. One initiative during the Council could have led to a more sensitive presentation on the rights of other creatures if it had been pursued more vigorously. In response to an appeal from the National Catholic Society for Animal Welfare in the USA, the Vatican undertook a symposium on animal rights in October 1962, under the chairmanship of Archbishop Pietro Palazzini, the secretary of the Sacred Congregation of the Council; the symposium aimed to compile Church teaching on animals and the need for laws to protect them. Unfortunately the fruits of the deliberations did not make their way into the Vatican documents.[1]

Minimal critique of modern industrialization in Vatican II

Like most of their contemporaries in politics and industry, the Council Fathers were quite favourable towards modern technology. They recognized that modern life is marked by technologies which give human beings increased control over nature. It is easy to be dazzled by the positive achievements of modern science and technology, especially when one benefits from it. One benefit that immediately strikes most people is the control which it has given over many of the infectious diseases which have ravaged human societies for millennia. *Gaudium et Spes*, no. 33 applauds these achievements when it says that 'through his labours and his native endowments man has ceaselessly striven to better his life. Today, however, especially with the help of science and technology, he has extended his mastery over nearly the whole of nature and continues to do it.'

Any real understanding of the dark side of industrialization is missing from these accolades. There is no appreciation of the distinction between natural and technical systems. Natural systems go through the life-cycle of birth, maturation and death. Yet the species is constantly regenerated and, over the millennia, a particular species will adapt itself more closely to the circumstances prevailing in its particular environment. Technical systems are quite different. There is no natural regeneration in the technical world, and so the recycling loop, so highly developed in the natural world, is usually severed. Even young children know that cars do not mate to produce new cars. Manufactured goods and technical systems wear out and rust and often finish up in junk yards.

The negative impact of many contemporary technologies on the biosphere was clearly visible in the 1960s, but the bishops attending Vatican II were not sensitive to this. They did not challenge humans to respect other life forms, obey ecological laws and work to establish more just human societies within the limits of the natural world. Only in *Sollicitudo Rei Socialis* in 1988 do we find any serious caution about the 'consequences of haphazard industrialization'. But even there the momentum to pollute the earth which is built into our modern industrial consumer society is not examined in any detail.

Populorum Progressio

Populorum Progressio ('The Development of Peoples') is one of the finest documents on development to come from the *magisterium* in recent decades. However, it, too, shows no sensitivity to the issues which Rachel Carson raised in *Silent Spring*. Moreover, it still subscribes to the domination ethic. It quotes the Genesis command to 'fill the Earth and subdue it' (no. 22) with no sense that this 'subduing' might be irreversibly and extensively destroying the living world instead of (as the document sees it) 'developing and perfecting' it.

The document contains no caution about the impact of industrialization on the biosphere. No. 25 states boldly that 'The introduction of industry is necessary for economic growth and human progress; it is also a sign of development and contributes to it. By persistent work and the use of his intelligence man gradually wrests nature's secrets from her and finds a better application for her riches.' This reflects the hubris of 'man the transformer'. Yet the 'greenhouse effect', the threat to the ozone layer from chlorofluorocarbons (CFCs), acid rain, soil erosion, agrochemicals, the pollution of rivers and seas with toxic substances like polychlorinated biphenyls (PCBs) or nuclear waste are a direct result of the industrial revolution. It is highly unlikely that some technological remedy will suddenly emerge to solve any one of the multitude of problems directly linked to our modern industrial processes. Even when advances in technology allow a more efficient use of fossil fuels and decrease the pollution created by cars, the spread of industrialization to Third World countries takes up the slack and adds to the worldwide problem of pollution.

Pope Paul VI's letter *Octogesima Adveniens* (the letter to Cardinal Roy), published in 1971, does speak about the environment. No. 21 says that 'Man is suddenly becoming aware that by an ill-considered exploitation of nature he risks destroying it and becoming *in turn the victim of this degradation*' (emphasis mine). But even here the threat is somewhat abstract. It is not made concrete by reference to what was happening to the forests, the air, the waters and the topsoil of the earth. In the final analysis, the outlook, expressed here is again anthropocentric. The destruction of species or ecosystems is not seen as in itself a moral and religious problem.

The 1971 Synod of Bishops touches briefly upon the issue. The document states that:

> Furthermore, such is the demand for resources and energy by
> the richer nations, whether capitalist or socialist, and such are
> the effects of dumping by them in the atmosphere and the sea
> that irreparable damage would be done to the essential
> elements of life on earth, such as air and water, if their rates of
> consumption and pollution, which are constantly on the
> increase, were extended to the whole of mankind.

This is one of the few texts in which the growth mania of the modern industrial consumer society is mentioned. However, the data are not clearly arranged and the analysis is not rigorous enough to challenge one of the most strongly held tenets of our modern society: that we must continue to have economic growth, otherwise we will stagnate and our way of life will collapse. It is also worth pointing out that the problems which are mentioned are mainly First World ones. Deforestation in the tropics, desertification, soil erosion and the chemical poisoning of the soil are not highlighted. In other words, there is no comprehensive vision of what is happening worldwide.

This document was written during the period when the Club of Rome — a group of European industrialists — initiated a study on the probable impact of continued industrial growth and population increase on available resources and on the ability of the environment to cope with the destabilizing effect of industrialization. It is now generally recognized that the investigators underestimated both the rate at which new mineral deposits would be discovered and the ability of the earth to cope. Still, if human society continues to consume the earth's non-renewable resources at an increasing rate and at the same time misuses or poisons renewable resources such as forests, soils and water, then at some point in the future the whole system will collapse. We have been given a breathing space — possibly a few decades — to develop a sustainable way of living. If we squander this time and do nothing until the day of reckoning is almost upon us, then we will have passed the point of no return.

Evangelii Nuntiandi ('Evangelization in the Modern World'), published in 1975, brought together many of the insights of the 1974 Synod of Bishops on evangelization. Once again this is an excellent document, and in many ways it has become a charter for modern missionary thinking. It addresses in a positive way the split between the Gospel and culture as an important evangelical problem of our times (no. 20). It speaks about family life, peace, justice, development and dialogue with other religions, but even this fine document is silent about the most serious threat to the earth and the human community in our times. This omission is all the more difficult to comprehend since the scars marking life on earth are so evident in the forests of Central and South America, Africa and Southeast Asia.

John Paul II

In his first encyclical, *Redemptor Hominis* ('The Redeemer of Humanity'), Pope John Paul II makes a number of references to the environment. In no. 8, he speaks of 'certain phenomena, such as the threat of pollution of the natural environment in areas of rapid industrialization'. No. 15 recalls that 'we seem to be increasingly aware of the fact that the exploitation of the earth, the planet on which we are living, demands rational and honest planning'. The interpretation of Genesis 1:28 which sees all creation as ordered to meet human needs is tempered somewhat by a realization that 'it was the Creator's will that man should communicate with nature as an intelligent and noble "master" and "guardian", and not as a needless "exploiter" and "destroyer" '.

This awareness is further defined in no. 16 where the Pope insists that 'The essential meaning of this "kingship" and "dominion" of man over the visible world, which the Creator himself gave man for his task, consists in the priority of ethics over technology, in the primacy of the person over things, and in the superiority of spirit over matter'. While this is a marked improvement on the domination ethic, this is still fundamentally anthropocentric. It encourages environmental preservation because it is ultimately in the interest of humans. It does not begin with an understanding of the totality of God's creation and then seek to decipher the role of humans within the total biosphere.

Environmental concerns did not figure prominently on the agenda of Pope John Paul II's pastoral ministry, especially during the early years of his pontificate. This is reflected in the preparations made for the 1984 Synod of Reconciliation. In the Hebrew Bible and the Christian scriptures, salvation involves a reconciliation between human beings and other creatures (Is 11:5–6; Gal 6:15; Rom 8:22–23). Given the present rate of destruction, what better place to have stressed this than at the Synod? Only a single speech — that of the Japanese Bishop Stephen Fumio Hamao — called for a reconciliation between humanity and the natural world. The bishop insisted that:

> Work for peace will be effective if all men become aware of
> their deep connection with nature, especially with all living
> beings. Man must not only dominate nature, but also seek
> harmony with it and admire in it the beauty, wisdom and love
> of the Creator. Thus men will be freed of their frenzy for
> possessions and domination and will become artisans for peace
> (*L'Osservatore Romano*, 10 October 1983).

Sad to say, this contribution — with its clear Buddhist overtones — was not carried over into Pope John Paul's Apostolic Exhortation *Reconciliatio et Poenitentia* ('Reconciliation and Penance'). In looking at a 'shattered world' in no. 2 the Pope speaks about the:

> trampling upon the basic rights of human beings;
> various forms of discrimination;
> violence and terrorism;
> use of torture and unjust and unlawful methods of repression;
> stockpiling of conventional and nuclear weapons and the arms
> race, with the spending on military purposes of sums which could
> be used to alleviate the undeserved misery of peoples;
> unfair distribution of the world's resources.

It is commendable to emphasize these divisions and conditions which lead to a breakdown of peace and to call for reconciliation, but it is difficult to understand why the alienation of human beings from the natural world was not included in the list.

The discussion of a sin which leads to death, or 'a sin which is death', as the Jerusalem Bible translates the Greek, could have been given contemporary relevance if the whole question of extinction and biocide had been taken up. This, surely, is the sin that, to quote *Time* (3 January 1989), causes 'The death of birth'. It is unfortunate also that in discussing rituals of reconciliation, no thought was given to rituals of reconciliation with the earth which has been so scarred and exploited.

Apart from one or two statements the ecological question is also overlooked in *Laborem Exercens* ('Human Labour'), a document which Pope John Paul II wrote on human endeavour in 1981. Even in no. 21, where the Pope speaks about the dignity of agricultural work, the progressive destruction of land through the use of agrochemicals and soil erosion is not referred to. The oversight is difficult to comprehend, because the ecological crisis is a direct result of human activity, especially since the beginning of the industrial revolution. Pope John Paul II did speak about the environment, however, at the United Nations Centre for the Environment in Nairobi in August 1985.

> It is a requirement of our human dignity, and therefore a
> serious responsibility, to exercise dominion over creation in
> such a way that it truly serves the human family. Exploitation
> of the riches of nature must take place according to criteria
> that take into account not only the immediate needs of people
> but also the needs of future generations. In this way, the
> stewardship over nature, entrusted by God to man, will not be
> guided by short-sightedness or selfish pursuits: rather, it will
> take into account the fact that all created goods are directed to
> the good of all humanity.

In this talk, the problem was addressed once again only from a human perspective. There is no mention of the rampant destruction of species. Previous mass extinctions, for example those that took place 55 million years ago at the end of the Cretaceous Period, were caused by climatic and geological changes. The massive extinction taking place today is, in the main, a direct result of human activity destroying the habitat of other creatures and polluting their environment.

Yet the damage is irreversible, and many scientists consider it the greatest threat to life since life first emerged on this planet 3.5 billion years ago. The biologist Edward O. Wilson points out that 'in at least one respect, this human-made megaextinction is worse than at any time in the geological past. In earlier mass extinctions . . . most of the plant diversity survived; now, for the first time, it is being mostly destroyed.'[2] Reversing the wave of extinction will require a thorough reappraisal of Western life styles and the kind of thinking which gives priority to economic pursuits over ecological imperatives. To date, no official Church statement that I am aware of has looked at extinction.

There has been no in-depth theological reflection on what extinction might mean for the community of the living and for God's sovereignty over creation. For a Church that glories in being pro-life, this is a serious omission.[3]

Population — a stumbling block

Many people feel that one reason why the leadership of the Catholic Church has given the ecological movement a wide berth is because of its position on population. Any comprehensive discussion of ecological problems inevitably includes a discussion of the rate of population growth. Chapter 2 above looked at the impact of rapid population growth on Third World countries, especially the Philippines, and argued that the Catholic Church is not facing up to the magnitude of this problem.

Nuclear power

Few ecologists are happy with the position which the Holy See has taken on nuclear power, as represented by Mgr Peressin in a conference organized by the International Atomic Energy Agency in Vienna, 21 September 1982. According to Mgr Peressin:

> The peaceful uses of nuclear energy had both advantages and disadvantages. The advantages of the very application of nuclear energy, whether in agriculture, food preservation, medicine or hydrology were widely recognized. The most important sector, however, was that of energy production for industrial and domestic use at a time when energy sources were becoming increasingly rare and when energy production costs were rising. Nuclear power could contribute to the economic developmemt of Third World countries and could help prevent the dangerous phenomena of deforestation and desertification due to excessively intensive exploitation of non-renewable energy sources. The benefits of peaceful uses of nuclear energy should thus be extended to all countries, in particular to developing countries . . .

> The use of nuclear power did, however, involve risks, associated either with accidents which might arise at nuclear power stations or with the storage of radioactive waste. Certain groups of naïve idealists and even certain personalities from the scientific, political, cultural or religious worlds condemn the use of nuclear power simply for that reason. It seemed more realistic not to overlook any effort to guarantee the safe operation of power stations and safe disposal of wastes and to minimize thereby the risks incurred on the

understanding that, as with any human enterprise, it was impossible to eliminate them totally. His delegation therefore welcomed the expansion of the Agency's nuclear safety programme: thanks to the efforts which had been made in that regard no fatal radiation accident had occurred at any nuclear facilities operated for non-military purposes. These efforts should be pursued, especially as far as the long-term storage of radioactive wastes was concerned, and information for the public should be more extensive and more complete with a view to preventing the creation of an atmosphere of fear and distrust.[4]

The best that can be said about the above text is that after Chernobyl, it appears remarkably naïve. Almost every statement in it is either incorrect or open to serious question.

Nuclear power is dangerous at every stage of the industry's operation, from the mining and milling of uranium to the disposal of nuclear waste. Some of the elements from mining are dangerous for up to 80,000 years. The volume of these poisonous tailings is increasing every year: by 1986 the eleven uranium mills in the United States alone had already accumulated 191 million tonnes of tailing on the ground. There is a growing fear that radioactive and chemical poison from this material will seep into the groundwater and permanently contaminate it over a wide area. At Hanford, one of the main storage centres in the United States, 422,000 gallons of radioactive liquid waste leaked out of the storage tanks. Tritium has been detected in groundwater, strontium-90 has been found in the Columbia River, and plutonium-239 in the nearby soil.[5]

People working in nuclear power stations also face health hazards. A report released in Bonn by a joint committee involving workers in the nuclear industry, trade union representatives and operators of the industry, recommends that certain types of cancer should be recognized as occupational diseases for workers in nuclear plants (*Philippine Daily Inquirer*, 30 April 1987). Workers at the Sellafield reprocessing plant in England have been found to have levels of plutonium in their blood 100 times in excess of normal levels.

The nuclear problem will continue to haunt the earth community: some of the elements are lethal for 250,000 years. Many people feel that it is a crime against future generations to develop nuclear power in an extensive way and to encourage its proliferation when no safe way has yet been found to store and dispose of nuclear waste. E. F. Schumacher, the author of *Small is Beautiful*, insists that 'no place on earth can be shown to be safe for disposing of nuclear waste'. Much of the low-level nuclear waste is dumped in some of the deepest parts of the ocean on the false assumption that no life exists there. Recent deep sea exploration has discovered life forms in every part of the ocean.

Once the radioactive material is absorbed into the biological chain it contaminates every organism in the food chain. Thus it moves from water to plankton, to algae, to fish and eventually to humans. Life-forms at the top of the food chain, like us, have the capacity to concentrate this radioactivity by a factor of 1,000 or more.

The speech by Mgr Peressin reflects the 'atoms of peace' naivety of the early 1950s, when President Eisenhower was assuring the world that nuclear power would produce electricity so cheaply that it would be uneconomical to install meters. This sort of naïvety was excusable in the early 1950s, but less so in the 1970s.

The truth is that even in economic terms, nuclear power is more costly than power generated from oil or coal. It is also much less versatile. In an article entitled 'The collapse of nuclear economics', Jim Jeffery disputes the figures of the Central Electricity Generating Board (CEGB) in Britain which claim that nuclear energy is cheaper than energy from fossil fuel. He maintains that electricity produced in coal- or oil-burning generating stations is significantly cheaper.[6] This is particularly true when one factor is the cost of eventually decommissioning nuclear plants. Proponents of nuclear power also conveniently gloss over the hidden subsidies which the civilian nuclear industry receives out of the taxpayers' money via the military connection. Both civilian and military programmes share the same research facilities and processing plants. In the UK, Sellafield is a prime example of this.

Attempts to distinguish the so-called peaceful use of nuclear power from the production and possible use of nuclear weapons are also naïve. Tony Benn, who was Secretary for Energy in successive Labour governments in Britain in the 1960s and 1970s, has harsh things to say about the whole industry. He states that in the United States, Britain, France, Israel, South Africa, India, Pakistan and the Warsaw Pact countries, the civilian nuclear programme is simply a cover for the development and enhancement of nuclear weapons. In the same article Mr Benn takes the British nuclear industry to task for repeatedly attempting to conceal its intimate connection with arms production.[7]

No one will deny that fossil fuels are limited in quantity, but so is uranium. Only by opting for fast-breeder reactors can our uranium resources be stretched to meet even a percentage of the future projected needs of a continually expanding industrial society. True there is a need for energy: but it should not be provided at such a risk to every succeeding generation of living organisms on this planet. The future scarcity of energy should spur us on to look at methods of conserving energy and at alternative means of producing energy from the sun, wind, biomass and water. Limited energy resources raise serious questions about the direction of our present industrial society. But recklessly committing ourselves to the nuclear option would surely be the road to collective suicide.

If the wish to expand nuclear power to every developing country were ever to be realized, then we could expect a series of disasters or near-disasters like the leaks of radiation from Sellafield and Three Mile Island or, most notably, the Chernobyl explosion to occur with frightening frequency. The Chernobyl accident left 31 people dead and over 200 people suffering from acute radiation poisoning, while 135,000 had to be evacuated from the area. It spewed out a cloud of radioactive material which spread across Europe from Greece to Scandinavia and from the USSR to the west coast of Ireland. Conservative estimates place the number of deaths likely to occur within the next few decades as a direct result of the Chernobyl accident at 29,000; some scientists like Professor John Gofman of the University of California estimate over one million victims. In August 1989, scientists in the western Soviet Republic of Byelorussia published reports on plant and animal abnormalities in areas of the republic exposed to the highest radiation. These included pine needles ten times larger than normal, oak and acacia trees with huge leaves, and genetic deformations among many rodents. Within a week the authorities in the republic launched an appeal to decontaminate an estimated 334,000 square kilometres; the cost of the clean-up is projected as 10 billion roubles ($A4.1 billion).[8]

The accident at Chernobyl was the result of human errors. This is the crucial factor in the whole nuclear debate. Should the human community commit itself irrevocably to a technology which is capable of such far-reaching and irreversible destruction? The more nuclear technology proliferates, the greater the possibility of similar accidents happening again, especially if the technology is exported to countries where there is insufficient scientific and technological training and where social unrest makes a nuclear installation a prime target for terrorists.

While the Bataan nuclear facilities were being built, a group of concerned Filipino scientists wrote to President Marcos asking him to desist from the project:

> We believe in the intellectual endowments of our Filipino
> scientists and engineers. Given the opportunity for research
> and funds to conduct studies in nuclear physics, we know that
> they will be more than capable. But such research, funds and
> training are not available in the country today. In case of any
> accident, we feel that we will not yet be in a position to cope
> with the situation. Nuclear technology is not our field. We
> hope it will never be.

Despite the hopes expressed above, nuclear power will not be a financial godsend for Third World countries. In fact, the main beneficiaries will be the First World corporations who sell the technology to Third World countries. The optimists fail to mention the huge capital costs of constructing and maintaining nuclear facilities. In the Philippines, the initial cost of the Bataan project was estimated to be around $600 million. When the project was finally suspended in April 1986 (in the wake of Chernobyl), the cost had reached $2.2 billion. Of this, around $50 million was paid by Westinghouse to a Marcos supporter in order to secure the contract.

Sellafield, Three Mile Island and especially Chernobyl refute the claims for the high standard of safety at nuclear plants. Former officials and technicians from Chernobyl were sentenced in 1988 to long prison terms for grossly violating safety procedures. The record of the International Atomic Energy Agency (IAEA) itself came under attack in a confidential report of the Agency published in 1988. Paul Brown, writing in the *Sydney Morning Herald* (1 June 1988), reports that:

> Dozens of installations are not inspected by the Agency for the diversion of material, and many it does inspect have so many problems with their procedures that the Agency cannot guarantee that diversions have not taken place. Among the countries where the Agency failed to reach its verification goals were West Germany and Belgium. The report contradicts evidence given to the European Parliament by Mr John MacMannus, director of the Agency's Operations Division, who testified that 'there has been no diversion of nuclear material to nuclear explosives'.

In 1957, a plutonium-producing atomic pile caught fire at Sellafield and released a cloud of radioiodine across Europe. Researchers in Ireland, Dr Patricia Sheenan and Dr Irene Hillary, insist that this caused numerous cancer-related deaths and birth deformities on the east coast of Ireland.[9] Across the Irish Sea *The Guardian* (4 October 1988) carried a report by Michael White entitled 'Nuclear Plant hit by "serious incidents" '. The subtitle stated that a congressional probe had uncovered a history of accidents at US nuclear installations.

Even the International Atomic Energy Commission (IAEA) is not above 'doctoring' the truth or masking it with jargon. Writing in *The Tablet* (25 October 1986), Vera Rich complained that the IAEA conference called in the wake of Chernobyl excluded the press from important sessions, and that euphemisms like 'the relocation of fuel' was used to refer to radioactive fission particles which fell on people in the Soviet Union and in many other parts of Europe.

In the wake of Chernobyl and Three Mile Island, people are rightly fearful of nuclear power. It has proved unsafe, quite apart from the problem of disposing of nuclear waste. Reprocessing plants like that at Sellafield discharge tonnes of low-level nuclear waste and at least 180 grammes of plutonium into the Irish Sea each year, making it the most radioactive sea in the world. Parents are understandably concerned about the health of the environment for their children.

Finally, in the terrorist world of hijacking, political assassination and suicidal guerrilla activity, some terrorist in the near future may well use nuclear blackmail, particularly if nuclear power continues to proliferate. These are real fears arising from people's desire to live. Those who believe in the integrity of creation as God fashioned it would do well to join forces to put out this Promethean fire before it gets completely out of control. Otherwise there may be no long-term future. It is hardly the role of the Holy See to accept the propaganda of the pro-nuclear lobby and attempt to dispel these very real fears.

Sollicitudo Rei Socialis

Happily, in 1988 *Sollicitudo Rei Socialis* did introduce the issue in papal teaching in a fairly substantial way. Nevertheless, it is as well to remember that almost every other institution in the world had moved on the issue before the Catholic Church; by 1988, the Brundtland Report had been published and people from such diverse backgrounds as Margaret Thatcher and Eduard Shevardnadze were making statements about the destruction of the environment.

Since this is the most extensive statement to date in papal teaching on the environment it is worth quoting in full.

> Nor can the moral character of development exclude respect for *the beings which constitute* the natural world, which the ancient Greeks — alluding precisely to the order which distinguishes it — called the 'cosmos'. Such realities demand respect, by virtue of a threefold consideration which it is useful to reflect upon.

> The *first consideration* is the appropriateness of acquiring a *growing awareness* of the fact that one cannot use with impunity the different categories of beings, whether living or inanimate — animals, plants, the natural elements — simply as one wishes, according to one's own economic needs. On the contrary, one must take into account the *nature of each being* and of its *mutual connection* in an ordered system, which is precisely the 'cosmos'.

> The *second consideration* is based on the realization — which is perhaps more urgent — that natural resources are limited; some are not, as it is said, *renewable*. Using them as if they were inexhaustible, with *absolute dominion*, seriously endangers their

availability not only for the present generation, but above all for the generations to come.

The *third consideration* refers directly to the consequences of a certain type of development on the *quality of life* in the industrialized zones. We all know that the direct or indirect result of industrialization is, ever more frequently, the pollution of the environment, with serious health consequences for the health of the population.

Once again it is evident that development, the planning which governs it, and the way in which resources are used must include respect for moral demands. One of the latter undoubtedly imposes limits on the use of the natural world. The dominion granted to man by the Creator is not an absolute power, nor can one speak of a freedom to 'use and abuse', or to dispose of things as one pleases. The limitations imposed from the beginning by the Creator himself and expressed symbolically by the prohibition not to 'eat of the fruit of the tree' (cf. Gen 2:16–17) shows clearly enough that, when it comes to the natural world, we are subject not only to biological laws, but also to moral ones, which cannot be violated with impunity.

A true concept of development cannot ignore the use of the elements of nature, the renewability of resources and the consequences of haphazard industrialization — three considerations which alert our conscience to the moral dimension of development.

It goes without saying that every Catholic who is working to preserve and improve the environment welcomes the fact that the Pope has added the moral authority of his office to this important issue. Still, it cannot be said that the environmental issue is central to the encyclical. I did not find that it captured either the magnitude of the problem or the urgency with which it must be faced. The encyclical is very concrete in its criticism of particular social, political and economic systems (no. 15); on the environmental issue, however, there are no realistic suggestions about conserving the earth or healing the damage which has already been done.

Even *Time* (2 January 1989) regards the environmental crisis as the most urgent problem facing both the earth and the human community. *Sollicitudo Rei Socialis* lacks that clarity. There, ecological problems are one among other equally pressing ones. The prodigious waste of non-renewable resources is recognized, but the fact that what is happening is in many ways irreversible is not hammered home and the moral responsibility of this generation for impoverishing each succeeding generation is not sufficiently underscored. There is no call to every Catholic individual and institution to spread the word about this frightful desecration of God's creation and to become actively involved in healing the earth.

The anthropocentric tone of the encyclical is set in the first line: 'the social concern of the Church directed towards an authentic development of man and society which would respect and promote all the dimensions of the human person, has always expressed itself in the most varied ways'. Ecological concerns are set firmly within this framework. The encyclical rightly challenges and often condemns development theories and strategies which give precedence to economic over social or moral considerations and in the process aggravate the plight of most people living in the Third World. The Pope recognizes that development for a fraction of humanity — the middle class in First World countries and the Third World elite — has been achieved through exploiting cheap labour and primary commodities from Third World countries. He overlooks the fact that it has also been achieved at the cost of precious topsoil, the elimination of forests with their unique flora and fauna and the poisoning of their rivers, springs, lakes and the air.

Eco-development

This path should be stated for what it truly is: the avenue of death. There is a growing consensus in development circles that, in future, development must be discussed with an awareness, not just of its impact on human societies, but on the total fabric of the earth itself. Long-term well-being for the planet and human beings depends on the continued well-being of the seas, the forests, the soil and the air. If human well-being, for example in the Philippines, is achieved at the expense of destroying the tropical forests, the corals, or the groundwater then it is illusory. Terms like eco-development and sustainable development, which have as yet not been adequately defined or put into practice, at least point the way for the future. This new concept of development must be grounded in an appreciation of ecological, biological and social factors.

The United Nations World Commission on Environment and Development in *Our Common Future* attempts to plough this furrow, with, it must be admitted, limited success — mainly because of its unwillingness to face the fact that it is the continued economic growth of First World countries which is destroying the biosphere. A 5 per cent annual increase in output means an eightfold leap in output by the year 2050. But, if the present level of output is destroying the earth and causing the 'greenhouse effect', what will happen if the output jumps eight times?

During pastoral visits to a number of countries in 1988, Pope John

Paul spoke about environmental degradation. During his visit to
Madagascar, 28 April to 1 May 1988, the Pope saw at first hand the
effects of deforestation and soil erosion. On his return to the capital
Antananarivo, he spoke to a group of assembled diplomats:

> Increasingly, world opinion is becoming conscious of the
> precious resource which is the earth, along with everything it
> protects . . .
>
> When the word environment is used: this means the
> environment in which man must live, it means the natural
> world which has been placed in his trust. And now we are
> aware of the threat to entire regions caused by inconsiderate
> exploitation or uncontrolled exploitation or uncontrolled
> pollution . . .
>
> Protecting the world's forests, stemming desertification and
> erosion, avoiding the spread of toxic substances harmful to
> man, animals and plants protecting the atmosphere, all these
> can be accomplished only through active and wise
> co-operation without borders or political powerplay.[10]

As this book was being prepared for production Pope John Paul
published his 1 January 1990 World Day of Peace Message, *Peace with
God the Creator, Peace with All Creation*. This is the first papal document
devoted exclusively to environmental concerns. It is written in a lively
style; its coverage is comprehensive; the analysis is incisive and the
text reverberates with a note of urgency. Throughout the document
the Pope insists that environmental degradation must be a concern of
every individual and every institution: ultimately, it has an essential
moral and religious dimension.

Ecological problems are named in a much more detailed manner
than in previous documents, which were often content to remain at a
philosophical and theological level. The Pope draws on Revelation to
begin his reflection, but he also speaks of the depletion of the ozone
layer, the 'greenhouse' effect, acid rain, soil erosion, the destruction of
marine resources, tropical deforestation and the prodigious waste of
resources on armaments.

Not content with enumerating ecological problems, the Pope looks
below the surface at the root causes of the devastation. 'First among
these is the indiscriminate application of advances in science and
technology.' This critique of technology constitutes a major shift in
emphasis in recent papal teaching that I am sure will not be welcomed by the captains of industry.

Equally unpalatable for many environmental consultants is the reminder that the standard of living which many people in the First World enjoy is obtained at the expense of Third World people and the earth itself. The Pope warns that 'modern society will find no solution to the ecological problem unless it takes a serious look at its life-style . . . Simplicity, moderation, and discipline, as well as a spirit of sacrifice, must become part of everyday life, lest all suffer the negative consequences of the careless habits of a few.'

This is an excellent document. Unfortunately, once again it refuses to acknowledge the pressure which rapid population growth is placing on resources and the biosphere itself.

Finally, though the document is dated 8 December 1989, a feast of Mary, there is no mention of Mary or the effects on women of ecological destruction. This is a curious oversight for a Pope who is deeply devoted to Mary. The Philippine bishops in their pastoral letter *What Is Happening to Our Beautiful Land?* see Mary, Mother of Life, challenging Filipinos to 'abandon the pathways of death and return to the way of life'. As we have seen, ecological destruction affects women in a special way. When the forests are destroyed they spend much more time collecting firewood and fetching water. Soil erosion reduces the food in their pots. When this happens, mothers meet the needs of their husbands and children first, often by eating less themselves. Many are constantly hungry and in a real way starve themselves to death.

Peace with God the Creator, Peace with All Creation is a landmark in the greening of the Church. One hopes and prays that the Pope's voice will be heard and acted upon in parishes, Church schools and dioceses around the world.

Pope John Paul's recent concern for the environment is not shared so enthusiastically by other key figures in the Vatican. Cardinal Joseph Ratzinger, prefect of the Congregation for the Doctrine of the Faith, in an interview published in *Il Sabato*, criticized environmentalists. He threw cold water on the ecumenical meeting in Assisi in 1986 organized by the World Wide Foundation. For Ratzinger the Greens are a blend of ill-defined romanticism with elements of Marxism and even stronger strains of liberalism — none of which he has much time for. According to Ratzinger, the Greens' synthesis is based on a

somewhat antitechnical, somewhat antirational concept of man as united to nature. It is a concept that has an antihumanist element. It presents man as having, by his thinking and action, destroyed the beauty and equilibrium that once existed. That would mean that man had moved backward in regard to himself. That seems to me the position of one who no longer recognizes himself in himself, who even has a kind of hate of himself and his history.[11]

A little breathless and a little late

Despite the Pope's recent statements it seems fair to say that the Catholic Church has not been involved in any extensive way in recognizing or responding to the ecological crisis. While few would be openly as negative toward the ecological movement as Cardinal Ratzinger, the Church's position is summed up in a phrase attributed to the late Fr Bernard Lonergan. On this issue Catholics, particularly the leadership within the Church, have arrived at this issue 'a little breathless and a little late'. After all, Rachel Carson published her famous book *Silent Spring* in the spring of 1962; yet the Vatican Council, which opened in October of the same year and continued for four years, had nothing to say on the issue. Rather than claiming that we have been in there working assiduously right from the beginning, it would be much more salutary and Christian humbly to admit our faults and failures and try to learn from them. We might ask: why is it that an issue of this magnitude passed us by for so long? Does it perhaps say something about the way information is gathered and communicated within the Church? Does it not also raise questions about the whole process of decision-making in overcentralized organizations?

Given Cardinal Ratzinger's comments on the Green movement and some other recent disturbing decisions emanating from Rome, it would appear that we are not out of the woods yet. Fr John Mutiso-Mbinda writes in *Sedos Bulletin* (15 December 1988) about the 'Collaboration between the Catholic Church and the World Council of Churches (WCC) in the Justice, Peace and the Integrity of Creation Programme' planned for Seoul, South Korea, 5–15 March 1990. He refers to the fact that when Dr Emilio Castro, General Secretary of the WCC, invited the Catholic Church to be a 'co-inviter', Cardinal Willebrands replied that 'because the Catholic Church and the World Council of Churches are, by nature, two different organisms, this has created difficulties in accepting to be one of the co-inviters'. It is difficult to cut through this ecclesiastical jargon and really know what the sentence means. From my perspective in Mindanao, where the environment is being devastated at an extraordinary rate on many fronts, it sounds like a good old-fashioned dose of un-Christian institutional pride. The Soviet Foreign Minister, Eduard Shevardnaze, was under no illusions about this when he spoke at the United Nations General Assembly in October 1988: 'Faced with the threat of environmental catastrophe, the dividing lines of the bipolar ideological world are receding. The biosphere recognizes no divisions into blocs, alliances or systems.'

In ecclesiastical terms this means that there are no Catholic lakes, Protestant rivers or Muslim forests. We all share a common earth and in the face of a threat to the survival of the planet we should unite our efforts and forget which institution should have precedence, and other ecclesiastical niceties.

Pope John Paul II envisages this kind of collaboration in *Sollicitudo Rei Socialis* no. 32: 'In this sense, just as we Catholics invite our Christian brethren to share in our initiatives, so too we declare that we are ready to collaborate in theirs, and we welcome the invitations presented to us'.

Bishops' statements

There are signs that many Christians, who have exercised a prophetic mission in the area of social justice, especially in Latin America and the Philippines, are now willing to do the same for environmental issues. The Guatemalan bishops' *The Cry for Land* links a concern for justice for campesinos with a clear recognition that 'the earth does not belong to us but to the Lord'.[12] Also in 1987, the bishops of the Dominican Republic published a pastoral letter entitled *The Protection of Nature is a Condition of Survival*.

> Our links with nature include our relations with others and God. For this reason the exploitation of natural riches should be carried out according to the needs of the whole human family, both present and future. The extreme poverty of the peasants is unjust, as is the waste of goods by those who possess more.[13]

1988 saw the publication of a pastoral letter by the bishops of the Philippines devoted exclusively to the destruction of the environment: *What Is Happening to Our Beautiful Land?* Looking around the country, the bishops say:

> Our small farmers tell us that their fields are less productive and are becoming sterile. Our fishermen are finding it increasingly difficult to catch fish. Our lands, forests and rivers cry out that they are being eroded, denuded and polluted. As bishops we have tried to listen and respond to their cry.[14]

The World Council of Churches

A concern for the integrity of creation has also been an important part of the agenda of the World Council of Churches (WCC) for almost two decades. It did not appear in a single moment of blinding insight, rather it evolved through a number of stages, all rooted in a concern for justice. At the Amsterdam meeting the Council challenged Christians to be concerned for a 'responsible (just) society'. This was seen as a necessary antidote to the fixation of much of Christian ethics with individual morality. Faithfulness to the biblical tradition demanded a commitment to work to transform social, political and economic institutions which were exploiting the poor, particularly in Third World countries. By 1975 the Assembly had moved on to call for a 'just, participatory and sustainable society'. This title emerged from a WCC-sponsored conference in Bucharest in 1974 on 'The Future of Man and Society in a World of Science-Based Technology'. In this perspective sustainability became a criterion of the social and economic order. If the present use of resources, particularly by a small segment of humanity, was destroying ecosystems, then it was seen as injurious to the well-being of all humanity living today and to all future generations.

While the term 'sustainability' captured some very important elements in the justice debate, especially the idea of the fragility of ecosystems, it also drew negative comments. Some felt that it was not biblically grounded, and Third World critics felt that it might be used to sustain the present unjust social and economic order. At the Vancouver Assembly in 1983 the theme had been broadened to include work for 'Justice, Peace and the Integrity of Creation'. The Programme Guidelines Committee of the Vancouver Assembly emphasized that the 'links as well as the tensions between the goals of justice, peace and the well-being of creation should be explored from a biblical, socio-economic and political perspective'.[15] In the wake of Vancouver, the Church and Society and the Faith and Order committees of the WCC were encouraged to explore together the meaning of the integrity of creation. This would mean looking at a viable theology of nature, a bio-centric ethics, the relationship between the kingdom and creation. Many of these issues were taken up at the First International Consultation on JPIC held at Glion, 7–15 November 1986. A number of practical consultations were also held on crucial issues: one of these in Manila in January 1986, discussed the crucial issue of 'New Technology, Work and the Environment'.

A European Ecumenical Assembly on this theme in Basel (15–21 May 1989) was co-sponsored by the Conference of European Churches and the Council of the European Episcopal Conference. Over 700 delegates from every country except Albania and from every Christian tradition met, reflected, prayed and worshipped around the theme 'Peace, Justice and the Integrity of Creation'. The message of the assembly called on Christians 'to turn back to the Creator who in love cares for all and each of His creatures'. The document declares that 'poverty and starvation are a scandal which permits us no rest', 'War must be abandoned as a method of settling conflicts', and 'To deal with nature in the way of peace requires us to reject economic and social structures which are a threat to life'.[16]

As mentioned above this is a vital area in which there is ample opportunity for co-operation between the Churches, as the meeting in Basel demonstrated.

Teilhard de Chardin (1881–1955)

At this point it is worth recalling briefly the contribution of a few Catholic thinkers who have helped lay the foundations for the emerging theology of creation in the Catholic tradition. Pride of place goes to Pierre Teilhard de Chardin. In *The Phenomenon of Man*, he traces the story of creation which has emerged from the combined work of many scientists and scientific disciplines during the previous two centuries.[17] He brings a religious dimension to the telling of the story of the emergent universe. The spiritual element is not added on to the physical, chemical and biological evolution which he traces through the aeons, but rather integral to every phase of the story of creation. In this way Teilhard attempted to overcome the dualistic mode of thought that is so prevalent in the Western humanist, religious and scientific tradition and which has effectively led to the downgrading of the material world.

From a theological perspective this vision moves creation back to the very centre of the theological stage, after almost five centuries during which redemption themes occupied the minds of Christian thinkers and spiritual writers almost exclusively. Teilhard does not re-establish the hierarchical and, ultimately, anthropocentric approach of the 'great chain of being' of the mediaeval scholastics. In fact, his dynamic, evolutionary understanding of the emergence of the universe also helped to give birth to a bio-centric, rather than merely human-centred ethic. Teilhard was vitally interested in rekindling human energies to assume more active responsibility for human and earthly affairs. Although humans only appeared two million years ago, for him they are central to the whole reality of the universe and are called to assume a central role in protecting the stability of the natural systems which are now under threat.

Teilhard himself did not perceive this threat to the environment which perceptive people were beginning to see in his time. He was fascinated by technology. Looking at the worldwide growth of modern technology during his lifetime, he felt that:

> if words have any meaning, is this not life some great body being born — with its limbs, nervous system, its perceptive organs, its memory — born in fact, of that great Thing which had to come to fulfil the ambitions aroused in the reflective being by the newly acquired consciousness that he was at one with and responsible to an evolutionary All.[18]

Thomas Berry

Fr Thomas Berry follows very much in the footsteps of Teilhard de Chardin. For over two decades he has been one of the few voices in the Catholic Church calling attention to the religious dimension of environmental issues. He has written and spoken about the extinction of species, the degradation of many of the most important ecosystems on earth, and the role of technology in the modern world. On the positive side he has emphasized the importance of religious traditions in empowering people to abandon the present way of death and to learn to live with the planet in a more intimate, satisfying and sustainable way. This must emerge from a 'new story' of the emergence of the universe and the place of human beings within the rest of creation. This story, told with modern scientific insight and religious sensitivity to the presence of the spirit in all reality, must, he says, become the touchstone of reality and value for the new ecological age into which humankind must move. Thomas Berry brings to his writings and lectures a wealth of knowledge of the history of religions, the Christian tradition, the great religions of Asia, and the cultures of the North American Indians, and a deep appreciation of the insights of modern science.

Until 1989 many of his essays were only available in the 'Riverdale Papers'. Now a selection of his writings on a wide range of environment-related topics is available in a single volume, *The Dream of the Earth*.[19] Thomas Berry has also been a source of encouragement and inspiration to many other Catholics who are involved in environmental issues, both in North America and the Philippines.

Matthew Fox

The best-known and most prolific writer in the area of creation theology is, undoubtedly, the American Dominican Matthew Fox. No one has done more to popularize creation theology or bring it to a wide audience through lectures, workshops, the Institute of Culture and Creation Spirituality in Oakland, California, and his books: *On Becoming a Musical Mystical Bear; A Spirituality Named Compassion; Whee! We, Wee, All the Way Home* and *Original Blessing*, to mention just a few.

In *Original Blessing*,[20] we find a popular exposition of many of the themes of creation theology. Fox contrasts what he calls the fall/redemption theology with a creation-centred theology, arguing that the fall/redemption theology has been excessively restrictive and that it has been responsible for sealing off our religious traditions from economic, social, political and even scientific concerns. Fall/redemption theology has left Christians with little to say to the world at large. Furthermore, in many ways this has crippled our religious and emotional imagination and has prepared the way for much of the exploitative and destructive tendencies in recent technology and modern living.

Fox calls Christians and the Churches back to a broader vision of 'original blessing' as a way of empowering people to search for a new wholeness with God, humanity, especially bruised humanity, and all creation. Fox's thought and mode of presentation have not always been well received. In his efforts to popularize creation theology, he has been criticized for selectively reading historical texts in an effort to find a 'creation-theology' in them.[21] In 1988 he was censured by ecclesiastical authorities. The censure has had the opposite effect to that intended; if anything, it has made him better known around the world. The growing worldwide concern for the environment ensures that Matthew Fox will have a receptive audience in many countries as Christians attempt to grapple with this vital issue.

The cost of discipleship

In a particularly sinister development, 1988 marked the year when people were called to give their lives for the earth. During the 1970s and 1980s in Latin America and the Philippines, men and women who have worked for justice for the oppressed have been brutally murdered, often by so-called Christians. No one is beyond the reach of a hired killer, as the bullet that killed Archbishop Romero of San Salvador made abundantly clear.

The killings have continued, and the targets now include people working to protect the environment. On 7 April 1988, Fr Carl Schmitz CP, a 70-year-old missionary who had worked among a neighbouring tribal group in southeast Mindanao, was brutally murdered by a member of a local paramilitary group. Before shooting him, his assailant accused Fr Carl of being sympathetic to the Communist rebels, the New People's Army (NPA). To those of us who knew Fr Carl, a tireless worker and a former China missionary, the accusation is preposterous. Local people claim that the real motive behind the murder was Fr Carl's efforts to protect what is left of the tropical rainforest where the tribal people live and to expose those involved in illegal logging.

Further north in Mindanao, a young priest, Fr Mario 'Mark' Estorba, a member of the Society of the Divine Word (SVD), was shot and killed in Butuan city during the first week of July 1988. Prior to his death, Fr Estorba had furnished the authorities with documentary evidence of atrocities committed by the logging companies against local settlers and the original tribal residents of the region.

Those protecting the environment are often harassed by sections of the military in league with the exploiters. During 1988, in two separate localities in Mindanao — Midsalip, Žamboanga del Sur and San Fernando. Bukidnon — members of basic Christian com-

munities literally protected what is left of the forest with their bodies
by placing a picket on the road leading to the forest. They called for a
stop to logging which is rapidly destroying both their forests and
farms through floods and massive erosion.

In both cases the 'picketers' were threatened with violence. In
Midsalip the logging company brought in a notorious bully-boy to
intimidate the men, women and children protecting the forest in an
effort to disperse them.

In Bukidnon, the protest was successful and the logging permit
was cancelled. But the victory was not without its cost. The peaceful
picketers were baton charged and violently dispersed by the military
and local police. Since logging has continued, the picket was once
again mounted in the area in December 1988. This time the military
have attempted to link the picketers with the New People's Army. In
the Philippines today this Communist smear is tantamount to a death
warrant. People who are maligned in this way become easy targets for
paid assassins or paramilitary agents who, after they commit their
crimes, are seldom brought to justice.

This new focus of violence continued to the end of 1988. On 22
December, in Xapuri, a town in the western Amazon state of Acre,
Brazil, Francisco 'Chico' Mendes was murdered. 'Chico' had been
acclaimed internationally for his efforts to protect the Amazon rainforest. His activities on its behalf had antagonized many powerful
logging operators and cattle ranchers. These are believed to be responsible for his murder.

In his Gospel, St John tells us that 'God so loved the World that he
gave his only Son, so that everyone who believes in him may not be
lost and may have eternal life' (John 3:16). Increasingly the Church is
summoned to cry out like the angel in the Book of Revelation, 'Do not
harm the earth or the sea or the trees, till we have sealed the servant's
of God upon their forehead' (Rev 7:3). Christians in local churches
are being called to imitate the Master and give their lives 'for the life of
the world'.

The Santa Cruz Mission

An ounce of practice is worth a tonne of theory. At the Santa Cruz
Mission we feel that the best way to communicate a message is by
example. We are combining education about the environment with
practical programmes to repair the damage already done in this area.
The Santa Cruz Mission, which began with a single school and chapel
among the T'boli people in the early 1960s, is now spread throughout
the province of South Cotabato and in 27 tribal communities. Over
450 lay missionaries are serving various tribal communities through
education, health care and agricultural programmes. Many of these
tribal communities have lost their lands and forests to migrants from

some of the other islands in the Philippines and from the entry into the area of large transnational agribusiness corporations like Dolé and Del Monte.

The missionaries at the Santa Cruz Mission are convinced that without security of land tenure and ecologically sound agriculture the tribal peoples will not survive. In many of the 27 mission centres the missionaries are helping to revive the skills of subsistence agriculture among the tribal peoples. This involves using traditional varieties of seeds, both for root crops and cereals, rotating crops, contouring and terracing to minimize erosion and avoiding the use of agrochemicals. Liturgies which celebrate God's gift of the land — such as earth and water liturgies — help generate the spiritual energies necessary for the enormous task of healing the earth in this region. Since the agriculture and reforestation programme began in 1984, hundreds of tribal farmers have been helped by the scheme.

Sustainable agriculture in the tropics demands the presence of the rainforest. Those of the Philippines have been devastated during the past 40 years. Now they only cover about 5 per cent of the country. The effects are disastrous — soil erosion, floods, drought, silting of rivers and estuaries. Once again the Mission has embarked on an ambitious reforestation programme using the traditional Philippine dipterocarp species as much as possible. Rainforests have an abundance of different plant and animal species. Reforestation should attempt to replicate this variety so that other creatures can once again live in the forest. Monocrop tree planations can be quite destructive of the local soil and tribal communities. They are also very vulnerable to a variety of pests. A single pest almost wiped out one non-indigenous species of tree, the ipil-pil, in 1986, as related above (p. 94).

The reforestation programme, while quite successful, is only scratching at the surface. The Santa Cruz Mission has already reforested over 400 hectares and completed another 1,500 hectares in 1989. But experts estimate that about 16 million hectares need to be reforested in the Philippines. This is a gigantic and expensive task. Local parish communities and basic Christian communities could do much to help reforest the country in the next decade if this were placed high on the list of pastoral tasks.

A recycling programme

It would be wrong to think that it is only Christians in Third World countries who can be involved in the apostolate of care for the earth. The *Christian Ecology Group News* (Spring edition 1987) carried a report on a Christian recycling company in Milton Keynes, England, called Community Recycling Opportunities Programme. The chief products recycled are cardboard, paper, glass, plastics, and beer and soft-drink cans. The venture, started as a parish-based operation by

Robert Brown, a Baptist minister, became a limited company in 1983. The company has four aims:

1. To promote the recycling of waste products with the Borough of Milton Keynes.
2. To give work experience and opportunities to the long-term unemployed.
3. To encourage and help local community groups to raise funds through recycling activities.
4. To set up an environmental awareness educational programme in both schools and in the community at large.

In 1986 the group recycled 1,200 tonnes of waste material, which represents about 3 per cent of all the domestic waste in the area of the city of Milton Keynes.

Writing about the programme in the CEGN newsletter, Robert Brown said that he felt that it was a very important religious work given the crisis which our planet now faces. He feels that it is time that the Church moved with force into this area. He says that he can testify to 'the healing power of cardboard'. Those who would otherwise be permanently unemployed are given meaningful work and thereby regain some of the human dignity lost through the stigma of long-term unemployment. Since the operation began, it has helped over half of the workers to find permanent employment elsewhere.

Conclusion

Part One of this book discussed how three interrelated ecological problems are impoverishing people and destroying God's creation. Part Two has attempted to look briefly at the various strands which woven together make up the Judaeo-Christian tradition. While there are undoubtedly problems with the somewhat excessively anthropocentric emphasis of this tradition, there is within it the seeds of a pro-environment theology. The tradition did not face the problems we, and the totality of creation, face today, mainly as a result of the scientific and technological revolution. Therefore one cannot come to the Bible or the Christian tradition hoping to find concrete answers for today's ecological problems. What one does find is an understanding of creation as good. It is created by a loving, caring God who challenges humans to be stewards of his creation. The doctrine of the cosmic Christ heightens this awareness of God's presence in the world and attests to his joy in seeing it flourish and reach its proper fulfilment.

While specific answers to modern questions are not to be found in the tradition, what I have said above emphasizes the flexibility of the tradition down through the centuries. It was able to incorporate within itself insights from Babylon, Persia, Canaan, Egypt, Greece, Rome and Western Europe. There is no reason today why it cannot incorporate within itself the understanding of the emergence of the cosmos which has come to us from the modern scientific under-standing of the earth and the animistic tradition. This new myth of understanding the emergence of the earth and the proper role of humanity in the totality of God's creation can inspire religious people to respond to the pain and degradation of the earth today. Within this overarching cosmic story the Judaeo-Christian tradition in all its facets will have an important role to play in empowering Christians to care for God's creation.

Emptying ourselves of our proud attitudes and learning from the tribal–shamanic tradition has deep scriptural overtones. In the modern world the tribal world is often dismissed and denigrated. The way of life of tribal people is seen as primitive and backward and needing the modernization and sophistication of Western-style development. In recent years, however, people are beginning to realize that tribal societies lived lightly on the earth and that they are one of the few successful human endeavours to live in a sustainable way. If the profusion and fruitfulness of life is to survive, then every society will have to learn to become sustainable. In Isaiah 53:3–5 the servant of Yahweh is despised and rejected, yet the wholeness of everyone, even those who mocked him, comes from his sacrifice. In much the same way the salvation of our civilization and Christian religious tradition may well depend on our ability to draw insights from the tribal religious experience which will help us recover the presence of God in creation and live lightly on the earth.

As the community of disciples who strive to walk in the footsteps of the Master, the Church is called to make Christ's redeeming love present in our world. The early Church did this through 'devoting themselves to the apostles' teaching, and fellowship, to the breaking of bread and prayers' (Acts 2:42). This text still embodies the challenge which Christians face in the modern world. Any adequate understanding of the apostles' teaching would include giving special attention to the theology of creation: the fellowship and sharing must now be expanded to cover the largest community which includes humanity and the totality of God's creation. The Church which has been healed through 'the wounds of Christ' (1 Pet 2:21–25) must become an active agent in healing the wounds of the human and earth community.

The Church is also experienced as a mother. The *Dogmatic Constitu-tion on the Church* of Vatican II sees the Church as a mother. 'The Church, moreover, contemplating Mary's mysterious sanctity, im-itating her charity, and faithfully fulfilling the Father's will, becomes herself a mother by accepting God's word in faith' (no. 64). This motherhood calls to mind the nurturing, caring dimension of the human reality touched on earlier in discussing the wisdom literature. If the Church could fulfil its motherly role as a teacher who respects the integrity of creation and as a healer dedicated to renewing the earth, then all humanity and the earth itself will be enriched by this maternal service.

Renew the face of the earth

There is an urgency in the task to protect the earth which is captured in the Christian notion of time embodied in the Greek word *kairos*. In the moment of *kairos*, there is a heightened awareness regarding the forces of good and evil which are at work in the world. Christians are called on to take sides, because it is clear which side God is on. While the ultimate outcome is assured, the resolution of the conflict in the present demands the active involvement of believers.

In the race to save the environment from further damage, there is no time to lose. On the time-clock of environmental disaster we are fast approaching midnight. In an address before the American Institute of Biological Sciences in August 1988, the biologist Thomas Lovejoy stated 'I am utterly convinced that most of the great environmental struggles will either be won or lost in the 1990s. By the end of the century it will be too late.'[23] This prediction presents the challenge in a very stark way, underlining the *kairos* moment we are living in.

A comprehensive response to this challenge demands that an ecological pastorate must become central to the ministry of the Church. On the practical level this will involve reaching out and co-ordinating with local and worldwide ecological organizations — The World Wide Fund for Nature, Greenpeace, the UN, Green consumer organizations and the emerging Green parties.

On the religious level this new ministry calls for a developed theology of creation and a spirituality which is sensitive to the presence of God in the natural world — locally and worldwide. Rituals that celebrate God's presence are vitally important in order to reconnect us in an integral way with the natural world. We should try to develop these for our homes, basic Christian communities, parishes, dioceses, national Churches and the worldwide Church. This will call on creative powers which at present lie dormant in the community of the Church.

Let me finish on a positive note. On the feast of Pentecost we call on the Holy Spirit: 'Come, O Holy Spirit fill the hearts of the faithful and enkindle in them the fire of your love. Send forth your spirit and they shall be created and you will renew the face of the Earth.' This is our challenge and this is our prayer. We know that the God who created this beautiful world mourns the destruction which is taking place in our times and that he is calling all Christians and the various

Churches to dedicate themselves to healing and caring for the earth. The worldwide growth in the ecological movement in the past decade and the more recent move to incorporate this into the ministry of the Church is a sign, to use the words of the poet Gerard Manley Hopkins:

> That the Holy Ghost over the bent
> World broods with warm breast and ah!
> bright wings.

A New Decalogue[1]

I the Lord am the God that made you; and as I made you, so have I made all living things, and a fit place for each living thing, and a world for all living things to share in interdependence.

And my reason for making all these are one with my reasons for making you; that each living thing may rejoice in its own being, and in the company of all beings, and in me the sum and essence and fulfilment of being, whose name is I AM THAT I AM: and that I may rejoice in each living thing, and in the company of all living things, which I have blest and hallowed with my love and to which I have lent a measure of that light by which you know that I am near.

All living things I have included in that covenant I made with your ancestors long ago; and by that covenant I gave them rights and a place, which you must not deny them, lest you displease your God.

And so that my creation may be cherished, and my covenant honoured, and my love made manifest, and you regain sight of who you truly are thus I command:

You shall not act in ignorance of the ecological consequence of your acts.

You shall not seek such ignorance, nor hide in such ignorance, hoping to say afterwards, 'Forgive me, for I knew not what I did'; for there will be no forgiveness of wilful ignorance or self-deception, either in this world or any other.

You shall not keep others in ignorance of the ecological consequences of their acts; for their ecological wrongdoing will be reckoned against you as if it were your own.

> You shall not act in any way which makes the
> world less able to sustain life:
> not by destroying the soil,
> not by destroying the living seas,
> not by laying waste the wild places,
> not by releasing poisons,
> nor by causing great changes in the climate.

You shall not act in any way that injures the buffers I have set about this world to protect its life;

the ozone layer of the atmosphere,
the carbon dioxide sink of the sea,
the chemical balance of the waters,
the interface between water and sky,
the vegetative cover of hillside and plain,
the multitude of species in a region,
the balance of species, each with each,
the adaptability of species, as contained in their genes.

You shall not encroach on a species' niche, or destroy its natural defenses, or reduce its numbers to the point where its survival is endangered.

And as I forbid these acts to you, so I forbid you to place others in a position where they must commit such acts; for their ecological wrongdoing will be reckoned against you as if it were your own.

I am the creator of the world; treasure it as your Father's treasure.

Honour the life of all living beings,
and the order of nature, and the wildness of the wilderness,
and the richness of the created world,
and the beauty of lands undefiled by your works;
and seek the holiness I have placed in these things,
the measure of light I have lent them;
and preserve these things well;
for these are my gifts to you from the dawn of time,
and their life will not be offered to you again.

And in the fulfilment of these commandments, be not half-hearted, and do not err on the side of your greed and your convenience: but act with all your ability to love,

and all your ability to discern;
and all your ability to understand,
and all your ability to foresee;

for I know your capacities, and I will know how well you use them.

And if you will listen carefully to my voice, and accept my guidance in these matters, and obey and honour and fulfil these commandments, not in the letter only but in the fullness of truth.

then I will bless your life,
and the lives of all about you,
and all that you hold dear.

I will bless you in your rising and your mid-day and your evening, and bless your sleep and sweeten all your dreaming:

> I will bless your settlements and your cultivations and the wild places you will never see;

> I will add to your riches and multiply your happiness;

> From generation to generation you will witness the unfolding of the future I myself have planned for the world from the beginning of time, and your hearts will overflow with the joy of it.   .

But if you will not attend to me, and instead live contrary to my way, your own acts and choices will become the means of your undoing.

Then it will seem to you that all the world has hardened and turned against you, though it is only that you have cast yourself out of the covenant of the world;

Famine and thirst, drought and flood and storm, blight and plague, division and strife, and slow painful death will walk among you;

Your house will be cast down, your fields laid waste, and all memory of your existence blotted out.

And on the day these punishments arrive, do not think to bargain with the Lord for mercy; for these punishment will come out of the laws I established at the dawn of time, the very laws through which I made you a place in my creation: and these laws are part of the covenant, which I have pledged never to set aside.

Therefore be holy, as I who love you and dwell within you am holy, I am the Lord.

What Is Happening to Our Beautiful Land?

A pastoral letter on ecology from the Catholic bishops of the Philippines[1]

Introduction

The Philippines is now at a critical point in its history. For the past number of years we have experienced political instability, economic decline and a growth in armed conflict. Almost every day the media highlight one or other of these problems. The banner headlines absorb our attention so much so that we tend to overlook a more deep-seated crisis which, we believe, lies at the root of many of our economic and political problems. To put it simply: our country is in peril. All the living systems on land and in the seas around us are being ruthlessly exploited. The damage to date is extensive and, sad to say, it is often irreversible.

One does not need to be an expert to see what is happening and to be profoundly troubled by it. Within a few short years brown, eroded hills have replaced luxuriant forests in many parts of the country. We see dried up river beds where, not so long ago, streams flowed throughout the year. Farmers tell us that, because of erosion and chemical poisoning, the yield from the croplands has fallen substantially. Fishermen and experts on marine life have a similar message. Their fish catches are shrinking in the wake of the extensive destruction of coral reefs and mangrove forests. The picture which is emerging in every province of the country is clear and bleak. The attack on the natural world which benefits very few Filipinos is rapidly whittling away at the very base of our living world and endangering its fruitfulness for future generations.

As we reflect on what is happening in the light of the Gospel we are convinced that this assault on creation is sinful and contrary to the teachings of our faith. The Bible tells us that God created this world, (Gen 1:1); that He loves His world and is pleased with it (Gen 1:4, 10, 12, 18, 21, 25 and 31); and that He created man and woman in His image and charged them to be stewards of His creation (Gen 1:27–28). God, who created our world, loves life and wishes to share this life with every creature. St John tells us that Jesus saw His mission in this light. 'I have come that they may have life and have it to the full' (John 10:10).

We are not alone in our concern. Tribal people all over the Philippines, who have seen the destruction of their world at close range, have cried out in anguish. Also men and women who attempt to live harmoniously with nature and those who study ecology have tried to alert people to the magnitude of the destruction taking place in our time. The latter are in a good position to tell us what is happening since they study the web of dynamic relationships which support and sustains all life within the earthly household. This includes human life.

A call to respect and defend life

At this point in the history of our country it is crucial that people motivated by religious faith develop a deep appreciation for the fragility of our islands' life-systems and take steps to defend the Earth. It is a matter of life and death. We are aware of this threat to life when it comes to nuclear weapons. We know that a nuclear war would turn the whole earth into a fireball and render the planet inhospitable to life. We tend to forget that the constant, cumulative destruction of life-forms and different habitats will, in the long term, have the same effect. Faced with these challenges, where the future of life is at stake, Christian men and women are called to take a stand on the side of life.

We, the Catholic Bishops of the Philippines, ask Christians and all people of goodwill in the country to reflect with us on the beauty of the Philippine land and seas which nourish and sustain our lives. As we thank God for the many ways He has gifted our land we must also resolve to cherish and protect what remains of this bounty for this and future generations of Filipinos. We are well aware that, for the vast majority of Filipinos, the scars on nature, which increasingly we see all around, us, mean less nutritious food, poorer health and an uncertain future. This will inevitably lead to an increase in political and social unrest.

We see the beauty and the pain of the earth

As you read this letter or listen to sections of it being read, scenes from your barrio may come to mind. In your mind's eye you may see well laid out rice paddies flanked by coconuts with their fronds swaying in the breeze. Or you may hear the rustle of the cogon grass on the hills behind your barrio. These scenes mean so much to us and are beautiful. Yet they do not represent the original vegetation with which God has blessed our land. They show the heavy hand of human labor, planning and sometimes short-sightedness.

For generations the hunting and food gathering techniques of our tribal forefathers showed a sensitivity and respect for the rhythms of nature. But all of this has changed in recent years. Huge plantations and mono-crop agriculture have pitted humans against nature. There are short-term profits for the few and even substantial harvests, but the fertility of the land has suffered and the diversity of the natural world has been depleted. So our meditation must begin by reflecting on the original beauty of our land, rivers and seas. This wonderful community of the living existed for millions of years before human beings came to these shores.

The forests

When our early ancestors arrived here they found a country covered by a blanket of trees. These abounded in living species — over 7,500 species of flowering plants, not to mention animals, bird and insects. These were watered by the tropical rains which swept in from the seas and gradually seeped down through the vegetation and soil to form clear flowing rivers and sparkling lakes which abounded in fish and aquatic life before completing the cycle and returning in the sea. An incredible variety of insects lived in the forest and were busy with all kinds of tasks from recycling dead wood to pollinating flowering plants. The community of the living was not confined to creatures who walked on the Earth. Birds flew through the air, their bright plumes and varying calls adding color and song to the green of the forests. Birds are also the great sowers. They contributed greatly to the variety of plant life which is spread throughout the forest. Finally small and large animals lived in the forest and feasted on its largesse. Our land born out of volcanic violence and earthquakes brought forth a bounty of riches. We stand in awe at the wisdom of our Creator who has fashioned this world of life, color, mutual support and fruitfulness in our land.

Our seas

The beauty did not end at the shoreline. Our islands were surrounded by blue seas, fertile mangroves and enchanting coral reefs. The coral reefs were a world of color and beauty with fish of every shape and hue darting in and out around the delicate coral reefs. *Perlas ng Silanganan* was an appropriate name for this chain of wooded islands, surrounded by clear seas, studded with coral reefs.

Creation is a long process

You might ask: Why is it important to remember the original state of our land? First of all, it reminds us of how God, in his wisdom and goodness, shaped this land in this part of the world. It did not happen overnight. It took millions of years of care and love to mould and reshape this land with all its beauty, richness and splendor, where intricate pathways bind all the creatures together in a mutually supportive community. Human beings are not alien to this community. God intended this land for us, his special creatures, but not so that we might destroy it and turn it into a wasteland. Rather He charged us to be stewards of his creation, to care for it, to protect its fruitfulness and not allow it to be devastated (Gen 1:28, 9:12). By protecting what is left of the rainforest we insure that the farmers have rain and plants for the food that sustains us.

Our forests laid waste

How much of this richness and beauty is left a few thousand years after human beings arrived at these shores? Look around and see where our forests have gone. Out of the original 30 million hectares there is now only 1 million hectares of primary forest left. Where are some of the most beautiful creatures who used to dwell in our forests? These are God's masterpieces, through which he displays his power, ingenuity and love for his creation. Humans have forgotten to live peacefully with other creatures. They have destroyed their habitat and hunted them relentlessly. Even now many species are already extinct and the destruction of species is expected to increase dramatically during the next decade as the few remaining strands of forest are wiped out by loggers and *kaingineros*. What about the birds? They used to greet us each morning and lift our spirits beyond the horizons of this world. Now they are silenced. In many places all we hear now are cocks crowing. Where is the soaring eagle circling above the land or the colorful kalaw [hornbill]?

The hemorrhage of our life blood

After a single night's rain look at the chocolate brown rivers in your locality and remember that they are carrying the life blood of the land into the sea. The soil, instead of being the seed bed of life, becomes a cloak of death, smothering, retarding and killing coral polyps. Soil specialists tell us that we lose the equivalent of 100,000 hectares of soil one meter thick each year. We are hardly aware of this enormous loss which is progressively eroding away our most fertile soil and thus our ability to produce food for an expanding population. Any comprehensive land reform must address this most serious threat to our food supply.

Deserts in the sea

How can fish swim in running sewers like the Pasig and so many more rivers which we have polluted? Who has turned the wonderworld of the seas into underwater cemeteries bereft of color and life? Imagine: only 5 per cent of our corals are in their pristine state! The blast of dynamite can still be heard on our coastal waters. We still allow *muro-ami* fishing methods which take a terrible toll both on the young swimmers and the corals. Mine tailings are dumped into fertile seas like Calancan Bay where they destroy forever the habitat of the fish. Chemicals are poisoning our lands and rivers. They kill vital organisms and in time they will poison us. The ghost of the dreaded Minamata disease hangs over towns in the Agusan river basin and the Davao gulf.

Recent destruction carried out in the name of progress

Most of this destruction has taken place since the beginning of this century, a mere wink of an eye in the long history of our country. Yet in that time we have laid waste complex living systems that have taken millions of year to reach their present state of development.

We often use the word progress to describe what has taken place over the past few decades. There is no denying that in some areas our roads have improved and that electricity is more readily available. But can we say that there is real progress? Who has benefited most and who has borne the real costs? The poor are as disadvantaged as ever and the natural world has been grievously wounded. We have stripped it bare, silenced its sounds and banished other creatures from the community of the living. Through our thoughtlessness and greed we have sinned against God and His creation.

One thing is certain: we cannot continue to ignore and disregard the Earth. Already we are experiencing the consequence of our short-sightedness and folly. Even though we squeeze our lands and try to extract more from them, they produce less food. The air in our cities is heavy with noxious fumes. Instead of bringing energy and life it causes bronchial illness. Our forests are almost gone, our rivers are almost empty, our springs and wells no longer sparkle with living water. During the monsoon rain, flash-floods sweep through our towns and cities and destroy everything in their path. Our lakes and estuaries are silting up. An out-of-sight, out-of-mind mentality allows us to flush toxic waste and mine tailings into our rivers and seas in the mistaken belief that they can no longer harm us. Because the living world is interconnected, the poison is absorbed by marine organisms. We in turn are gradually being poisoned when we eat seafood.

We can and must do something about it

It is already late in the day and so much damage has been done. No one can pinpoint the precise moment when the damage becomes so irreversible that our living world will collapse. But we are rapidly heading in that direction. Even now there are signs of stress in every corner of our land. As we look at what is happening before our eyes, and think of the horrendous consequences for the land and the people we would do well to remember that God, who created this beautiful land, will hold us responsible for plundering it and leaving it desolate. So will future generations of Filipinos. Instead of gifting them with a fruitful land, all we will leave behind is a barren desert. We, the Bishops, call on all Filipinos to recognize the urgency of this task and to respond to it now.

As Filipinos we can and must act now. Nobody else will do it for us. This is our home; we must care for it, watch over it, protect it and love it. We must be particularly careful to protect what remains of our forests, rivers, and corals and to heal, wherever we can, the damage which has already been done.

The task of preserving and healing is a daunting one given human greed and the relentless drive of our plunder economy. But we must not lose hope. God has gifted us with creativity and ingenuity. He has planted in our hearts a love for our land, which bursts forth in our songs and poetry. We can harness our creativity in the service of life and shun anything that leads to death.

Signs of hope

Despite the pain and despoliation which we have mentioned, there are signs of hope. Our forefathers and our tribal brothers and sisters today still attempt to live in harmony with nature. They see the Divine Spirit in the living world and show their respect through prayers and offerings. Tribal Filipinos remind us that the exploitative approach to the natural world is foreign to our Filipino culture.

The vitality of our Filipino family is also a sign of hope. Parents share their life with their children. They protect them and care for them and are particularly solicitous when any member of the family is sick. This is especially true of mothers; they are the heartbeat of the family, working quietly in the home to create an atmosphere where everyone is accepted and loved. No sacrifice is too demanding when it comes to caring for a sick member of the family. The values we see in our families of patient toil, concern for all and a willingness to sacrifice for the good of others are the very values which we must now transfer to the wider sphere in our efforts to conserve, heal and love our land. It is not a mere coincidence that women have been at the forefront of the ecological movement in many countries. The tree planting program of the Chipko in India, popularly known as the 'hug a tree' movement and the Green belt movement in Kenya spring to mind.

We call to mind that, despite the devastation which has taken place in our forests and seas, we Filipinos are sensitive to beauty. Even in the poorest home parents and children care for flowers. We are also encouraged by the growth in environmental awareness among many Filipinos. Small efforts which teach contour plowing, erosion control, organic farming and tree planting can blossom into a major movement of genuine care for our Earth. We are happy that there have been some successes. Both the Chico dam project was suspended and the Bataan nuclear plant mothballed after massive local resistance. This year the people of San Fernando, Bukidnon and Midsalip, Zamboanga del Sur defended what remains of their forest with their own bodies. At the Santa Cruz Mission in South Cotabato serious efforts are underway to reforest bald hills and develop ecologically sound ways of farming. The diocese of Pagadian has chosen the eucharist and ecology as its pastoral focus for this year. These are all signs for us that the Spirit of God, who breathed over the waters, and originally brought life out of chaos is now prompting men and women both inside and outside the Church to dedicate their lives to enhancing and protecting the integrity of Creation. In order that these drops and rivulets will join together and form a mighty stream in the defense of life we need a sustaining vision to guide us.

Our vision

We will not be successful in our efforts to develop a new attitude towards the natural world unless we are sustained and nourished by a new vision. This vision must blossom forth from our understanding of the world as God intends it to be. We can know the shape of this world by looking at how God originally fashioned our world and laid it out before us.

This vision is also grounded in our Faith. The Bible tells us that God created this beautiful and fruitful world for all his creatures to live in (Gen 1:1–2:4) and that He has given us the task of being stewards of His creation (Gen 2:19–20).

The relationship which links God, human beings and all the community of the living together is emphasized in the covenant which God made with Noah after the flood. The rainbow which we still see in the sky is a constant reminder of this bond and challenge (Gen 9:12). This covenant recognizes the very close bonds which bind living forms together in what are called ecosystems. The implications of this covenant for us today are clear. As people of the covenant we are called to protect endangered ecosystems, like our forests, mangroves and coral reefs and to establish just human communities in our land. More and more we must recognize that the commitment to work for justice and to preserve the integrity of creation are two inseparable dimensions of our Christian vocation to work for the coming of the kingdom of God in our times.

Christ our life (Col 3:4)

As Christians we also draw our vision from Christ. We have much to learn from the attitude of respect which Jesus displayed towards the natural world. He was very much aware that all the creatures in God's creation are related. Jesus lived lightly on the earth and warned his disciples against hoarding material possessions and allowing their hearts to be enticed by the lure of wealth and power (Matt 6:19–21; Luke 9:1–6). But our meditation on Jesus goes beyond this. Our faith tells us that Christ is the center point of human history and creation. All the rich unfolding of the universe and the emergence and flowering of life on Earth are centered on him (Eph 1:9–10; Col 1:16–17). The destruction of any part of creation, especially the extinction of species, defaces the image of Christ which is etched in creation.

Mary, Mother of Life

We Filipinos have a deep devotion to Mary. We turn to her for help and protection in time of need. We know that she is on the side of the poor and those who are rejected (Luke 1:52). Our new sensitivity to what is happening to our land also tells us that she is on the side of life. As a mother she is pained and saddened when she sees people destroy the integrity of creation through soil erosion, blast-fishing or poisoning land. Mary knows what the consequences of this destruction are. Therefore as Mother of Life she challenges us to abandon the pathway of death and to return to the way of life.

Taken together the various strands of our Christian vision envisage a profound renewal which must affect our people, our culture and our land. It challenges us to live once again in harmony with God's creation. This vision of caring for the Earth and living in harmony with it can guide us as, together, we use our ingenuity and many gifts to heal our wounded country.

This is what we suggest

In the light of this vision we recommend action in the following areas.

What each individual can do

Be aware of what is happening in your area. Do not remain silent when you see your environment being destroyed. Use your influence within your family and community to develop this awareness. Avoid a fatalistic attitude. We are people of hope, who believe that together we can change the course of events. Organize people around local ecological issues. Support public officials who are sensitive to environmental issues. Become involved in some concrete action. There is much that can be done by individuals to reforest bald hills and prevent soil erosion.

What the Churches can do

Like every other group, the Church as a community is called to conversion around this, the ultimate pro-life issue. Until very recently many religions, including the Catholic Church, have been slow to respond to the ecological crisis. We, the bishops, would like to redress this neglect. There is a great need for a Filipino theology of creation which will be sensitive to our unique living world, our diverse cultures and our religious heritage. The fruits of this reflection must be made widely available through our preaching and catechetical programs. Our different liturgies must celebrate the beauty and pain of our world, our connectedness to the natural world and the on-going struggle for social justice. We would like to encourage the administrators of our Catholic schools to give special importance to the theme of peace, justice and the integrity of creation in their schools.

Since programs, however laudable, will not implement themselves, we suggest the setting up of a Care of the Earth ministry at every level of Church organization; from the basic Christian communities, through the parish structure and diocesan offices right up to the national level. This ministry could help formulate and implement policies and strategies which flow from our new and wider vision. The idea is not so much to add another activity to our pastoral ministry, but rather that this concern should underpin everything we do.

What the Government can do

We ask the government not to pursue short-term economic gains at the expense of long-term ecological damage. We suggest that the government groups together into an independent Department all the agencies which deal at present with ecological issues. This Department should promote an awareness of the fragility and limited carrying capacity of our islands' eco-systems and advocate measures designed to support ecologically sustainable development. Obviously the Department should have an important contribution to make to related Departments like Education (DECS), Health, Natural Resources (DENR) and Agriculture. There is also a need to encourage research into the eco-systems of our land and the problems they face in the future. The Department should publish a state of the environment report for each region and for the country as a whole each year. Above all the Department needs legislative teeth to insure that its policies and programs are implemented.

Non-governmental organizations

NGOs have a very important role to play in developing a widespread ecological awareness among people. They can also act as a watch-dog to ensure that the government and those in public office do not renege on their commitment to place this concern at the top of their list.

Conclusion

This brief statement about our living world and the deterioration we see all around us attempts to reflect the cry of our people and the cry of our land. At the root of the problem we see an exploitative mentality, which is at variance with the Gospel of Jesus. This expresses itself in acts of violence against fellow Filipinos. But it is not confined to the human sphere. It also infects and poisons our relationship with our land and seas.

We reap what we sow; the results of our attitude and activities are predictable and deadly. Our small farmers tell us that their fields are less productive and are becoming sterile. Our fishermen are finding it increasingly difficult to catch fish. Our lands, forests and rivers cry out that they are being eroded, denuded and polluted. As bishops we have tried to listen and respond to their cry. There is an urgency about this issue which calls for widespread education and immediate action. We are convinced that the challenge which we have tried to highlight here is similar to the one which Moses put before the people of Israel before they entered their promised land: 'Today I offer you a choice of life or death, blessing or curse. Choose life and then you and your descendants will live' (Deut 30:19–20).

Approved at Tagaytay, 29 January 1988

Note: Data on the Philippine Environment are available in a series of pamphlets, prepared by Lingkod Tao Kalikasan. For more information please write to: Lingkod Tao Kalikasan, c/o Sister Ma. Aida Velasquez OSB, PO Box 3153, Manila.

Notes

Chapter 1   International debt

[1]Rosalinda Pineda-Ofreneo and Karen Tanada, *Primer on Women and Debt*, prepared for the National Congress on Women and Debt (23 July 1989).

[2]Ibid.

[3]*Britain and the Philippines* (fact sheet) (Philippine Resource Centre, 1–2 Grangeway, Kilburn, London NW6 2BW; May 1989).

The Freedom from Debt Coalition Primer lists companies which were given preferential treatment by the Marcos regime. The Marcos government assumed the debts of crony corporations, including Rudolfo Cuenca's Construction and Development Corporation of the Philippines (CDCP), which had a debt of $323 million; Robert Benedicto's NASUTRA and PHILSUCOM ($265 million); the Cojuangcos' Philippine Long Distance Telephone (PLDT) ($654 million); and Herminio Disini's National Power Corporation ($794 million) (p. 10).

Ibid., p. 12: a former investment banker, James Henry, in his article 'The debt hoax: where the money went', revealed that the capital flight had a direct bearing on the foreign debt, and that it benefited two parties — the Third World's elite and the foreign commercial banks.

[4]Ibid.

[5]*Philippine Daily Inquirer* (5 March 1989).

[6]Jose Ernesto Ledesma, 'A beginner's guide to the IOL', Philippine Human Rights Update (15 May–14 June 1989).

[7]Rosalinda Pineda-Ofreneo and Karen Tanada, op. cit., p. 5.

[8]Ibid.

[9]Pontifical Commission 'Justitia et Pax', *At the Service of the Human Community: an Ethical Approach to the International Debt Question:* in *L'Osservatore Romano* (2 February 1987).

[10]See Appendix 2 above, p. 207.

[11]Susan George, 'Environment news', *Panoscope* (London; 16 May 1988).

[12]J. Winston Porter, *Chemical Engineering Progress* (28 September 1986).

[13]Andrew Feeney, *Multinational Monitor* (USA; July 1986).

[14]John Durie, 'Debt going cheap but takers scarce', *The Australian* (15 August 1989).

[15]Jared Kotler, 'Debt-for-equity swaps could "mortgage the region's future" ', *Latinamerica Press* (15 September 1988).

[16]John Durie, 'Investors grow fat on Third World debt', *The Australian* (3 August 1989).

[17]John Durie, op. cit. (15 August 1989).

[18]Jared Kotler, op. cit., p. 4.

[19]In January 1988, Mexico suspended debt-for-equity swaps when the government determined that these activities were contributing to an annual inflation rate of 135 per cent: *Concern Focus*, issue 82 (Center for Concern, Washington, DC; January 1988).

   Debt-for-equity swaps also caused inflationary pressures in the Philippines, according to *Debt-for-Development Alternative in the Philippine Context: Some Policy Notes* (Policy Study Group, Philippine Rural Reconstruction Movement, May 1989). By May 1988, $461 million had been released to investors. The governor of the Central Bank confirmed that the debt-for-equity swap had fuelled inflation to 9.23 per cent. This has resulted in a limit of $180 million per year being placed on debt-for-equity swaps.

[20]Ibid., p. 2. Cf. also Erick Foronda, 'Bolivia's debt-for-nature swap comes under fire', *Latinamerica Press* (20 October 1988); Amanda Davita, 'Bolivia's debt swap: not only birds and trees', *Panoscope* (November 1988).

[21]Rosalinda Pineda-Ofreneo and Karen Tanada, op. cit., p. 4.

[22]Pontifical Commission 'Justitia et Pax', op. cit.

[23]*The UK Banks and the Philippine Debt* (Philippine Resource Centre, 1–2 Grangeway, Kilburn, London NW6 2BW).

[24]At a conference on sustainable development (Sydney, 18–20 July 1989) Susan George estimated that the Third World debt crisis had cost the Australian economy around 70,000 jobs.

[25]Susan George, *A Fate Worse Than Debt* (Penguin, Harmondsworth, Middx, 1988), pp. 237–45.

[26]Ibid., p. 234.

[27]*Sollicitudo Rei Socialis* (1988), no. 43.

[28]'Forgive us our debts', *The Tablet* (22 August 1987).

[29]'Columbans and the world debt crisis', unpublished paper circulated among Columban missionaries by Fr Noel Connolly (1988).

[30]Eugene Thalman, 'A biblical response to the global debt', *Impact*, vol. 21, no. 9 (Manila; September 1986).

[31]*Relieving Third World Debt* (US Catholic Bishops' Conference, Washington, DC, October 1989), p. 11.

[32]Ibid., pp. 12–13.

Chapter 2   Will there be too many mouths to feed?

[1]The data presented here are based on an unpublished paper by Fr Rex Mansmann, 'Insights into the population issue: Tablo'. The research was conducted in the latter part of 1987 by the fieldworkers in Tabo and the health personnel of the Santa Cruz Mission under the supervision of Sister Cecilia Lorayes.

[2]Ibid., p. 18.

[3]Ibid., pp. 19–20.

[4]Gareth Porter and Delfin Galapin, Jr, *Resources, Population and the Philippines' Future* (paper no. 4; World Resource Institute, 1735 New York Avenue, Washington, DC 20006, 1988), p. 2.

[5]Ibid., p. 1.

[6]Ibid., p. 2.

[7]Ibid., pp. 2, 3.

[8]Ibid., pp. 6, 7.

[9]Paul Ehrlich, *The Population Bomb* (Ballantine, New York, 1969).

[10]Robert Repetto (ed.), *The Global Possible* (Yale University Press, New Haven, CT, 1985), p.7.

[11]Lester Brown *et al.* (eds), *State of the World 1989* (WorldWatch Institute, 1776 Massachusetts Avenue NW, Washington, DC 20036, 1989), p. 13.

[12]'Endangered Earth: Planet of the Year', *Time* (2 January 1989).

[13]James V. Schall, *Welcome, Number 4,000,000,000!* (Alba Books, Caufield, OH 44406, 1977).

[14]*Sollicitudo Rei Socialis* (1988), no. 25 (St Paul Publications, Homebush, NSW 2140, Australia).

[15]Robert Repetto, op. cit., p. 145.

[16]*Global 2000 Report to the President, 1980*, report prepared by the Council on Environmental Quality and the Department of Energy (Penguin, Harmondsworth, 1982).

[17]Quoted in Edward Goldsmith and Nicholas Hildyard (eds), *The Earth Report* (Mitchell Beazley, London, 1988), p. 156.

[18]D. C. Hall and J. V. Hall, 'Concepts and measures of natural resource scarcity', *Journal of Environmental Economics and Management*, vol. 11 (1984), pp. 363–79.

[19]*Familiaris Consortio* (1981) (Daughters of St Paul, 2650 F. B. Harrison, Pasay, Metro Manila).

[20]Robert Repetto, op. cit., p. 9.

[21]Mercedes Concepcion, 'The Filipino Catholic response to population policy', *Pro Mundi Vita Studies: Religions and Population Policies* (September 1988; Brussels).

[22]Quoted in *National Catholic Reporter* (3 May 1985).

[23]Ibid.

[24]Cf. Mercedes Concepcion, op. cit. A majority of Filipino Catholic women think that the Church approves of artificial birth control.

[25]Quoted by Peter Hebblethwaite in *National Catholic Reporter* (3 December 1988).

[26]Quoted in Clifford Longley, 'Is the Inquisition alive in Rome?', *The Times* (25 July 1989).

[27]Quoted in Clifford Longley, 'Challenging the rule of Rome', *The Times* (24 July 1989).

[28]Jack Dominian, '*Humanae Vitae* revisited', *The Tablet* (27 October 1984). A few years ago, in an unguarded moment, the Duke of Norfolk remarked that the trouble with the approved 'natural' family planning methods is that 'they don't bloody well work': quoted in Clifford Longley, 'Conceptions of conscience', *The Times* (26 July 1989).

[29]Even this statement needs to be qualified. The discussion here refers to teaching which has come from the papal *magisterium* within the Church. As the New Testament and the history of the Church make abundantly clear, this is not the only teaching mode within the Church, though in recent years it has often been erroneously identified with the total teaching function of the Church. The Vatican II Decree on the Laity recognizes that the whole people of God shares in the prophetic mission of Christ (no. 2).

[30]*Lumen Gentium*, no. 25: Walter M. Abbott SJ (ed.), *The Documents of Vatican II* (America Press, USA/Geoffrey Chapman, London, 1966).

[31]Mercedes Concepcion, op. cit.

[32]Quoted in *Far Eastern Economic Review* (20 October 1988).

[33]*National Catholic Reporter* (3 May 1985). Writing in *The Month* (March 1987), Jack Mahoney SJ speaks about an 'infallibility by association', which gradually accrued to all papal teaching, especially during the pontificate of Pius XII.

[34]Eugene Hillman, *National Catholic Reporter* (26 August 1988).

[35]Nicholas Ayo, 'Birth-control revisited', *The Furrow* (October 1987), pp. 696–704.

[36]Lester Brown (ed.), *The State of the World 1985* (W.W. Norton, New York, 1985), p. 216.

[37]*Philippine Daily Inquirer* (27 October 1986).

[38]G. J. Hughes SJ, 'Natural law ethics and moral theology', *The Month* (March 1987).

[39]Ibid., pp. 100–1.

[40]Frank Lynch (1976): quoted in Chester L. Hunt, 'Philippines population growth shatters development plans', *Solidarity* (May–June 1988), pp. 91–102.

[41]Robert Repetto, op. cit., p. 154.

[42]Jesus Varela, 'Twenty years of "Humanae Vitae" '. *CBCP Monitor* (September–October 1988), pp. 7–11. The bishop says 'there is a widespread interest in Natural Family Planning as a human solution to the demographic problem (if at all it is that kind of problem that alarmist demographers are painting it to be)'.

[43]Chester L. Hunt, op. cit.

[44]James B. Reuter SJ, 'This is war', *CBCP Monitor* (March–April 1989), pp. 29–39.

[45]Robert Repetto, op. cit., p. 154.

[46]Rafael Salas, 'Population: the Mexico Conference and the future', statement to the International Conference on Population (Mexico City, 6 August 1984): quoted in Lester Brown, op. cit. (1985), p. 203.

[47]*Our Common Future* (Oxford University Press, Oxford, 1987), p. 95 (emphasis mine).

Chapter 3   When the trees are gone

[1]Norman Myers, *Conservation of the Tropical Moist Forest* (National Academy of Sciences, Washington, DC, 1980).

[2]'Save the forests: save the planet. A plan for action', *The Ecologist*, vol. 17, no. 4/5 (1987).

[3]*Philippines Forest Cover Statistics* (1988), Haribon data sheet, compiled by A. Burcer, NAMRIA (Mapping and Resource Information Authority) of the DENR.

[4]Ooi Jin Bee, *Depletion of the Forest Resources in the Philippines* (Field Report Series no. 18; Asean Economic Research Unit, University of Singapore, 1987).

[5]Norman Myers, *The Primary Source: the Tropical Forests and Our Future* (W. W. Norton, New York, 1984), p. 106.

[6]James Clad and Marites Vitug, 'The politics of plunder', *Far Eastern Economic Review* (24 November 1988).

[7]Dean Worcester, *The Philippines Past and Present*, vol. II (Macmillan, New York, 1914); quoted in Jun Terra, 'A requiem for the Philippine forests' (see below, note 11).

[8]Nestor Baguinon, *Development and Conservation of Indigenous Non-Dipterocarp Trees and Shrub Species* (National Conference on Genetic Resources and Development, Tagaytag City, 2–6 September 1987).

[9]*The Ecologist* (1987), op. cit.

[10]Catherine Caufield, *In the Rainforest* (Picador, London, 1985), pp. 209–18.

[11]Jun Terra, 'A requiem for the Philippine forests' (unpublished; 1989) (Nature, c/o 29 Kensington Gardens Square, London W2 4BG).

[12]B. Vandermeer, 'Corn cultivation on Cebu: an example of an advanced stage in migratory farming', *Journal of Tropical Geography* (1963), pp. 172–7.

[13]El Niño is a recurring climatic phenomenon which affects most severely the Pacific coast of Latin America; climatologists now think that it also affects climatic conditions in the eastern Pacific and Australia. While the phenomenon is not fully understood, El Niño involves a reduction in the trade winds in the southern Pacific. This leads to a build-up of warm water on the surface of the ocean, thus preventing colder, nutrient-rich waters from the Antarctic region from reaching the surface. Birds and fish in the area are immediately affected. In 1984 El Niño was blamed for causing floods in California and a seven-month drought in much of the western Pacific. Because it is first noticed in December, it is called *El Niño* ('the child') after the Christ child.

[14]Peter Bunyard, 'Gaia: the implications for industralized societies', *The Ecologist*, vol. 18, no. 2/3 (1988).

[15]'For the rights of tribal people', *Survival International*, no. 18 (1987).

[16]From Friends of the Earth, Japan (16 July 1989): *The World Rainforest Report* (Rainforest Information Centre, PO Box 368, Lismore, NSW 2480, Australia; August 1989).

[17]Senator Graham Richardson's office, Parliament House, Canberra, ACT 2600, Australia: *World Rainforest Report* (see above).

[18]Tracey Aubin, 'Ban "would harm rainforest" ', *Sydney Morning Herald* (27 July 1989).

[19]*The Ecologist* (1987), op. cit.

[20]Catherine Caufield, op. cit., pp. 178–81.

[21]OISCA Bulletin Board, Organization for Industrial, Spiritual and Cultural Advancement International, Tokyo: taken from a Foreign Affairs memorandum, Canberra, Australia (9 December 1986), p. 4.

[22]Ibid., p. 4.

[23]Ibid., p. 25.

Chapter 4   And God saw that it was good

[1]Sean McDonagh, *To Care for the Earth* (Geoffrey Chapman, London/ Bear, Santa Fe, NM, 1986), pp. 68–76.

[2]Mike Samuels and Hal Zina Bennett, *Well Body, Well Earth* (Sierra Club Books, San Francisco, 1983), p.18.

[3]Quoted in Sean McDonagh, op. cit., p. 149.

[4]Bruce Chatwin, *Songlines* (Picador, London, 1987), p. 13.

[5]Phyllis Bird in Norman Gottwald (ed.), *Images of Women in the Old Testament* (Orbis Books, Maryknoll, NY, 1983), pp. 252–89.

⁶Frederick Turner, *Beyond Geography: the Western Spirit against the Wilderness* (Viking, New York, 1980).

⁷Biblical quotations marked NJB are from the New Jerusalem Bible (Darton, Longman and Todd, London/Doubleday, New York); those marked RSV are from the Revised Standard Version.

⁸Much of what follows is found in Sean McDonagh, op. cit., pp. 111–12.

⁹Jürgen Moltmann, *God in Creation: a New Theology of Creation and the Spirit of God* (Harper and Row, San Francisco, 1985), p. 75.

¹⁰Lynn White, 'Historical roots of our ecological crisis', *Science* (1967), pp. 1203–7.

¹¹Ted F. Peters in *The Cry of the Environment* (Bear, Santa Fe, NM, 1984), pp. 415–16; William Dyrness, 'Stewardship of the earth in the Old Testament' in Wesley Granberg-Michaelson (ed.), *Tending the Garden* (Eerdmans, Grand Rapids, MI, 1987).

¹²Jürgen Moltmann, op. cit., p. 31.

¹³Keith Thomas, *Man and the Natural World* (Pantheon, New York, 1983), pp. 17–30.

¹⁴Bernard W. Anderson, *The Living World of the Old Testament* (Longmans, London, 1958), p. 174.

¹⁵Norman Myers in *The Guardian* (9 October 1987).

Chapter 5   The covenant tradition

¹Wendell Berry, *The Gift of Good Land* (North Point Press, San Francisco, 1981).

²Quoted in Ted Trainer, *Developed to Death* (Green Print, London, 1989), p. 109.

³In Gunter Friedrichs and Adam Schaff (eds), *Microelectronics and Society* (Pergamon, London, 1982), pp. 26–27; quoted in Geoff Lacey, *What Technologies are Appropriate* (Pax Christi, PO Box 31, Carlton, South Victoria 3053, Australia; 1989).

⁴Geoff Lacey, op. cit., p. 9.

⁵Ibid.

⁶World Charter for Nature (United Nations, 1983).

⁷Edward Goldsmith and Nicholas Hildyard (eds), *The Earth Report* (Mitchell Beazley, London, 1988), p. 94.

⁸Norman Myers, 'The peace campaigner's latest military manual', *The Guardian* (8 November 1988).

⁹Quoted in Preman Niles, *Restating the Threats to Life* (Risk Book series; WCC Publications, Geneva, 1989), p. 18.

¹⁰Jonathan King, *Troubled Water* (Rodale Press, Emmaus, PA, 1985), p. 28.

¹¹Ted Trainer, op. cit., p. 145.

[12]See Appendix 2 above, p. 214.

[13]FAO Genetic Conservation Training Programme, Crop Ecology and Genetic Resources Unit, 'Genetic conservation' (FAO PI.F7460): quoted in *Renewing the Earth, CAFOD Campaign 1989–91* (CAFOD, 2 Romero Close, Stockwell Road, London SW9 9TY).

[14]Dr F. Rajotte, 'Some theological and ethical points of concern on the issue of the patenting of genetically engineered living organisms' (World Council of Churches, Geneva).

Chapter 6 Prophets, Psalms and wisdom literature

[1]Sam Hall, 'Whaling: the slaughter continues', *The Ecologist*, vol. 18, no. 6 (1988), pp. 207–13.

[2]Walther Zimmerli, 'The place and limit of the Wisdom literature in the framework of the Old Testament theology', *Scottish Journal of Theology*, vol. 17 (1964), p. 148: quoted in Robert K. Johnston, 'Wisdom literature and its contribution to a biblical environmental ethic' in Wesley Granberg-Michaelson (ed.), *Tending the Garden* (Eerdmans, Grand Rapids, MI, 1987).

[3]Gustavo Gutiérrez, *On Job: God Talk and the Suffering of the Innocent* (Claretian Publications, Quezon City, Philippines, 1986), p. 74.

[4]James Lovelock, *GAIA* (Oxford University Press, Oxford, 1981), p. 9.

[5]Ibid.

[6]Rosemary Radford Ruether, *New Woman/New Earth: Sexist Ideologies and Human Liberation* (Seabury Press, New York, 1975), p. 204.

[7]Preman Niles, *Restating the Threats to Life* (Risk Book series; WCC Publications, Geneva, 1989), p. 19.

[8]Yves Congar, 'The Spirit of God's femininity', *Theology Digest* (Summer 1982), pp. 415–16.

Chapter 7 'I have come that they may have life'

[1]Andrew Linzey and Tom Regan, *Compassion for Animals* (SPCK, London, 1988), p. 86.

[2]Ernest Becker, *The Denial of Death* (Free Press, London, 1973).

[3]Patricia Wilson-Kastner, 'Does the world have a future?' in *Church and Society Documents* (August 1988) (World Council of Churches, Geneva).

[4]Denis Carroll, *Towards a Story of the Earth* (Dominican Publications, Dublin, 1987), p. 33.

[5]Joint pastoral letter by the Guatemalan Bishops' Conference (1987): published in *Newsletter*, no. 4 (1988) (Inter-Church Committee on Human Rights in Latin America, Suite 201, 40 St Clair Avenue, East Toronto, Ontario, Canada M4T 1M9).

[6]Lewis Mumford, *The Pentagon of Power* (Harcourt Brace Jovanovich, New York, 1970), pp. 172–3: quoted in Geoff Lacey, *What Technologies Are Appropriate?* (Pax Christi, PO Box 31, Carlton, South Victoria 3053, Australia; 1989), p. 17.

[7]Jürgen Moltmann, *God in Creation: a New Theology of Creation and the Spirit of God* (Harper and Row, San Francisco, 1985), p. 123.

Chapter 8   Christian witnesses through the ages

[1]Denis Carroll, *Towards a Story of the Earth* (Dominican Publications, Dublin), p. 38.

[2]Susan Bratton Power, 'The original desert solitary: early Christian monasticism and wilderness', *Environmental Ethics*, vol. 10, no. 1 (Spring 1988), pp. 31–53. Much of what follows on pp. 166–7 above is drawn from this article.

[3]Ibid., p. 35.

[4]Ibid., p. 36.

[5]Andrew Linzey and Tom Regan, *Compassion for Animals* (SPCK, London, 1988), p. 34.

[6]Denis Carroll, op. cit., pp. 40–1.

[7]Andrew Linzey and Tom Regan, op. cit., p. 9.

[8]John Macquarrie, 'Paths in spirituality' in Michael Maher (ed.), *Irish Spirituality* (Veritas, Dublin, 1983), p. 7.

[9]Patrick Logan, *The Holy Wells of Ireland* (Colin Smythe, Gerrards Cross, Bucks, 1980).

[10]Marian Keaney, *Irish Missionaries* (Veritas, Dublin, 1985), p. 38.

[11]Dermot Moran, 'Nature, man and God in the philosophy of John Scotus Eriugena' in Richard Kearney (ed.), *The Irish Mind* (Wolfhound Press, Dublin, 1985), pp. 99–100.

[12]Ibid., pp. 17–18.

[13]Alexander Carmichael (ed.), *The Sun Dances: Prayers and Blessings from the Gaelic* (Floris Books, Edinburgh, 1960), p. 35.

[14]René Dubos, *Wooing the Earth* (Charles Scribner's Sons, New York, 1980).

[15]St Francis of Assisi, 'The Canticle of Brother Sun' in M. A. Habig (ed.), *St Francis of Assisi: Omnibus of Sources* (Franciscan Herald Press, Chicago, IL, 1983), pp. 130–1.

[16]Hildegard of Bingen, translated by Gabriele Uhlein, *Meditations with Hildegard of Bingen* (Bear, Santa Fe, NM, 1982), pp. 56, 65, 51.

Chapter 9   The environment in the modern Catholic Church

[1]From a letter by T. M. Bartram MBE, of Somerton, Somerset, England, printed in *The Catholic Herald* (22 February 1963).

[2]Edward Wilson, 'Extinction' in Edward Goldsmith and Nicholas Hildyard (eds), *The Earth Report* (Mitchell Beazley, London, 1988).

[3]The 1988 report from the Pontifical Academy of the Sciences that some 35,000 species face extinction before the year 2000 came late in the day, and underestimates the level of extinction.

[4]International Atomic Energy Agency, General Conference, 26th regular session (20–24 September 1982), record of 240th plenary meeting, held at the Neue Hofburg, Vienna.

[5]Edward Goldsmith and Nicholas Hildyard, op. cit., p. 188.

[6]J. W. Jeffery, 'The collapse of nuclear economics', *The Ecologist*, vol. 18 (January–February 1988), pp. 9–14.

[7]Tony Benn, *The Ecologist*, vol. 16, no. 4/5 (1986).

[8]'Appeal for Chernobyl clean up', *Sydney Morning Herald* (23 August 1989), quoting *The Independent*.

[9]Sean McDonagh, *To Care for the Earth* (Geoffrey Chapman, London/Bear, Santa Fe, NM, 1986), pp. 52–4.

[10]Cliff Baxter, 'Pope's appeal for world conservation', *The Catholic Weekly* (Sydney: 9 August 1989).

[11]Gary MacEoin, 'Ratzinger knocks Green party, dialogue with Jews', *National Catholic Reporter* (6 November 1987).

[12]*The Cry for Land*, joint pastoral letter by the Guatemalan Bishops' Conference (1987): published in *Newsletter*, no. 4 (1988) (Inter-Church Committee on Human Rights in Latin America, Suite 201, 40 St Clair Avenue, East Toronto, Ontario, Canada M4T 1M9), p. 4.

[13]Catholic Bishops of the Dominican Republic, *The Protection of Nature Is a Condition of Survival* (1987): quoted in *Renewing the Earth*, CAFOD Campaign 1989–91 (CAFOD, 2 Romero Close, Stockwell Road, London SW9 9TY), p. 36.

[14]See Appendix 2 above, pp. 215–16.

[15]A. J. Van Der Bent, 'The wholeness of creation in ecumenical perspective — a documentary survey', *Exchange: Bulletin of Third World Christian Literature* (December 1988) (c/o IIMO–Department of Missiology, Rapenburg 61, 2311 GJ Leiden, Netherlands), pp. 9–20.

[16]Mimeographed copy of the final document.

[17]Pierre Teilhard de Chardin, *The Phenomenon of Man* (paperback edn; Fontana, London, 1965).

[18]Ibid., p. 270.

[19]Thomas Berry, *The Dream of the Earth* (Sierra Books, San Francisco, 1988).

[20]Matthew Fox, *Original Blessing* (Bear, Santa Fe, NM, 1983).

[21]Oliver Davies, 'Eckhart and Fox', *The Tablet* (5 August 1989), pp. 890–1.

[22]Lester Brown *et al.* (eds), *State of the World 1989* (WorldWatch Institute, Washington, DC, 1989), p. 192.

Appendix 1   A new Decalogue

[1]Marshall Massey, 'Uniting Friends with nature' (talk given at Mount View Meeting, Denver, CO), *Friends Bulletin* (1985), pp. 24–39.

Appendix 2   *What Is Happening to Our Beautiful Land?*

[1]Catholic Bishops' Conference of the Philippines, *What Is Happening to Our Beautiful Land?* (Catholic Bishops' Conference of the Philippines, 470 General Luna Street, Intramuros, Manila 2800; January 1988); published as *The Cry of Our Land* (available from CAFOD, 2 Romero Close, Stockwell Road, London SW9 9TY).